A FIELD GUIDE TO

HAWKS

OF NORTH AMERICA

THE PETERSON FIELD GUIDE SERIES ®

A FIELD GUIDE TO

HAWKS

OF NORTH AMERICA

Second Edition

WILLIAM S. CLARK
AND BRIAN K. WHEELER

Illustrations by
BRIAN K. WHEELER

SPONSORED BY THE NATIONAL AUDUBON SOCIETY,
THE NATIONAL WILDLIFE FEDERATION, AND
THE ROGER TORY PETERSON INSTITUTE

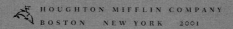

HOUGHTON MIFFLIN COMPANY
BOSTON   NEW YORK   2001

For information about permission to reproduce selections from
this book, write to Permissions, Houghton Mifflin Company,
215 Park Avenue, New York, New York 10003

Visit our Web site: www.houghtonmifflinbooks.com.

PETERSON FIELD GUIDES and PETERSON FIELD GUIDE SERIES
are registered trademarks of Houghton Mifflin Company.

Library of Congress Cataloging in Publication Data

Clark, William S., date.
A field guide to hawks, North America /
William S. Clark and Brian K. Wheeler ;
illustrations by Brian K. Wheeler. — 2nd edition.
p. cm. — (The Peterson field guide series)
ISBN 0-395-67068-3 (cl) — ISBN 0-395-67067-5 (pbk.)
1. Birds of prey — North America — Identification.
I. Wheeler, Brian K., 1955– II. Title. III. Series.

QL696.F3 C59   2001
598.9'097—dc21   2001024477

Book design by Anne Chalmers
Typeface: Linotype-Hell Fairfield; Futura Condensed (Adobe)

Printed in the United States of America

WCT 10 9 8 7 6 5 4 3 2 1

Acknowledgments

We wish to thank the many people who assisted us in the preparation of this revision to our raptor field guide. We greatly appreciate the help given us by the Houghton Mifflin staff: Lisa White, our editor, and the copyeditor, Lisa Sacks.

This project benefited from the constructive criticism of the text and artwork by John Schmitt and Ken Meyers. Their input is greatly appreciated.

The following people, in alphabetical order, assisted us in our field work or provided a base from which to operate or gave us helpful comments or some combination of these. They are Bill Alther, Bud Anderson, Sharon Bartles, Pete Bloom, Peter Capaino, Jack and Dolly Clark, Jeff Dodge, John Economidy, Paul Fritz, Ned and Linda Harris, Joe and Elaine Harrison, Stuart Houston, Jimmy Jackson, Stuart Keith, Jerry Liguori, Michael McNall, Frank Nicoletti, Leif Robinson, John Schmitt, Dan Varland, Clayton White, and Jim Wolford.

Many museums graciously permitted study of their raptor specimens for this revision or for preparation of the original guide or both; they are American Museum of Natural History, National Museum of Natural History, British Museum of Natural History, Field Museum, Delaware Museum, Denver Museum, Los Angeles County Museum, Academy of Natural Sciences of Philadelphia, San Diego Museum of Natural History, Western Foundation of Vertebrate Zoology, Alberta and British Columbia Provincial Museums, Winnipeg Museum, and the museums at the following colleges and universities: Alberta, Arizona, Arkansas, California (Museum of Vertebrate Zoology), Harvard (Museum of Comparative Zoology), Kansas, Louisiana State, Miami (Florida), Michigan, Minnesota (Bell Museum), New Mexico, Oklahoma, Principia College, Puget Sound, Saskatchewan, Southeastern Kansas, Texas A & M, Tulane, Washington, Wisconsin, and Yale (Peabody Museum).

The following people provided information on the one-time vagrants: Henry Armistead, Jim Ayers, James Flynn, Mike O'Brian, Bruce MacTavish, and David Wingate.

We thank Paul Lehman for providing up-to-date information on the range maps.

Tony Beck, George Jett, Kevin Karlson, and Jerry Liguori provided color slides for use in the guide.

We especially thank WSC's sister, Ellie Clark, and BKW's wife, Lisa Wheeler, for their support and encouragement during preparation of this revision.

William S. Clark
Brian K. Wheeler

Contents

LIST OF PLATES

A FIELD GUIDE TO

HAWKS

OF NORTH AMERICA

The legacy of America's great naturalist, Roger Tory Peterson, is preserved through the programs and work of the Roger Tory Peterson Institute of Natural History. The RTPI mission is to create passion for and knowledge of the natural world in the hearts and minds of children by inspiring and guiding the study of nature in our schools and communities. You can become a part of this worthy effort by joining RTPI. Just call RTPI's membership department at 1-800-758-6841, fax 716-665-3794, or e-mail (webmaster@rtpi.org) for a free one-year membership with the purchase of this Field Guide.

INTRODUCTION

The purpose of this field guide is to present the latest tried and proven field marks (see Field Marks below) for accurate field identification of the 35 regularly occurring and 12 vagrant diurnal raptor species in North America. By knowing and using these field marks, anyone should, with a little practice, be able to accurately identify most flying and perched diurnal raptors when they see them clearly.

A growing number of people would like to be able to identify raptors accurately in the field, especially birders and those who watch, count, hunt with, or study raptors. However, field identification of hawks, kites, eagles, vultures, and falcons is notoriously difficult because they are wary and difficult to approach, exhibit a variety of plumages, and alter their shape with different flight modes.

Additionally, although the bird field guides, including those in the Peterson series, constantly incorporate new information and are adequate for the identification of most bird species, space limitations prevent them from fully describing and illustrating all of the plumages and field marks of diurnal raptors.

This work is the culmination of our efforts over the past twenty-plus years toward making the art of raptor field identification more scientific by discovering and describing new field marks and behavioral characteristics.

We have both spent considerable time in the field watching and photographing raptors in North America and have conducted raptor identification seminars and led field excursions to watch and identify raptors. We discovered many new field marks when we continued observing raptors *after* we had identified them and asked ourselves, What can we tell others about this species that would help them correctly identify it?

We have also spent considerable time studying raptor specimens in collections, visiting museums in all regions of North America to check field marks, look for individuals with unusual plumages, and gather measurement data from labels. Some new field marks came to light as we studied photographs and examined museum skins. All of the field marks presented herein have been field tested by us and by others, and they work in almost all cases, but there will always be the odd raptor that lacks a certain field mark and is thus more difficult to label properly in the field.

We searched most of the recent North American ornithological literature, including the regional, state, and provincial journals, for articles on raptor identification, distribution and status, plumages, natural history, behavior, and other subjects.

SPECIES ACCOUNTS

The accounts for the regularly occurring species appear in the sequence used in the seventh edition of the *American Ornithologists' Union Check-list of North American Birds* (AOU 1998); the accounts for the vagrant species appear at the end. We have followed traditional treatments by including the New World Vultures; we do not believe that they are storks, as the methodology used in the studies that suggested they are storks has been shown to be flawed. We consider them the ecological equivalents of Old World Vultures, which are most certainly raptors, and therefore include them in this guide.

GROUP HEADING. Preceding the accounts for each group of similar species is a group account, which may be a subfamily, in the case of the Osprey; a genus, such as *Accipiter* or *Falco;* or a group of similar species not in the same genus, such as kites, vultures, or falcons. The species accounts of that group follow. The species accounts are written in the following format. Each account includes the information described below. **Note** indicates important information for the reader.

COMMON AND SCIENTIFIC NAMES. The common and scientific names used in this guide are the same as those used in the seventh AOU checklist, except for the scientific name of the Gray Hawk, which we retain as *Buteo*. We agree that *Asturina* could be valid, but if it is, it should also contain Red-shouldered and Roadside Hawks. Note our comments under **SUBSPECIES** for these species. We have treated the Harlan's Hawk as distinct from the Red-tailed Hawk, but only for field identification purposes, without commenting on its taxonomic status (which, however, should be reexamined).

DESCRIPTION. A brief initial description of each species indicates size, general type (e.g., accipiter, falcon, etc.), and range. Field marks common to all plumages are enumerated, with mention of sex and age differences and color morphs, if applicable to that species. Next are detailed descriptions of each different age, sex, color morph, and geographically different plumage.

FIELD MARKS. Each species has features that distinguish it from every other species. These are called field marks. Examples are the dark mark (patagial mark) on the Red-tailed Hawk's underwings, the red head of adult Turkey Vultures, and the gull-like wing shape of Ospreys. Diagnostic field marks are italicized.

PLUMAGES. Raptors replace their plumages annually, during the summer in most species. Adult and immature plumages are described and portrayed for all species; most species have only one immature plumage: juvenile. All other recognizably different, regularly occurring plumages, such as sexually different and older immature plumages and color morphs, are also completely described and portrayed. See also Molt below. We prefer the term "morph" in place of the often used "phase," as the latter word implies a character that changes with time.

UNUSUAL PLUMAGES. Occurrences of albinism, partial albinism, melanism, and dilute plumage are noted, as well as instances of hybrids between species.

SIMILAR SPECIES. Similar species are listed, including cross-references to the proper color plate or plates, and distinguishing field marks are enumerated. These, however, are listed for only one of the two species; the other's account includes the sentence "See under that species for differences."

FLIGHT. Three methods of flight are described: active, soaring, and gliding flight. Other interesting flight modes, such as hovering or kiting, are described for some species.

MOLT. This section describes when and how raptors molt their feathers. Some adults complete their molt annually on the breeding grounds before and after breeding (molt is usually suspended while breeding). Others, especially long-distance migrants, molt some feathers on the breeding grounds but suspend molt during the autumn migration and complete their molt on the winter grounds. Some of the larger species do not replace all of their flight feathers in one year; they usually require two years or more to renew all feathers. The molt of juveniles (first prebasic molt) differs from that of adults in some species. Some species begin to molt in their first spring, when they are almost a year old, whereas others, particularly migrants wintering in the tropics or South America, begin to molt earlier on the winter grounds and replace some or most of their body feathers and sometimes also a few tail and flight feathers. A few species begin a partial first prebasic molt (usually of body feathers only) within two or three months after fledging. Molt is usually suspended during migration.

Age terminology is related to molts. All species are in juvenile plumage when they leave the nest. Many species reach adult plumage in their first (first prebasic) molt; others, particularly the larger eagles, require three or four annual molts to reach adult plumage, with several immature plumages in between. See the List of Terms for the definitions of the immature plumages Basic I through Basic IV. See Humphrey and Parkes (1959) for a discussion of molts, plumages, and terminology.

Understanding the molt sequences of the flight feathers is important to properly age large raptors in immature plumages. Edelstam (1984), Miller (1941), and Jollie (1946) discuss wing and tail molt in raptors. In accipitrid raptors, primary molt begins with number 1, the innermost, and proceeds outward in sequence. In falconids, primary molt begins with number 4 and proceeds both inward and outward. When all primaries are not replaced in one year, the sequence of molt continues where it left off when molt begins again the next spring. However, in accipitrids, molt of primary 1 occurs again during this molt season, beginning a new wave of primary molt. Secondary molt of accipitrid juveniles begins at three molt centers, S_1, S_5, and S_1_3 or 14. It proceeds inward from S_1 and S_5 and outward from S_1_3 (also inward to replace the tertiaries). In falconid raptors, secondary molt begins with S_4 or S_5 and proceeds both inward and outward. After the secondaries have been replaced once, the pattern of molt is apparently random.

Molt of the tail feathers is more irregular, however, and usually begins with T_1, the central pair. Usual sequence is T_2, T_3, T_6, T_4, then T_5, with much variation in the order. Molt is often asymmetrical, especially on older birds.

BEHAVIOR. Behaviors that aid in identifying a species, such as hunting behavior and prey selection, are described. Other interesting behaviors are also described for many species.

VOICE. We make little mention of vocalizations because we feel that it is difficult to portray calls adequately using letters, such as *kek* or *tewp*. Voice is one of the better field marks available for field identification, but vocalizations are best learned from field study and from recordings, such as the bird song guides in the Peterson Field Guide Series. When a species is particularly vocal, that fact is noted in the Behavior section.

STATUS AND DISTRIBUTION. Range, including breeding and wintering ranges and migration routes or permanent range, is presented, together with out-of-range occurrences and relative abundance.

RANGE MAPS. The summer and winter ranges are illustrated for most species. The range maps were produced using published distributional data, personal correspondence from knowledgeable people, and range maps from published bird field guides. Range maps are useful on a large scale for general distribution but have inherent limitations: they do not show density, habitat preference, detectability due to behavior, nor do they provide the precise limits of summer and winter ranges as these are usually not well known and vary with time. The text should be consulted for habitat preferences and exceptions. Consult state, provincial, and regional bird books for finer detail on the status and distribution of raptors.

FINE POINTS. More detailed information on field identification is presented.

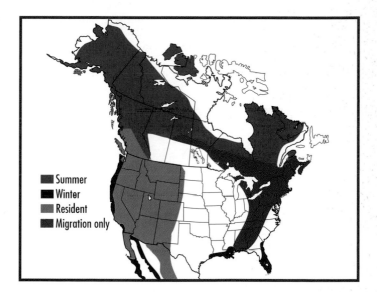

SUBSPECIES. All of the races in North America north of Mexico as recognized by the AOU in the fifth edition of the *Check-list of North American Birds* are given, together with the approximate breeding range of each. Many species are monotypic. Subspecific labels have not been used with the various recognizably different "forms" of a species because individuals within the range of one subspecies sometimes have the characteristics of another. Furthermore, it is sometimes impossible to separate many subspecies in the field, and some recognized subspecies fail to satisfy the criteria of subspecies (e.g., Krider's Hawk does not occupy a range exclusive of other races of the Red-tailed Hawk but is nevertheless a recognizable form of the Red-tail). In most cases, the forms described correspond to subspecies. In some, however, the subspecies cannot be distinguished in the field and are thus not differentiated in the text or plates.

ETYMOLOGY. The origins of the common and scientific names are noted.

MEASUREMENTS. The average and range of values for length, wingspread, and weight are presented in both English and metric units. The total length measurement used is the distance from the top of the head to the tip of the tail. Wingspread is the distance between wingtips of a raptor whose wings are fully extended. Weight is reported to the nearest gram. The data are given separately for each sex for some species in which male and female sizes show little or no overlap. Measurements were taken on live birds whenever possible. When few live data were available, these were augmented by data from museum specimens, or, as a last resort, from published sources.

PLATES. The 40 plates have been grouped in the center of the book for quick access. Legends on the facing pages contain summaries of the major field marks. Field marks printed in italics are diagnostic for species identification; those in roman type pertain to age and sex determination within the species. However, some age- and sex-related field marks are also species determining and thus are in italics (e.g., the red head of the adult Turkey Vulture). Legend pages also include cross-references to text. The sequence of species on the plates corresponds as nearly as possible to the AOU check-list order, considering that multiple species are drawn on many plates.

The plates and the text were produced to complement each other. We worked together throughout their production and attempted to show all the important field marks of each species and to picture as many forms of each species as possible, but always depicting adult, juvenile, dark morph, and sexually different plumages. Some field marks that could not be depicted on the color plates are shown on the color photographs.

We have emphasized identification of both flying and perched raptors in this revised edition. Drawings of detached heads, wings, and tails showing field marks were used to save space. To facilitate comparison, many similar species were drawn in the same flight profile on different plates (e.g., the accipiters).

PHOTOGRAPHS. Color photographs are included with the text to complement the plates by illustrating or emphasizing field marks and depicting a color morph, age or sex class, or position or attitude that is not illustrated on the plates.

Basic points to keep in mind regarding the identification of raptors are

- The field marks used for perched and flying raptors may be different. For example, wing shapes and underwing patterns of soaring raptors are not visible on perched raptors, when the relative position of wingtip and tail tip can be used as field marks.
- Females are larger than males in most species, noticeably so in some species.
- Adult and immature plumages are quite different in most species.
- In several species adult males and females have different plumages.
- Adults and juveniles of many species have different proportions. Adult wings are usually narrower and longer, but in some species of buteonines, adult wings are wider. In most species the adult tail is shorter.
- Juveniles in fresh plumage usually show pale tips to flight and tail feathers and to greater wing coverts; the latter form narrow pale lines on wings. These tips usually wear off in winter.
- Non-juvenile raptors in summer and early autumn often show signs of molt in wings and tail or gaps in wings and uneven trailing edges of wings and tip of tail.
- Flight and tail feathers are darker on uppersides as compared to undersides and darker on outer webs compared to inner webs. As a result, flight and tail feathers appear darker on the uppersides.
- Some raptors show pale areas on backlit underwings (windows or panels).
- Rufous underparts in fresh plumage of some raptors, e.g., juvenile Northern Harriers, are usually faded by sunshine and weather to buffy, creamy, or even whitish within a few months.
- Raptors that show rounded wingtips when soaring often show somewhat pointed wingtips when gliding.
- When raptors are seen up close, more detail and shadings of color are noticeable; the same raptor seen at a distance appears much more black and white, with loss of definition and color.
- Raptors, and other birds as well, often appear different colored under different lighting conditions. All flying raptors, even ones with white underparts, appear darker against whitish skies.

Raptor Types

All of the raptors treated in this guide can be assigned to one of the general types described below on the basis of wing and tail shape, color, size, and behavior.

VULTURES. The three vulture species are large raptors with featherless heads, long wings, and generally blackish coloration. They spend considerable time soaring and gliding.

OSPREY. The Osprey is a large gull-like raptor found near water. The distinctive wing shape and dark eye line are conspicuous.

KITES. The three widespread pointed-wing kites are medium-sized raptors. They are falconlike in silhouette, but are more buoyant in flight and have unique tails. One is solid white, one is dark and flared, and the last is swallowlike.

HARRIER. The single harrier species has long, narrow wings and a long tail, and its buoyant flight is with wings held in a strong dihedral.

ACCIPITERS. The three species of "true hawks," small to large raptors with long tails and relatively short, rounded wings, are found most often in forested areas. Their typical active flight is three or more rapid wingbeats interspersed with periods of gliding. Wingtips reach only halfway down the tail on perched birds.

BUTEOS. The six species of "buzzards," medium to large raptors with long, broad wings and relatively short, wide tails, are found in open and forested habitats. They all soar frequently; many sit on exposed perches. Wingtips usually reach to or nearly to the tail tip on perched birds.

EAGLES. The two eagle species are very large, mostly dark brown raptors with proportionally longer wings. They soar and glide with wings held nearly horizontal.

FALCONS. The five species of regularly occurring falcons are small to large raptors with long, pointed wings, long tails, and large, squarish heads. They are swift on the wing and occur in open habitats. Wingtips usually reach over halfway down the tail on perched falcons.

HOW TO USE THIS BOOK

When you see an unfamiliar raptor, *before* opening the guide, you should determine its general type from the descriptions above (at first, you may have to open the guide to this section to determine general type). Make written notes of all important field marks observed, including color and contrasting marks (such as a pale superciliary line, shape and color of marks or panels on underwing, and number and relative thickness of tail bands). Also observe and note the raptor's behavior. Make these notes before consulting the field guide because the bird may soon be out of your sight.

Which field marks to look for on any species will depend on whether the bird is perched or flying. On perched birds, note the color and pattern of the back and underparts, the color of the eye, and the head pattern, as well as the presence or absence of tail banding and leg feathering and how far the wingtips extend toward the tail tip. On flying birds, look for the underwing pattern, the shape and relative length of head, tail, and wings, any distinguishing marks (such as belly bands, dark secondaries, and dark patagial or carpal patches), the presence and shape of wing panels, and the pattern of tail banding.

When you have noted all marks and behavior, and only then, open this field guide to the color plates. These are arranged in order more or less by the raptor types described above, with the vultures shown on the first two plates and so forth. Quickly scan the illustrations of all species of the appropriate type, reading the important field marks for each species (including those referring to age and sex). Note the similar species, and check the plates for these. Next, turn to the color photographs. Look at the photos for the species being considered and read the explanatory captions. If a positive identification has not been made, or if more information is desired, consult the text at this stage.

Study the text, color plates, and color photos at home to become familiar with the diagnostic field marks to look for on each species. If possible, take photographs of raptors that you are not able to identify. Try to photograph the bird from different angles. Often only one photo of many taken could show a diagnostic field mark.

A word of caution is in order: even when you use this or any other field guide, you should not expect to identify every hawk accurately. Experienced hawk watchers know that they must record a few hawks as "unidentified," most often because they could not see the bird clearly enough. On the other hand, some experienced hawk watchers are able to identify hawks correctly beyond the range where most field marks can be seen. How do they do it? Such people record most identification clues subconsciously; they bring into play the familiarity that comes from experience. They spot subtle differences in shape, proportion, and behavior. This impression of a species is often called "jizz" or "gestalt." It is difficult to teach or describe this ability because the clues are subtle and are subconsciously noted. They also vary from one location to the next and under different wind and light conditions.

We recommend that you continue to watch raptors after they have been identified. You will learn more about their identification and will observe the behavior of some of nature's most impressive creatures — a rewarding experience indeed.

Much remains to be learned about raptor identification. We would appreciate any suggestions and constructive criticism for future editions of this book. Please send your comments to the authors, c/o Houghton Mifflin Company, 222 Berkeley Street, Boston, Massachusetts 02116-3704.

Good luck in your hawk watching.

Adult plumage. The final breeding plumage of a bird. Also called "definitive basic" plumage.

Albinism. Rare abnormal condition when all of the feathers, beak, cere, talons, and eyes of a bird are without pigmentation. Feathers are white, and beak, cere, and talons are ivory. See **partial albinism** and **dilute plumage.**

Allopreening. When one bird preens the feathers of another, usually its mate. Also called "mutual preening."

Auriculars. The feathers covering the ears (Fig. 4).

Axillars or Axillaries. Feathers at the base of the underwing, also called the "armpit" or "wingpit" (Fig. 1).

Back. See Figs. 2 and 5.

Band. A stripe of contrasting color, usually in tail. See **tail banding.**

Barring. See Fig. 6.

Basic I. The second plumage of a bird that takes more than one year to attain adult plumage (e.g., eagles). Usually but not always acquired at one year of age and usually worn for a year. Basic II and III, etc. are the following plumages.

Beak. See Fig. 5., see also **mandibles.** Also called **"bill."**

Belly. See Fig. 5.

Belly band. See Fig. 1.

Bib. Pattern of uniformly dark breast that contrasts with paler belly.

Bill. See Fig. 5, see also **mandibles.** Also called **"beak."**

Breast. See Fig 1.

Buzzard. Name for raptors in the genus *Buteo* and related genera. This name has been mistakenly applied in North America to vultures.

Carpal. The underwing at the wrist, usually composed of all of the primary underwing coverts (Fig. 1).

Cere. A small area of bare skin above the upper mandible (Fig. 5).

Cheek. See Fig. 4.

Collar. A pale band across hindneck.

Coverts. The small feathers covering the bases of the flight feathers and tail both above and below (Fig. 5).

Crown. Top of head (Fig. 6).

Dihedral. The shape created when a bird holds its wings above the horizontal, further defined as: (1) Strong dihedral: wings held more than 15 degrees above level; (2) Medium dihedral: wings held between 5 and 15 degrees above level; (3) Slight dihedral: wings held between 0 and 5 degrees above level; (4) Modified dihedral: wings held between 5 and 15 degrees above level but held nearly level from wrist to tip.

Dilute plumage. An abnormal plumage in which the dark colors are replaced by lighter, usually creamy colors (but not white) most likely due to a reduction in the dark pigment melanin. Also called **"leucistic."**

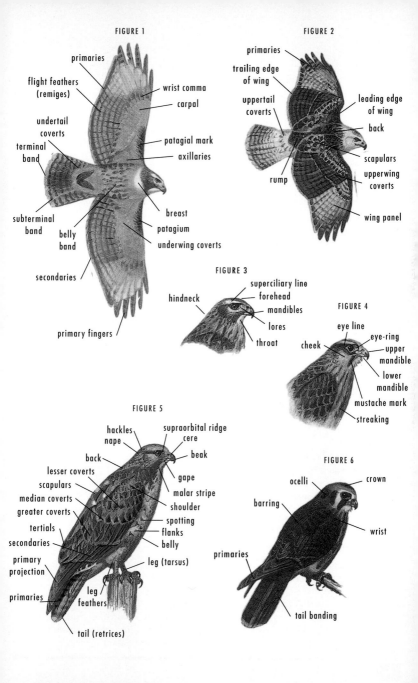

FIGURE 1

primaries
flight feathers (remiges)
wrist comma
carpal
undertail coverts
terminal band
patagial mark
axillaries
subterminal band
belly band
breast
patagium
underwing coverts
secondaries
primary fingers

FIGURE 2

primaries
trailing edge of wing
uppertail coverts
leading edge of wing
back
scapulars
rump
upperwing coverts
wing panel

FIGURE 3

hindneck
superciliary line
forehead
mandibles
lores
throat

FIGURE 4

eye line
eye-ring
upper mandible
cheek
lower mandible
mustache mark
streaking

FIGURE 5

hackles
nape
supraorbital ridge
cere
back
beak
lesser coverts
gape
scapulars
malar stripe
median coverts
shoulder
greater coverts
spotting
tertials
flanks
secondaries
belly
primary projection
leg (tarsus)
primaries
leg feathers
tail (retrices)

FIGURE 6

ocelli
crown
barring
wrist
primaries
tail banding

Emargination. An abrupt narrowing on the outer web of an outer primary, see also **notch**.

Eye line. Noticeable line that extends behind eye, sometimes also in front of eye, usually dark (Fig. 4).

Eye-ring. The bare skin around the eye, somewhat wider in front of the eye in falcons (Fig. 4). Also called "orbital ring'" and "scleral ring."

Face skin. The lores when bare of feathers.

Facial disk. A saucer-shaped disk of feathers around the face, thought to direct sound to the ears. Most noticeable on harriers.

Feather edge. The sides of a feather. Pale edges usually give the effect of streaking.

Feather fringe. The complete circumference of a feather. Pale fringes usually give a scalloped appearance.

Flank. See Fig. 5.

Fledgling. A raptor that has just left the nest, fledged.

Flight feathers. The primaries and secondaries (Fig. 1).

Forehead. See Fig. 3.

Gape. The opening between the mandibles when the bill is open.

Glide. Flight attitude of a bird when it is coasting downward. The wingtips are pulled back, more so for steeper angles of descent. Tails are usually closed.

Greater wing coverts. Rows of feathers overlapping the primaries and secondaries (Fig. 5).

Hackles. Erectile feathers on the nape.

Hawk. A raptor of the genus *Accipiter,* but also used generically for all diurnal raptors.

Hindneck. See Fig. 3.

Hover. To remain in a fixed place in the air by flapping the wings. More properly called "wind hover."

Immature. Nonspecific term that means "not adult." It is used in some references to mean "juvenile," and in others to mean the plumages between juvenile and adult.

Juvenile plumage. First complete plumage, acquired in the nest and usually different from the adult plumage.

Kite. To remain in a fixed place in moving air on motionless wings. See also **hover**.

Leading edge of wing. See Fig. 2.

Leg. See Fig. 5.

Leg feathers. See Fig. 5.

Length. Distance from top of head to tip of tail.

Lesser wing coverts. Small wing feathers near the leading edge of the wing (Fig. 5).

Leucistic. An abnormal plumage in which the dark colors are replaced by lighter, usually creamy colors (but not white), most likely due to a reduction in the dark pigment melanin. Also called *"dilute plumage."*

Lores. The area of the face between the eye and the beak (Fig. 3).

Lower mandible. See Fig. 4.

Malar stripe. A dark mark on the cheek under the eye (Fig. 5).

Mandible. The upper or lower half of the beak (Fig. 3).

Median wing coverts. Single row of feathers between the lesser and greater coverts (Fig. 5).

Melanism. Rare abnormal condition causing a raptor's feathers to be unusually darker due to excess dark pigments called melanin.

Molt. Means by which a bird replaces its feathers.

Monotypic. Having no subspecies.

Morph. Term used for recognizably different forms of a species, usually color related, as in "dark morph" and "light morph." See also **phase.**

Mustache mark. A dark mark directly under the eye that appears on most falcon species (Fig. 4).

Nape. The back of the head (Fig. 5).

Nominate race. The subspecies that has the generic name, e.g., *Buteo lineatus lineatus.*

Notch. Abrupt narrowing of the inner web of an outer primary.

Ocelli. Dark or light spots on the nape and hindneck that resemble eyes (Fig. 6).

Partial albinism. Abnormal condition when a few to almost all feathers of a raptor lack pigmentation and appear white. Feathers can be part white and part normal. Eyes, cere, and beak colors are usually normal; some talons can be ivory. See **albinism** and **dilute plumage.**

Patagial mark. See Fig. 1.

Patagium. The area on the front of the wing between the wrist and the body (adjective is patagial) (Fig. 1).

Phase. Term formerly used for "color morph." Phase implies a temporary condition; color morphs are permanent. See **morph.**

Plumage. All of the feathers of a bird, collectively.

Primaries. The outer flight feathers (Figs. 1, 2, 5, and 6). Primaries are referred to as P1, P2, etc., numbered from innermost one outward.

Primary fingers. Outermost primaries that project separately (Fig. 1).

Primary projection. The distance on the folded wing of perched birds from the tip of the longest primary to the tips of the secondaries (Fig. 5).

Raptor. Any bird of prey; any member of the Falconiformes or Strigiformes, although sometimes used to refer only to the diurnal birds of prey.

Rectrices. Tail feathers (Fig. 5).

Remiges. Flight feathers (Fig. 1).

Rump. The lowest area of the back (Fig. 2).

Scapulars. Row of feathers between back and upperwing coverts of each wing (Figs. 2 and 5).

Scavenger. Bird that eats carrion, offal, and other decaying material.

Secondaries. The inner flight feathers (Figs. 1 and 5). Secondaries are referred to as S1, S2, etc., numbered from outermost one inward.

Shoulder. See Fig. 5.

Soar. Flight attitude of a bird when wings, and usually tail, are fully spread. Used to gain altitude in rising air columns.

Spotting. See Fig. 5.

Streaking. See Fig. 4.

Subadult plumage. First adult plumage, when some immature characteristics are retained.

Subterminal band. See Fig. 1.

Superciliary line. Contrasting line above the eye, usually pale (Fig. 3).

Supraorbital ridge. Bony projection over the eye that gives raptors their fierce appearance (Fig. 5).

Tail. See Fig. 5.

Tail banding. See Fig. 6.

Tail coverts. Feathers that cover the base of the tail feathers, both above and below. See also **uppertail coverts** and **undertail coverts** (Figs. 2 and 1).

Talon-grappling. Behavior involving two flying raptors that lock feet and tumble with their wings extended.

Tarsus. Leg above the toes to the next joint. May or may not be covered by feathers (Fig. 5).

Terminal band. See Fig. 1.

Tertials. Short innermost secondaries (Fig. 5).

Throat. See Fig. 3.

Trailing edge of wing. See Fig. 2.

Underparts. Breast and belly (Figs. 1 and 5).

Undertail coverts. See Fig. 1.

Underwing. The underside of the open wing.

Underwing coverts. See Fig. 1.

Upper mandible. See Fig. 4.

Uppertail coverts. See Fig. 2.

Upperwing coverts. Primary and secondary coverts (Figs. 2 and 5).

Wing chord. Distance from the tip of the longest primary to the wrist with the feathers in normal shape (i.e., curved, not flattened).

Wing coverts. Feathers that cover the bases of the flight feathers. The four sets of wing coverts are marginal, lesser, median, and greater (Figs. 1, 2, and 5). See **upperwing coverts** and **underwing coverts.**

Wing linings. Underwing coverts (Fig. 1).

Wing loading. Weight divided by the wing area; a measure of the buoyancy of flight. The lower the wing loading, the more buoyant the flight.

Wing panel. A light area in the primaries, usually more visible from below when wing is backlit (Fig. 2).

Wingspread. Distance between wingtips with wings fully extended. Also called "wingspan."

Wrist. Bend of wing (Fig. 2).

Wrist comma. Comma-shaped mark, usually dark, at the bend of the underwing. Seen on underwings of most buteos (Fig. 1).

PLATES

1 . BLACK VULTURE *Coragyps atratus*   **P. 102**

Black vulture. Short square tail, *whitish legs,* and *white primary patches*. They often glide on level wings. Rapid choppy wingbeats are with stiff wings. Wingtips reach tail tip.

[a] OLDER JUVENILE. Like juvenile, except for *beak tip becoming yellow* and some wrinkles on lower neck.

[b] ADULT. *Gray head is unfeathered and wrinkled,* and *tip of beak is yellow*. Note *white legs* and *short primary projection*.

[c] JUVENILE. Similar to adult, but smooth head is covered with fine black down and *tip of beak is dark*. Feathered nape extends farther up hindneck than does that of adults.

[d] HEAD-ON SILHOUETTE. Soars with wings in a slight dihedral.

[e] ADULT. Appears overall black except for *whitish primary panels*. Gray head and neck appear more obvious than those of Turkey Vultures.

[f] ADULT. Appears overall black except for *whitish primary panels and legs*. White legs extend to tail tip.

2 . TURKEY VULTURE *Cathartes aura*   **P. 105**

Brownish black vulture. Adults have *red heads;* juveniles have dusky heads. *Legs are pink and white. Silvery flight feathers contrast with blackish coverts.* Blackish brown upperwings (not shown) show paler brown primaries. They often glide with wings in a modified dihedral. Flight is with slow soft, deep wingbeats. Wingtips reach tail tip.

[a] HEAD-ON SILHOUETTE. Soars with wings in a strong dihedral, often rocking or teetering.

[b] BASIC I. First-plumage adults are like adults except that tip of beak is dusky (gradually becoming smaller and disappearing) and *red face* has fewer whitish warts.

[c] ADULT. *Head is entirely red,* with white warts on face; beak is ivory; and body is brownish black. Neck and back show purplish iridescence. Note *pinkish legs and long primary projection*.

[d] OLDER JUVENILE. Like juvenile except face is now pinkish and pale area on base of beak is larger.

[e] JUVENILE. Similar to adult but head dark, nasal area pinkish, crown and nape down covered, and *dark beak shows pale area on base*. Upperparts have buffy feather edges. Neck and upperparts not iridescent.

[f] JUVENILE. Almost like adult in flight, but head is entirely dark and flight feathers are slightly darker.

[g] ADULT. Long wings are *two-toned*. Note *red head* and long tail. Head and neck appear less obvious than those of Black Vultures. *Legs extend only halfway down tail*.

Huge black vulture, larger than any eagle. Overall black except for *orangish head* (except juveniles) and *white wing areas.* Wingtips extend beyond tail tip on perched condors. Legs are whitish with red around upper tarsi joint. Short tails have square corners on tips. Adult plumage is acquired in six or seven years. Older immatures are intermediate in characters between juvenile and adult.

[a] ADULT. Overall black, except for *orangish head* and *white axillaries and lesser and median underwing coverts.* Legs are whitish, with red around upper joint of tarsi. Note the bare red area in midbreast.

[b] JUVENILE. Similar to adult, but head is dark and *white axillaries and underwing coverts have a variable amount of dusky mottling.*

[c] HEAD AND NECK OF ADULT. Mostly featherless orange head and pinkish neck often appear puffy. Note the black area across forehead and in front of eyes and the large red area on front of lower neck. Eyes are scarlet; beak is horn-colored.

[d] HEAD AND NECK OF BASIC II. Similar to head and neck of juvenile but lower neck becoming pink, appearing as a pale ring around the neck.

[e] HEAD AND NECK OF JUVENILE AND BASIC I. Head and neck are dark and covered with short dark down and are not as puffy like those of adults. Beak is dark, and eyes are gray-brown.

[f] ADULT. Overall black except for *orangish head, narrow white bar on upperwings,* and whitish *cast to inner secondaries.*

[g] JUVENILE. Similar to adult but head is dark and uppersides are browner, with secondaries lacking a whitish cast and *narrow whitish bar* on coverts much less noticeable.

1 . OSPREY *Pandion haliaeetus* **P. 113**

Large, pale, long-winged and long-legged raptor. Note *gull-like crooked wings* and *white head with dark eye-stripes*. Appear somewhat pigeon-headed due to lack of supraorbital ridges. At a distance, they often show orangish cast to uppertail.

[a] JUVENILE. Similar to adult but upperparts appear scaly, white areas of crown show dark streaks, and eyes are orangish.

[b] ADULT. Adults show dark brown back and upperwing coverts that lack pale feather edges and have unstreaked white areas in crown and yellow eyes. Note *dark eye-stripe* and *white stripe between shoulder and body*. Females usually have more boldly marked necklaces, but sexes overlap in this character. Wingtips extend just beyond tail tip.

[c] HEAD-ON SILHOUETTE. *Glides with wings held in gull-like crook.*

[d] ADULT. Showing gull-like wing attitude. White body and *dark carpal patches* are distinctive. *Dark eye-stripes* are noticeable on flying birds.

[e] JUVENILE. Similar to adult but with wide white tips to flight and tail feathers. Black lines at base of secondaries are not as prominent as those of adults. In early autumn, can show pale rufous on underwing coverts.

---

2 . HOOK-BILLED KITE *Chondrohierax uncinatus* **P. 119**

Distinctive kite with *large hooked beak* and *paddle-shaped wings that narrow at the body*. Pigeon-headed look is due to lack of supraorbital ridges. *Lores are uniquely green and yellow.*

[a] DARK-MORPH ADULT MALE. Overall blackish, with wide white tail band. Adult female has subtly darker crown.

[b] DARK-MORPH JUVENILE. Overall brownish black with subtly darker crown, pale feather edges, and two pale tail bands.

[c] ADULT MALE. Overall slate gray with white barring on belly. Dark uppertail shows wide gray band. Adults' eyes are whitish.

[d] ADULT FEMALE. Crown and nape are slate brown, with contrasting *rufous cheeks and collar*. Upperparts are dark brown, and rufous underparts have whitish barring. Eyes are whitish.

[e] JUVENILE. Crown and nape are blackish, with contrasting *whitish cheeks and collar*. Whitish underparts show a variable amount of narrow dark brown barring. Upperside of tail shows equal-width brown and dark bands. Juvenile's eyes are brown. Wingtips fall short of tail tip.

[f] ADULT MALE. Appears overall dark gray, with whitish banding on outer primaries, white barring on undersides, and wide white tail bands. *Note paddle-shaped wings.*

[g] HEAD-ON SILHOUETTE. Glides with wings cupped.

[h] JUVENILE. Appears overall pale, with boldly marked flight feathers and equal-width dark and light tail bands. *Wings pinch in at body.*

[i] ADULT FEMALE. Underparts and underwing coverts appear rufous, and flight feathers are heavily barred and show a rufous cast.

1[a]

1[b]

1[c]

1[d]

1[e]

2[a]

2[b]

2[c]

2[d]

2[e]

2[f]

2[g]

2[h]

2[i]

1 . SWALLOW-TAILED KITE *Elanoides forficatus*   **P. 123**

Unmistakable black-and-white kite. Bold black-and-white plumage, long pointed wings, and *long deeply forked tail* are diagnostic. Adults and juveniles in flight seen from above are not shown here; they can be seen in the photo section.

[a] JUVENILE. Similar to adult but with fine dark streaks on crown and breast (usually not visible). Iridescence is greenish. Eyes are dark brown.

[b] ADULT. Black-and-white plumage and *long deeply forked tail* are distinctive. Iridescence is purplish. Note *white patches on back* and pigeon-headed look. Eyes are dark brown.

[c] ADULT. Bold black-and-white plumage, long pointed wings, and *long deeply forked tail* are diagnostic.

[d] JUVENILE. Like adult but with shorter tail.

2 . WHITE-TAILED KITE *Elanus leucurus*   **P. 127**

Whitish falcon-shaped kite. Appears rather gull-like in color and flight. Always distinguished by *black shoulders* when perched; wingtips almost reach tail tip. Adults and juveniles in flight seen from above are not shown here; they can be seen in the photo section.

[a] ADULT. Head, underparts, and tail are white; crown, nape, back, upperwing coverts, and *central tail feathers are gray. Black shoulder* is obvious. Note scarlet eye and black area in front of eye.

[b] BASIC I. First winter kites are similar to adults but their eyes are orangish and flight feathers and greater secondary upperwing coverts have whitish tips. Tails usually show a *narrow dusky subterminal band.*

[c] MOLTING JUVENILE. A more or less complete body molt begins about three months after fledging. Rufous on breast disappears soon after fledging due to both fading and molt.

[d] JUVENILE. Fresh plumage soon after fledging, with strong rufous wash across breast; gray-brown crown and nape; and buffy or white tips to gray-brown back, wing coverts, and flight and tail feathers. Tail shows *narrow dusky subterminal band.* Eye is brown.

[e] ADULT. Appears overall white except for blackish primaries and *black carpal patches.* Secondaries can appear a shade or two darker than coverts. Upperwings are gray with black coverts (not shown). *Tail is completely white.*

[f] JUVENILE. Similar to adult but with rufous wash across breast, narrow dusky subterminal tail band, and pale gray secondaries.

[g] HEAD-ON SILHOUETTE. Soars with wings in a dihedral.

Paddle-winged kite with *thin, deeply hooked beak.* Wingtips extend beyond tail tip. Adult plumage is acquired in three years. Basic I kites are almost like juveniles; Basic II are similar but have darker underparts and adult eye colors by sex.

[a] HEAD-ON SILHOUETTE. Glides with wings cupped.

[b] ADULT MALE. Overall slate gray, with *scarlet eyes* and *bright reddish orange cere, face skin, and legs,* brighter when breeding. Undertail coverts are white. Black tail has white base with sharp line of contrast and square corners.

[c] ADULT MALE. Overall slate gray. Darker flight feathers contrast with paler wing coverts. Uppertail coverts are white.

[d] CUTOUT OF UNDERWING OF BASIC III (SUBADULT) MALE. Similar to that of adult male, but with bold white banding.

[e] ADULT MALE. Overall slate gray. Tail has white base, square corners, and narrow pale band on tip. Note *paddle-shaped wings.*

[f] ADULT FEMALE. Overall dark brown, with rufous feather edging on upperparts and whitish streaks or spotting on dark underparts. Eyes are a darker red than those of adult males. Cere and face skin are yellow, becoming orange-yellow when breeding. Legs are orangish. Tail is like that of adult male. This is an older adult female with dark gray head and darker underparts.

[g] BASIC II MALE. Basic II female is similar, but with darker red eyes; eyes of males are scarlet. Cere and face skin are yellow-orange on males, brighter when breeding. Face pattern is with whitish superciliary lines and small whitish cheek patches and throat. Legs are orangish.

[h] ADULT FEMALE. Dark brown underparts are streaked or mottled whitish. Undersides of wings show pale flight feathers that are narrowly banded, with a wide dark band on trailing edge, and, usually, pale patches at base of outer primaries. Note *paddle-shaped wings.*

[i] JUVENILE. Similar to adult female, but superciliary lines and cheek patches are larger and buffy, eyes are dark brown, lores are grayish, and cere and legs are yellow. Pale edges on upperparts are more extensive. Dusky tail has wide white base with less defined border with dusky.

[j] JUVENILE. Similar to adult female, but superciliary lines and cheek patches are larger and buffy, eyes are dark brown, lores are grayish, and cere and legs are yellow. Pale edges on upperparts are more extensive, and flight feathers and greater coverts have pale tips that form narrow pale lines on upperwings.

[k] JUVENILE. Similar to adult female, but buffy underparts have dark brown streaking. Undersides of wings show pale flight feathers that are narrowly banded, with a narrow dark band on trailing edge. Note *paddle-shaped wings.*

PLATE 5

[a]

[b]

[c]

[d]

[e]

[f]

[g]

[h]

[i]

[j]

[k]

Dark falcon-shaped kite. Note *short outer primary* and *flared tail*. All ages show black spot in front of and black ring around eyes. Adult plumage is acquired in two years. *Wingtips exceed tail tip.*

[a] ADULT MALE. Adults have gray bodies with *whitish secondary bars* and scarlet eyes. Males have whitish heads, black tails, and gray undertail coverts. Wingtips extend beyond tail tip.

[b] ADULT FEMALE. Adults have dark ceres. Adult females have grayish heads, blackish tails with pale outer feathers that have wide dusky tips and pale feather shafts, and whitish barring on undertail coverts.

[c] ADULT MALE. Adults are gray above with *wide whitish secondaries*. Tail tip often appears notched.

[d] ADULT MALE. Adults are gray below with a *narrow white band on tips of secondaries*. Males have whitish heads, black tails, and gray undertail coverts, and usually show rufous in primaries. Note *flared tail* and *short primary projection*.

[e] CUTOUT OF ADULT FEMALE UNDERTAIL. Females have blackish tails with pale outer feathers that have wide dusky tips.

[f] EARLY STAGE SUBADULT (BASIC I) MALE. Subadults appear adultlike from above but lack whitish secondaries and rufous in primaries. Note notch in wing due to molt of inner primaries.

[g] EARLY STAGE SUBADULT (BASIC I) MALE. Subadults show whitish and buffy spots on body, lack adults' whitish secondary bar, and have retained juvenile tails. Subadults have scarlet eyes.

[h] LATE STAGE SUBADULT (BASIC I) FEMALE. Subadults lack adults whitish secondary bar and have juvenile tails. Some individuals have completed the body molt and appear all gray. Note the new inner primaries.

[i] EARLY STAGE SUBADULT (BASIC I) MALE. Subadults in early summer usually show pale spots on underparts, have juvenile tail and flight feathers, and juvenile rufous-brown underwing coverts. They often show active molt in the inner primaries.

[j] LATE STAGE SUBADULT (BASIC I) MALE. Later in summer, subadults have completed the body and covert molt and have uniform gray underparts and underwing coverts. Note white on retained outer primaries. Note *short outer primary* and *flared tail*.

[k] JUVENILE. Juveniles have dark heads with *short whitish superciliaries*, dark eyes, and yellow ceres. Brown backs show rufous feather edges and white spots. Buffy underparts show wide rufous streaks.

[l] JUVENILE. Darker juvenile with heavily marked underparts and dark tail with partial bands.

[m] JUVENILE. Darker juvenile with typical underwing and lacking white bands on folded tail.

[n] JUVENILE. Juveniles show streaked underparts and rufous-brown coverts. Variant with large whitish panel in primaries.

[o] JUVENILE UNDERWING CUTOUT. Variant showing whitish panel and base of secondaries and paler coverts. Note *short outer primary*.

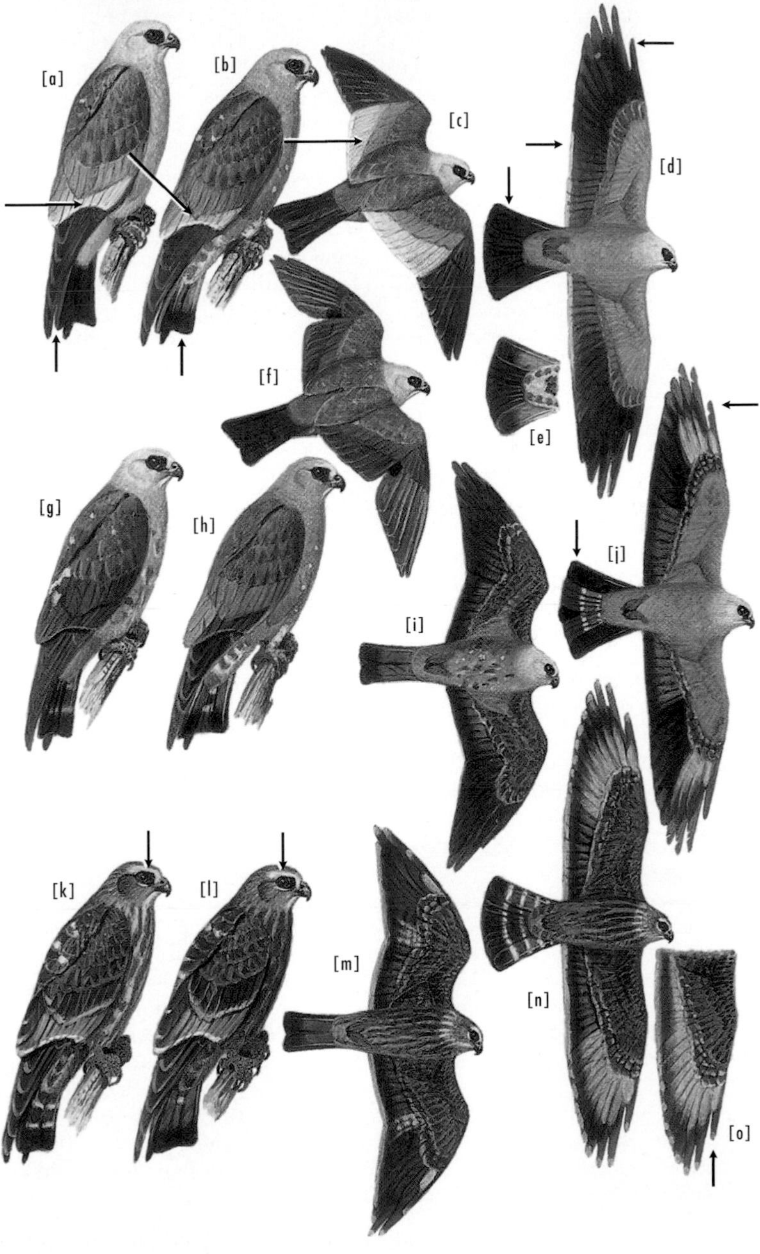

PLATE 6

[a]

[b]

[c]

[d]

[e]

[f]

[g]

[h]

[i]

[j]

[k]

[l]

[m]

[n]

[o]

Large, usually dark-bodied eagle. Bill and cere are usually the same color, never tricolored. All immatures show pale gray lores and yellow gapes. Orangish tarsi are bare above feet. Wingtips almost reach tail tip on perched adults and older immatures, but fall quite short of tip on perched juveniles. Adult plumage is acquired in four or five years.

[a] ADULT. Adults have *white heads,* tail coverts, and *tails* and *bright yellow-orange ceres and beaks.* Eyes are pale yellow.

[b] BASIC IV (SUBADULT). Some first-plumage adults retain some immature characters, especially fine black streaking on the head, dark tips on tail feathers, and a few whitish body feathers and wing coverts.

[c] BASIC III. Appears almost adultlike, but white head has dark streaking and often narrow dark eye lines, white on neck does not extend as far as that of adults, white tail has dark tips and edges, and dark brown body and wing coverts show some white spotting. *Orangish yellow beak shows some dark smudging.*

[d] BASIC II. This is a variant with dark belly and back, and therefore similar to Basic III, but head is darker, beak and cere are more mottled dusky, and eyes are often pale brown.

[e] BASIC II. Most are similar to Basic I with *white belly and triangle* on back, but beak and cere are orangish, eyes are paler, and dark eyestripes are narrower.

[f] BASIC I. Differs from juvenile by *wide buffy crown and superciliaries* that contrast with dark brown cheeks, *white belly* that contrasts with dark brown breast, dark brown upperwing coverts, and shorter tail. This is a paler variant with extensive pale areas on crown, throat, back, belly, and wing coverts. Note pale cere and base of beak.

[g] BASIC I. Differs from juvenile by *wide buffy crown and superciliaries* that contrast with dark brown cheeks, *white belly* that contrasts with dark brown breast, dark brown upperwing coverts, and shorter tail. Note the faded retained juvenile secondaries and wing coverts.

[h] JUVENILE (SUMMER). Juveniles are overall dark, with dark brown eyes and *blackish cere and beak.* Recently fledged juveniles in fresh plumage show crown and superciliary that are only a bit paler than dark brown cheeks and *dark tawny belly* that is only a bit paler than dark brown breast. This variant has an all dark tail.

[i] JUVENILE (WINTER, SPRING). Juveniles are overall dark, with dark brown eyes and *blackish cere and beak.* By winter juveniles show paler brown crown and superciliaries and noticeably *paler tawny belly* that contrasts with dark brown breast. Note tawny back with no white spotting and tawny upperwing coverts that contrast with darker secondaries. Uppertail varies from pale gray with dark tip and edges as shown to all dark to dark with pale oval patch.

PLATE 7

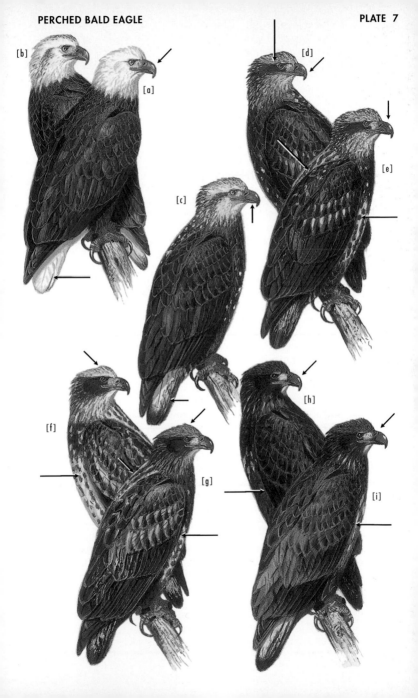

Large, usually dark-bodied eagle. *Head and neck protrude more than half the tail length on flying eagles.* Eagles have proportionally longer wings than most other raptors. Trailing edge of wings is nearly parallel to leading edge, except on juveniles and Basic I eagles. Juveniles have wider wings and longer tails than do older eagles. *Juveniles and Basic I and II eagles show white axillaries* and, usually, white bar on underwing coverts. There are no plumage differences between northern and southern eagles. Adult plumage is acquired in four or five years.

[a] ADULT. Adults with *white heads,* tail coverts, *and tails* and bright yellow-orange ceres and beaks are distinctive. Note long wings.

[b] BASIC IV (SUBADULT). Some first-plumage adults retain some immature characters, especially fine black streaking on the head, dark tips on tail feathers, and a few whitish body feathers and wing coverts.

[c] BASIC III. Appears almost adultlike but *white head* has dark streaking and usually narrow dark eye lines, white on neck does not extend as far as that of adults, *white tail* has dark tips and edges, and dark brown body, wing coverts, and axillaries show some white spotting. Outer primaries are almost always new. Rarely a juvenile secondary can be retained on one or both wings.

[d] BASIC II. Similar to Basic I, usually with *white belly,* but beak and cere are more orangish, eyes are paler, and dark eye-stripes are narrower. Trailing edge of narrow wings is usually smooth, as molt of the secondaries is usually finished, however, one or two longer, pointed juvenile secondaries (S4 or S9 or both) can occasionally be retained. Outer primary is almost always juvenile. Dark legs contrast with white belly.

[e] BASIC I. Differs from juvenile by wide buffy crown and superciliaries, *white belly* that contrasts with dark brown breast, and shorter tail. Distinctive *ragged trailing edge of wings* is due to mix of new darker, shorter and retained longer, pointed secondaries. Underside of tail is usually mottled pale gray with dark band on tip and *dark edges.* Dark legs contrast with white belly.

[f] JUVENILE. Juveniles have dark underparts, but tawny belly contrasts with dark brown breast. Undersides of some flight feathers usually show whitish wash, especially inner primaries and secondaries. Trailing edge of wings, compared to older eagles, is more rounded and serrated, with all secondaries about the same length as their neighbors. Underside of long tail is usually mottled pale gray with dark band on tip and *dark edges* but can be completely dark.

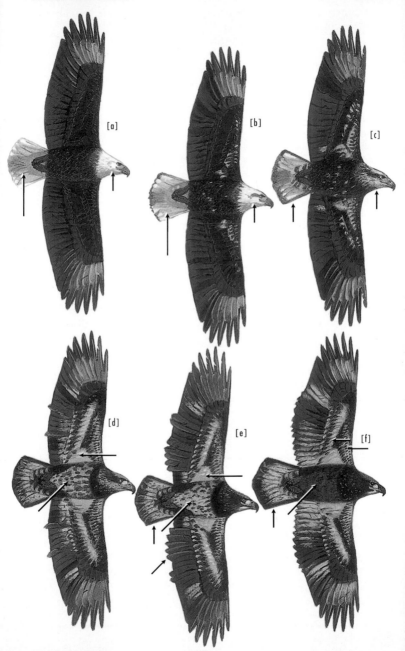

1 . WHITE-TAILED EAGLE *Haliaeetus albicilla*   P. 288
Vagrant. Large dark-bodied eagle. Bill and cere are usually the
same color, never tricolored. *Wingtips of flying eagles show seven
"fingers"* (vs. six on Bald Eagles). Wingtips reach or almost reach
tail tip on perched adults and older immatures, but fall short of
tip on perched juveniles. Adult plumage is acquired in four or five
years, and plumages of each age are somewhat similar to those of
Bald Eagles.

[a] ADULT. *Head and neck vary from light brown to creamy.* Head usually
shows narrow dark eye lines. Color of neck bleeds into upper
breast and back, lacking a sharp line of contrast. Eyes are yellow,
and beak and cere are lemon yellow.

[b] JUVENILE. Overall dark with tawny mottling on body and wing coverts.
Eyes are dark brown, and beak is blackish. All immatures show
pale gray lores and yellow gapes.

[c] ADULT. Head and neck vary from light brown to creamy, with color
bleeding onto upper breast and back, lacking a line of contrast.
Short white tail has a wedge-shaped tip. Underwings and belly
are dark brown. *Undertail coverts are dark brown.*

[d] JUVENILE. Juveniles have tawny underparts with dark brown spotting,
usually a bit heavier on the breast, but without a sharp line of
contrast between breast and belly. Trailing edge of wings, compared to older eagles, is more rounded and serrated, with all secondaries, except for shorter inner two, about the same length as
their neighbors. Whitish axillaries are usually noticeable. Undersides of longer whitish *tail shows white spikes on dark tip* and dark
edges.

2 . STELLER'S SEA EAGLE *Haliaeetus pelagicus*   P. 291
Vagrant. Huge dark-bodied eagle. They are unmistakable, with
huge beaks; adult's white wing patches; and *long, wedge-shaped
white tails.* Trailing edge of wings is more curved than those of
Bald and White-tailed Eagles. Wingtips fall quite short of tip of
long tail on perched eagles. Adult plumage is acquired after four
or five years.

[a] ADULT. *Huge beak, cere, and orange-yellow face skin* are distinctive.
Note the *white shoulders.*

[b] JUVENILE. Overall dark brown with dark brown eyes. *Huge yellow beak
is tinged with brown. Cere and face skin are yellow.*

[c] ADULT. Mostly dark with white on leading edges of underwings and
long white tail is extremely wedge-shaped. Note *huge orange-yellow beak* and white legs.

[d] JUVENILE. Similar in shape to adults, but white on underwings is on
base of primaries and axillaries, legs are dark, and *long, wedge-
shaped white tail* usually shows dark tips.

1[a]

1[b]

1[c]

1[d]

2[a]

2[b]

2[c]

2[d]

Long-winged, long-tailed, medium-sized raptor that shows *white uppertail covert patch in all plumages*. Dark hood and slow quartering low flight with wings held in a strong dihedral are diagnostic. Wingtips of perched harriers fall quite short of tail tip. All show *owllike facial disk*. Both sexes have a similar Basic I plumage, and juveniles differ by sex in eye color.

[a] SUBADULT (BASIC I) MALE. Similar to adult male, but gray areas on head, neck, breast, back, and wing coverts have a brownish cast and underparts are more heavily marked with brownish rufous.

[b] ADULT MALE. Head, neck, and upper breast are gray, giving a hooded look. Eye is orange-yellow. Back is a darker sooty gray, and wing coverts are a mix of gray and dark sooty gray. Whitish underparts show small rufous spots. Note long legs.

[c] SUBADULT (BASIC I) MALE. Similar to adult male. Undersides of flight feathers often show black banding, and markings on underparts and underwing coverts are heavier and browner. Wingtips of harriers often appear pointed. Note *white uppertail coverts*.

[d] ADULT MALE. Appears whitish from below, with gray hood, black tips on outer primaries, and *black band on tips of secondaries*. Rufous spotting on underparts only seen up close. Note long wings and tail.

[e] SUBADULT (BASIC I) FEMALE. Very similar to adult females, but their eyes are usually pale brown, underparts are more rufous, and neck and upperparts average darker. Note *owllike facial disk*.

[f] ADULT FEMALE. Dark brown head and neck have rufous-buff streaks. Back and wing coverts are dark brown, with rufous-buff mottling on median coverts. Eyes are yellow. Note *owllike facial disk*.

[g] ADULT FEMALE. Appears buffy from below, with completely streaked underparts and small barred area on flanks. Note dark head and neck giving a *hooded look*. Secondaries have noticeable white bands; compare to juvenile in Fig. n. Note long wings and tail.

[h] FLIGHT SILHOUETTE. Flight is with wings held in a strong dihedral.

[i] JUVENILE MALE HEAD (SPRING). Eyes become yellowish over winter.

[j] JUVENILE MALE HEAD (WINTER). Eyes gray-brown to greenish-yellow.

[k] JUVENILE FEMALE HEAD (SPRING). Eyes become brown over the winter, and underparts have faded to buffy or creamy by spring.

[l] JUVENILE FEMALE (FALL/WINTER). Similar to adult females but have rufous underparts and lack rufous-buff streaks on neck and dark spots on leg feathers. Note *owllike facial disk*.

[m] JUVENILE FEMALE. Similar to adult females but have rufous underparts and lack rufous-buff neck streaks. Note *white uppertail coverts*.

[n] JUVENILE FEMALE. Juveniles have rufous underparts with streaking restricted usually to upper breast and flanks and lacking flank barring. Note *dark patch on underwings* and long wings and tail.

Smallest hawk. Legs are sticklike. Most figures below are of race *velox*. Wingtips reach less than halfway down tail.

[a] ADULT MALE. Head always appears rounded; hackles are never raised. *Crown and nape are same color. Tail tip has square corners and narrow white terminal band.* Breeding males show orangish legs.

[b] ADULT FEMALE. *Crown and nape are same color.* Back color of females is browner than that of males, especially in spring and summer. *Tail tip has slightly rounded corners and narrow white terminal band.*

[c] ADULT FEMALE, *PEROBSCURUS*. Similar to *velox* but darker. Some adults have rufous breasts and thighs and rufous on undertail coverts.

[d] ADULT FEMALE, *SUTTONI*. Similar to *velox*, but breast, flanks, and thighs are uniformly rufous.

[e] ADULT FEMALE. *Wrists are pushed forward* on soaring hawks. Note squarish corners of tail tip.

[f] HEAD-ON SILHOUETTE. Soars and glides with wings level.

[g] ADULT FEMALE. *Small, rounded head barely projects beyond wrists on gliding birds. Crown and nape are the same color.*

[h] ADULT FEMALE. *Small, rounded head barely projects beyond wrists on gliding birds.*

[i] JUVENILE HEAD. Eye color is orangish by spring. Note long narrow pale superciliary line.

[j] JUVENILE MALE. Usually has narrow dark brown streaking on underparts. *Tail tip shows square corners and narrow pale terminal band* and often shows a notch when folded. Outer tail feathers are nearly as long as others.

[k] JUVENILE FEMALE. Juvenile females usually have wide rufous streaking on underparts that extends onto the belly and bold rufous barring on the flanks, however, some females show malelike narrower dark streaking. *Tail tip shows slightly rounded corners and narrow pale terminal band.* Outer tail feathers are nearly as long as others.

[l] JUVENILE FEMALE, *PEROBSCURUS*. Averages darker than *velox*, with pale superciliary line reduced or absent, especially on females. Leg feathers are mostly rufous, and undertail covers usually have rufous markings.

[m] JUVENILE FEMALE, *SUTTONI*. Similar to *velox* but with flanks and thighs solid rufous.

[n] JUVENILE FEMALE. *Wrists are pushed forward* on soaring hawks. Flight feathers of most females *lack a crisp narrow dark band* on tips of underwings.

[o] JUVENILE MALE. *Small, rounded head barely projects beyond wrists on gliding birds.* Upperparts appear uniformly dark brown, with little or no pale spotting or feather edges.

[p] JUVENILE MALE. *Small, rounded head barely projects beyond wrists on gliding birds. Tail tip shows square corners and narrow pale terminal bands* and often shows a notch when folded.

COOPER'S HAWK *Accipiter cooperii* P. 160

Medium-sized hawk. Females are separably larger than males. Legs are thick. Wingtips reach less than halfway down tail.

[a] ADULT MALE. Adult males have gray cheeks and napes. *Head appears square* when hackles are raised. *Dark crown contrasts with paler nape.* Note wide *white band on rounded tail tip*.

[b] ADULT FEMALE. Adult females have rufous cheeks, sometimes with a gray cast, gray napes, and grayish upperparts that usually fade to brownish by spring and summer. Head appears rounded when hackles are not raised. *Dark crown contrasts with paler nape.* Note *wide white band on tail tip*.

[c] FIRST-PLUMAGE ADULT (SUBADULT) FEMALE. Females in their first adult plumage have rufous cheeks and napes, bright yellow, occasionally orangish, eyes, and may show retained juvenile feathers.

[d] ADULT MALE. Soars with *leading edge of wings straight out from body*, emphasizing long head and neck. Note *rounded corners* and *wide white band on tip of long tail*.

[e] FIRST-PLUMAGE ADULT (SUBADULT) MALE. Glides with wrists forward, but *head still projects far beyond wrists. Dark crown contrasts with paler back.* Males in first adult plumage have gray napes, rufous cheeks, orangish eyes.

[f] ADULT MALE. Glides with wrists forward, but *head still projects far beyond wrists. White tips of outer tail feathers are short of tip of long tail.*

[g] HEAD-ON SILHOUETTE. *Soars usually with wings in a dihedral*, but glides with wings level.

[h] JUVENILE MALE. Juveniles have narrow dark brown streaks on underparts; some western hawks have heavily streaked belly and narrow dark streaks on undertail coverts. *Head appears square when hackles are raised. Pale superciliaries are usually faint or absent.*

[i] JUVENILE FEMALE. Upperparts are brown with rufous feather edges and pale areas. Head appears rounded when hackles are not raised. *Outer tail feathers are shorter than others.* Eyes are greenish yellow in autumn. *Streaking often ends on belly.*

[j] JUVENILE HEAD. Juveniles have bright yellow eyes by spring. Some can show pale superciliaries.

[k] JUVENILE. *Soars with leading edge of wings straight out from body*, emphasizing long head and neck. Most juveniles show *unmarked bellies,* and many, like this hawk, show *tawny cheeks.* All juvenile Cooper's show a crisp narrow dark band on the trailing edge of underwings.

[l] JUVENILE. Glides with wrists forward, but *head still projects far beyond wrists.* Note rounded corners and wide white band on tail tip.

[m] JUVENILE. Glides with wrists forward, but *head still projects far beyond wrists.* Some western hawks show streaked belly and barred flanks. *White tips of outer tail feathers are short of tip* of long tail.

PLATE 12

Largest hawk. Females are somewhat larger than males. Long wings give flying Goshawks a buteo-like appearance. *Pale superciliaries are conspicuous* in all plumages. Most figures are of race *atricapillus*. Wingtips reach less than halfway down tail.

[a] ADULT FEMALE. *Distinctive black head shows wide whitish superciliary lines.* Upperparts of adults are blue-gray, usually somewhat darker on females. *Grayish underparts* show fine dark vermiculations and narrow black shaft streaks. Tip on long tail is wedge-shaped.

[b] SUBADULT FEMALE. Hawks in Basic I plumage resemble adults but have darker upperparts and orangish eyes; females usually show coarser barring on underparts. Note *black head with wide white superciliary lines.*

[c] SUBADULT MALE. Hawks in Basic I plumage resemble adults but have darker upperparts; males often show bold barring only on the breast. Undersides of flight feathers show bold dark banding. Tail bands are more prominent than are those of adults. Note retained juvenile secondaries and also retained feathers on uppertail and upperwing coverts.

[d] ADULT MALE. Grayish underparts show fine dark vermiculations. Flight feathers show faintly banded primaries and unbanded secondaries. White undertail coverts are spread widely during display flights.

[e] ADULT MALE. *Uppersides of adult's wings are two-toned:* blackish flight feathers contrast with blue-gray coverts. Wingtips appear rather pointed during active flight. Tip on long tail is wedge-shaped.

[f] HEAD-ON SILHOUETTE. Soars and glides with wings held level.

[g] ADULT, *LAINGI.* Overall darker than adult *atricapillus*, with narrower, less obvious superciliary line. Upperparts are uniformly dark, lacking two-toned appearance.

[h] JUVENILE HEAD. Eye color is usually orangish by spring.

[i] JUVENILE. Typical juvenile with *wide buffy superciliary lines, pale bar on wing coverts,* and heavily streaked underparts. Note *narrow pale "highlights" between tail bands.* Creamy *undertail coverts usually have dark spotting or streaking.* Wingtips reach less than halfway down tail.

[j] JUVENILE. Paler individual with narrow dark streaking on underparts and lightly marked undertail coverts.

[k] JUVENILE, *LAINGI.* Overall darker than juvenile *atricapillus*, with narrower, less obvious superciliary line. Lacks pale band on wing coverts.

[l] JUVENILE. *Wings are longer than those of other accipiters,* with wide, *bulging secondaries that taper to narrower primaries.* Undertail coverts show dark blobs.

[m] JUVENILE. Upperwings show pale bar on wing coverts. Wingtips appear rather pointed during active flight. Note *irregular tail bands, with narrow pale "highlights" between them.* Tip of long tail is wedge-shaped.

COMMON BLACK-HAWK *Buteogallus anthracinus* P. 170

Large dark buteonine with wide wings and long legs. They soar and glide with wings level.

[a] ADULT FEMALE HEAD. Adult females often show a white bar under each eye. On adults, *orange-yellow cere color bleeds onto the base of the otherwise black beak,* and lores appear orange-yellow. Adults' eyes are dark brown.

[b] ADULT MALE. Adults are overall black except for a *wide white band through the middle of the tail.* Occasionally a frosty cast to the upperparts is noticeable. *Long legs are orange-yellow.* Wingtips fall somewhat short of tail tip. Note the *short primary projection* beyond the long secondaries.

[c] ADULT. Adults appear overall black from above except for the *wide white band* through the middle of the tail and the narrow white terminal tail band. Occasionally a frosty cast to the upperparts is noticeable. *Rufous to buffy markings* on the flight feathers and the resultant dark band on tips can be seen in good light. Tail appears short because of the wide wings.

[d] ADULT FEMALE. Adults appear overall black from below except for *small white marks* at the bases of the outer primaries, *wide white band* through the middle of the tail, and narrow white terminal tail band. *Rufous to buffy markings on flight feathers* and the resultant dark band on tips can be seen in good light. Some females show a narrow white partial band near base of tail. Tail appears short because of the wide wings.

[e] JUVENILE. Juveniles are overall dark brown with heavily streaked rufous-buffy underparts. Note *strong face pattern* of buffy superciliaries, dark eye lines, buffy cheeks, and wide dark malar stripes that extend down the sides of the neck onto the sides of the upper breast. Juveniles' eyes are medium brown. Lores are pale gray. *Blackish tail shows irregular white bands* and narrow white tip. Wingtips fall short of tail tip.

[f] JUVENILE. Juveniles appear dark brown from above, except for *buffy primary panels* and *heavily banded whitish tail.* Wings of juveniles are narrower and tail is longer than those of adults. *Blackish tail shows irregular white bands* and narrow white tip.

[g] JUVENILE. Juveniles appear buffy below with paler *buffy primary panels,* heavily streaked underparts, and *dark brown tail with irregular white bands.* Note *wide dark malar stripes that extend down sides of neck onto upper breast* and dark flanks.

1 . HARRIS'S HAWK *Parabuteo unicinctus*   **P. 175**

Distinctive dark, long-legged, long-tailed buteonine. Wings appear somewhat *paddle-shaped. Rufous wing coverts* and *extensive white at base of tail* are diagnostic. Wingtips reach only halfway down long tail.

[a] **ADULT.** Adults appear overall dark brown, except for *rufous areas on shoulders and leg feathers.* Note *wide white tip of long tail.*

[b] **ADULT.** Adults appear overall dark brown, except for *rufous underwing coverts* and *large white area at base and wide tip of tail.*

[c] **HEAD-ON SILHOUETTE.** Glides on cupped wings.

[d] **JUVENILE.** Juveniles appear similar to adults but have whitish undersides of primaries and whitish streaking on underparts, heavier on the belly. White band on tail tip is narrower than that of adults. This a dark-bellied variant with uniform rufous leg feathers.

[e] **JUVENILE.** Juveniles appear similar to adults but have pale streaking on their heads and whitish streaking on their underparts, heavier on the belly. Males average paler on underparts. Leg feathers are finely barred rufous and white. White band on tail tip is narrower than that of adults.

[f] **JUVENILE.** Juveniles appear adultlike except for pale markings on secondaries, pale tips on greater coverts, and narrower white tail tip.

2 . GRAY HAWK *Buteo nitidus*   **P. 178**

Crow-sized, long-tailed accipiter-like buteo. *White U visible at base of uppertail* noticeable on flying hawks. Wingtips of perched hawks reach only halfway down long tail.

[a] **ADULT.** Adults are overall gray, with *underparts finely barred white and gray. Long tail shows one wide and one narrow white band.* Note bright orange-yellow cere and legs.

[b] **ADULT.** Adults appear dark gray from above, with *white U at base of tail* and one wide and one narrow white band in long black tail.

[c] **ADULT.** Adults appear pale from below, with *narrow black tips on outer primaries* and long tail with one wide and one narrow white band.

[d] **JUVENILE.** Crown, nape, and upperparts are dark brown. Note *striking pattern* of dark eye lines and malar stripes on white face. Cere is bright yellow, and *long tail has 6 or more progressively wider, chevron-shaped dark bands.*

[e] **JUVENILE.** Juveniles appear dark brown above with *white U at base of long tail* and *6 or more progressively wider bands* toward tip. Note distinct dark eye line.

[f] **JUVENILE.** Juveniles appear much like juvenile Cooper's Hawks in flight, with leading edge of wings held perpendicular to body but have longer wings, fainter dark markings on underwings, and *6 or more progressively wider bands* and *square corners on tail.* Faint but distinct crescent-shaped pale panels are often visible near wingtips of backlit wings.

1 . ROADSIDE HAWK *Buteo magnirostris*   **P. 297**
Vagrant. Crow-sized, long-tailed, accipiter-like buteo. *Belly is
barred* in all. Wings appear *paddle-shaped* and *buffy U at base of
tail* is noticeable. Wingtips reach about halfway to tail tip.

[a] ADULT. Head is gray to gray-brown, and upperparts are brown with a
gray cast in fresh plumage. *Dark brown to gray-brown breast forms
a bib.* Tail has equal-width dark and light brown bands.

[b] JUVENILE. Similar to adult but has *wide pale superciliary lines*,
orangish eyes, yellower legs, brown head and back lacking gray
cast, and more and narrower equal-width tail bands.

[c] ADULT UPPERWING. Some n. Mexican adults show rufous in primaries.

[d] ADULT. Head and upperparts are gray-brown to brown. *Note buffy U
on uppertail coverts* and equal-width dark and light tail bands.

[e] ADULT. *Dark breast and barred belly are diagnostic.* Some adults have
fine whitish streaks in bib. Note *paddle-shaped wings*.

2 . RED-SHOULDERED HAWK *Buteo lineatus*   **P. 182**
Medium-sized buteo with long tail and legs. Wingtips reach three-
quarters of way down tail on adults; somewhat less on juveniles.

[a] ADULT, *LINEATUS*. Note *rufous shoulder, black-and-white checkered wing
coverts, black tail with narrow white bands,* and long legs. Adult
lineatus has noticeable brown streaking on rufous barred underparts.

[b] ADULT, *ALLENI/TEXANUS*. Similar to *lineatus* but lacking dark streaks on
underparts. Heads average paler and backs grayer.

[c] ADULT, *EXTIMUS*. Similar to *lineatus*, but rufous underparts are noticeably paler, head and back are gray, and it is noticeably smaller.

[d] ADULT, *ELEGANS*. Similar to *lineatus* but more brightly colored. Head is
tawny, rufous breast lacks white barring, gray back and scapulars
have whitish markings, and tail bands are wider.

[e] JUVENILE, *LINEATUS*. Brown head shows buffy superciliaries and cheeks,
dark malar area, and creamy throat. Rufous shoulder sometimes
noticeable. Note *three pale bands on folded secondaries* and long
legs. Juvenile *lineatus* has only dark streaking, no barring, on
creamy underparts. Creamy leg feathers and undertail coverts
usually have sparse dark spotting. Tail often shows wider dark
band on tip (not shown). *Dark uppertail shows narrow pale bands.*

[f] JUVENILE, *ALLENI/TEXANUS*. Similar to *lineatus*, but underparts are also
barred, heavier on breast, leg feathers are usually barred, and tail
usually lacks rufous on base and wide unbanded tip.

[g] JUVENILE, *EXTIMUS*. Similar to *lineatus*, but underparts are narrowly
streaked, heavier on breast (bib), leg feathers are barred, and tail
lacks rufous on base and wide unbanded tip.

[h] JUVENILE, *ELEGANS*. Upperparts and tail are adultlike. Head has tawny
superciliaries and cheeks and dark throat. Underparts are heavily
barred.

(Flying figures only; perched hawks are shown on Plate 16.)

Medium-sized buteo with long tail. Adults have rufous under-parts and underwing coverts and *bold black-and-white markings on flight feathers; their black tail shows 3 or 4 narrow white bands.* Juveniles are browner, with brown streaking or barring on pale underparts. Wings are pressed forward when soaring. They show *crescent-shaped primary panels* in all plumages.

[a] ADULT, *LINEATUS*. Underparts and underwing coverts appear rufous; undersides of *flight feathers are boldly marked black and white.* Note *whitish crescent-shaped primary panel* on backlit wing. Adult *lineatus* has brown head and brown streaking on underparts. *Long black tail has 3 or 4 narrow white bands.*

[b] ADULT, *EXTIMUS*. Similar to *lineatus*, but head is gray and rufous under-parts are paler and lack dark streaking.

[c] ADULT, *LINEATUS*. *Bold black-and-white pattern* on flight feathers and *white crescent-shaped primary panel* are distinctive. *Rufous lesser wing covert patches* are usually noticeable.

[d] ADULT, *ELEGANS*. Somewhat similar to *lineatus* but overall more brightly colored. Head is tawny, breast is uniform rufous, lacks white bar-ring, and white tail bands are wider.

[e] HEAD-ON SILHOUETTE. Soars with wings level.

[f] HEAD-ON SILHOUETTE. Glides with wings cupped: wrists up and tips down.

[g] JUVENILE, *LINEATUS*. Buffy underparts of juvenile *lineatus* have a vari-able amount of dark streaking and are never barred. Creamy un-derwings show *crescent primary panels* on backlit wings. *Long dark tail shows narrow pale bands*, usually with a wider dark band on tip.

[h] JUVENILE, *LINEATUS*. Upperparts of juveniles are dark brown, with *tawny primary panels*, and *dark tail with narrow pale bands* is distinctive. Three rows of pale spots on upper secondaries can often be seen, but rufous on lesser wing coverts usually cannot be seen.

[i] JUVENILE, *ALLENI/TEXANUS*. Similar to *lineatus*, but underparts are more heavily marked with arrowhead-shaped barring, as well as streaks, heavier on breast; leg feathers are usually barred; and tail usually has wide unbanded area on tip.

[j] JUVENILE, *ELEGANS*. Similar to adult *lineatus* (Fig. c) on uppersides, with *rufous shoulders.*

[k] JUVENILE, *ELEGANS*. Somewhat similar to other juveniles but has more heavily marked underwing coverts and underparts, white *cres-cent-shaped primary panels*, and *adultlike tail pattern.*

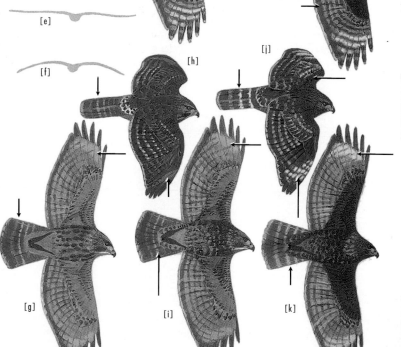

Crow-sized, short-legged buteo. *Wingtips of flying hawks are relatively pointed for a* buteo. Wingtips of hawks reach three-quarters of way down tail.

[a] ADULT, LIGHT MORPH. Head, back, and wing coverts are unmarked dark brown. White underparts have a variable amount of rufous-brown barring. *Dark tail has one wide pale gray band.* Note short legs.

[b] ADULT, LIGHT MORPH. Some adults show dark bibs. This variant shows no markings on undertail coverts. Adults have medium brown eyes.

[c] ADULT, DARK MORPH. Overall dark brown. Tail as in light-morph adult. Note short legs.

[d] ADULT, DARK MORPH. Body and coverts are dark brown. Flight feathers and tail are same as those of light-morph adults. *Wingtips of gliding hawks are noticeably pointed.*

[e] ADULT. Adults appear uniformly dark brown on uppersides, with *one prominent wide pale gray tail band.* Many show a narrower pale gray basal band as well. Black wingtips are often noticeable.

[f] ADULT, LIGHT MORPH. Pale underwings are usually unmarked (but can have rufous coverts), except for wide dark band on tips and trailing edges. This variant shows a dark bib.

[g] HEAD-ON SILHOUETTE. Soars and glides with wings held level.

[h] JUVENILE, LIGHT MORPH. Dark brown upperparts can show narrow pale feather edges on scapulars and wing coverts. Some show little or no streaking on underparts. This variant shows an accipiter-like tail pattern. Note *dark secondaries lacking pale markings.*

[i] JUVENILE, LIGHT MORPH. Most juveniles show dark streaking on underparts and brown uppertail with narrow dark bands, subterminal widest. More heavily marked hawks show dark barring on flanks and leg feathers. Note *dark secondaries lacking pale markings.*

[j] JUVENILE, DARK MORPH. Overall dark brown. Some juveniles only show faint rufous markings on breast. Tail as in light-morph juvenile.

[k] JUVENILE, DARK MORPH. Body and coverts are dark brown. Flight feathers and tail are same as those of light-morph juveniles. Some dark juveniles show rufous streaking on underparts.

[l] JUVENILE. Juveniles appear dark brown on uppersides, with faint pale markings on upperwing coverts. This variant shows an accipiter-like tail pattern. Wingtips of gliding hawks are noticeably pointed.

[m] JUVENILE, LIGHT MORPH. Pale underwings are relatively unmarked except for dusky band on tips and trailing edges. This hawk shows almost unmarked underparts.

[n] JUVENILE, LIGHT MORPH. Most juveniles show streaking on underparts, often with a clear area in midbreast. This variant shows barring on outer primary tips and barred flanks.

Crow-sized buteo with relatively long wings. Occurs in both dark and light morphs. Most often seen in flight. *Wingtips of flying hawks are relatively pointed. Wingtips of perched hawks reach tail tip.*

[a] ADULT LIGHT MORPH. White underparts are unmarked. Brown tail has indistinct pattern of wide dark subterminal band and several other narrower dark bands. Note *rufous patch on side of neck* and *white forehead and lores.*

[b] ADULT DARK MORPH. Overall dark brown. Tail as in light-morph adult, but dark bands can be wider. Note *white forehead and lores.*

[c] ADULT LIGHT MORPH. White body and wing coverts are unmarked; coverts contrast with grayish secondaries and inner primaries. White undertail shows dark subterminal band and several, often indistinct, narrower ones. Note *oval white patches on primaries* and *dark cheeks and narrow white throat.*

[d] ADULT DARK MORPH. Tail as in light-morph adult, but dark bands are wider. Note *oval white patches on primaries.*

[e] HEAD-ON SILHOUETTE. Glides with wings held level or slightly raised and with *wingtips curved noticeably upward.*

[f] ADULT LIGHT MORPH. Adults appear uniformly dark brown on upper-sides, with indistinct banding on tail. *Wingtips of gliding hawks are noticeably pointed.*

[g] JUVENILE LIGHT MORPH. Note strong face pattern. Back and wing coverts are brown, with some faint narrow pale feather edging on coverts, and contrast with darker flight feathers. Creamy underparts are unmarked except for a few narrow dark streaks on sides of breast. Brown tail has indistinct pattern of wide dusky subterminal band and several other narrower incomplete bands.

[h] JUVENILE LIGHT MORPH. Creamy body usually shows only a few narrow dark streaks on sides of upper breast. Unmarked creamy wing coverts contrast little with whitish bases of secondaries. *Grayish secondaries contrast somewhat with white primaries.* White undertail shows dusky subterminal band and several, often indistinct, narrower ones. (Mexican juveniles show distinct, equal-width dark bands.)

[i] JUVENILE DARK MORPH. Overall dark brown, except for pale patches on cheeks and throat and white spotting on belly. Juveniles have pale to medium brown eyes. Brown tail has 5 to 7 equal-width dark bands.

[j] JUVENILE DARK MORPH. Paler dark juvenile with white streaks on belly and wing coverts, sometime breast. Bands on undertail can be adult-like, with subterminal wider. Note *oval white patches on primaries.*

[k] JUVENILE DARK MORPH. Typical dark juvenile with white spotting on breast and wing coverts. *Grayish secondaries contrast somewhat with white primaries.* Undertail shows 5 to 7 equal-width dark bands. Note *oval white patches in primaries.*

Slender, long and pointed-winged buteo. All but darkest or rufous-morph adult males show breast darker than belly, forming a bib. *Underwings usually appear two-toned:* pale coverts contrast with darker flight feathers; *this is the only adult* buteo *with dark undersides of flight feathers.* Wingtips extend beyond tail tip on perched adults. Adult plumages vary in a cline from light to rufous to dark; they are attained after two annual molts. Adults have white bases on outer primaries. Adults' *tails are gray with narrow dark brown bands, subterminal much wider.*

[a] LIGHT-MORPH ADULT MALE. Palest adults with gray faces, *orange-rufous to rufous breasts* (forming dark bib), and unmarked or lightly marked whitish bellies are almost always males. Note rufous on nape. Light-morph adults have white foreheads and throats.

[b] LIGHT-MORPH ADULT. Darker adults with brown faces, *rufous-brown breasts*, and spotted bellies can be either male or female but are more often the latter. This is a variant showing a lightly marked belly, which can be quite heavily marked.

[c] LIGHT INTERMEDIATE ADULT FEMALE. Darker adults with dark brown heads and *breasts* and heavily barred bellies are usually females. Males this heavily marked can also have brown or rufous breasts.

[d] HEAD-ON SILHOUETTE. Soars and glides with wings in a strong dihedral.

[e] LIGHT-MORPH ADULT. All light-morph adults have a noticeable dark bib and two-toned underwings. Note pointed wingtips and relatively long tail with wide subterminal band.

[f] RUFOUS-MORPH ADULT MALE. Similar to light-morph adult male but with rufous belly, hence lacks dark bib. *White undertail coverts contrast with rufous belly.*

[g] RUFOUS-MORPH ADULT. Females and some males have dark brown head and breast and rufous belly. *White undertail coverts contrast with rufous belly.*

[h] RUFOUS-MORPH ADULT MALE. Underparts of males appear uniformly rufous, lacking dark bib. Underwing coverts vary from rufous to creamy but always appear two-toned. White undertail coverts contrast with rufous belly. Wingtips appear very pointed when bird is gliding.

[i] DARK INTERMEDIATE ADULT. Appears overall dark brown but with rufous barring on lower belly and leg feathers and *small white areas on forehead* and throat. *White undertail coverts contrast with dark belly.*

[j] DARK-MORPH ADULT. Darkest adults are overall dark brown or black, except for pale lores and *undertail coverts that contrast with dark belly* but are rarely also dark.

[k] DARK-MORPH ADULT. Darkest adults are overall dark brown or black, with *pale undertail coverts that contrast with dark belly* but are rarely also dark. Underwing coverts are usually dark brown and rufous but can occasionally be completely dark.

Slender, long and pointed-winged buteo. All show strong face pattern of wide buffy superciliaries, narrow dark eye line, and buffy cheeks and throat separated by *wide malar stripes that extend into dark patches on sides of upper breast.* Juvenile and Basic I plumages vary in a cline from pale and lightly marked (light morph) to streaked (rufous or intermediate morph) to mostly dark (dark morph) on underparts, leg feathers, and underwing coverts. Basic I plumage has wider wings and wider subterminal bands on wings and tail. *Underwings usually appear two-toned:* pale coverts contrast with darker flight feathers but are not as contrasting as those of adults. *Wingtips reach or almost reach tail tip.*

[a] LIGHT-MORPH JUVENILE. Underparts are buffy in fresh plumage. Juvenile tail shows equal-width narrow dark bands, but subterminal band often a bit wider. This is a lightly marked variant. Pale scapulars form a V on back of perched juveniles.

[b] LIGHT-MORPH JUVENILE. Paler one-year-old juveniles often have white heads and underparts. Pale feather edges on back and upperwing coverts have worn off, but pale V on scapulars is still noticeable.

[c] HEAD-ON SILHOUETTE. Soars with wings in a strong dihedral.

[d] LIGHT-MORPH JUVENILE. Juveniles have dark patches on sides of upper breast; underparts appear overall buffy. *Underwings are somewhat two-toned.* This is a lightly marked variant.

[e] LIGHT-MORPH BASIC I. One-year-old-plus hawks in autumn have almost acquired Basic I plumage. New flight and tail feathers are darker, with wider dark subterminal bands. Underparts and underwing coverts appear buffy in late summer, as shown. Note pale areas on retained, faded juvenile outer primaries.

[f] INTERMEDIATE (RUFOUS) JUVENILE. Juveniles with moderate markings on underparts will most likely become rufous-morph adults. Pale scapulars form a V on backs of perched juveniles.

[g] LIGHT INTERMEDIATE JUVENILE. Typical juvenile with some dark markings on underparts and two dark patches on sides of upper breast.

[h] INTERMEDIATE-MORPH JUVENILE. Juveniles with moderate markings on underparts and underwing coverts will most likely become rufous-morph adults. Wingtips appear very pointed on gliding birds.

[i] DARK-MORPH JUVENILE. Underparts are mostly dark brown with some buffy or white mottling and pale throat.

[j] DARK INTERMEDIATE JUVENILE. Underparts are heavily streaked.

[k] DARK-MORPH BASIC I. Darker variant with underparts almost uniformly dark, having few buffy or white spots, mainly on breast.

[l] DARK INTERMEDIATE JUVENILE. Variant with darkish belly and streaked breast.

[m] DARK-MORPH JUVENILE. Underparts are mostly dark brown. *Underwings appear uniformly dark. Pale undertail coverts contrast with darker belly.*

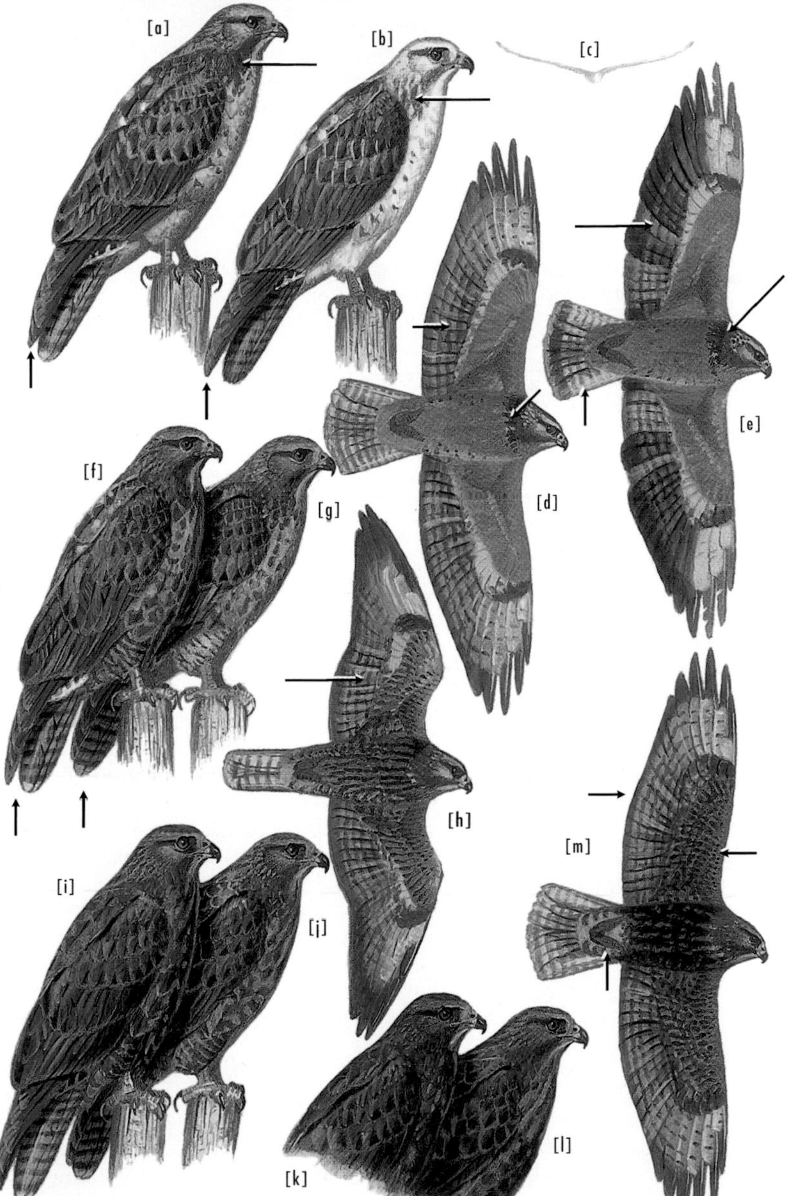
[a]
[b]
[c]
[d]
[e]
[f]
[g]
[h]
[i]
[j]
[k]
[l]
[m]

Large, long-winged buteo. Three immature plumages are juvenile, Basic I, and Basic II. Wings narrow noticeably at body on trailing edges in all plumages. *Wingtips project far beyond tail tip.*

[a] ADULT. Head and back are gray, except for white throat. Note *rufous shoulder patches and rufous wash on scapulars.* White underparts often show fine dark barring on belly, flanks, and leg feathers. *White tail has wide black subterminal band.*

[b] ADULT. Head and back are gray. Upperwings are blackish, with *small rufous patches. Uppertail coverts and rump are white. White tail has wide black subterminal band* and five or more fine dark bands and appears short because of broad wings.

[c] ADULT. Some (younger?) adults have grayish throats. Adults have pale yellow to pale greenish yellow ceres.

[d] ADULT. Gray cheeks and narrow white throats are noticeable. Many adults have unmarked white underparts. *Underwings usually appear two-toned: dark primaries contrast with white coverts and paler secondaries.* Note white bases on outer two or three primaries. *White tail has wide black subterminal band.*

[e] SUBADULT (BASIC II). Similar to adult but head, neck, and back are blackish; belly, flanks, and leg feathers have narrow dark barring; and uppertail often appears somewhat off-white to pale gray.

[f] SUBADULT (BASIC II). Similar to adult but head, neck, and back are blackish; rump is mottled black and white; and *uppertail often appears a mix of off-white and pale gray.*

[g] BASIC I. Head lacks juveniles' pale face patches. *Shoulder patches are rufous,* but scapulars lack rufous wash. Breast is usually white, and black belly and flanks have whitish and rufous mottling. Leg feathers vary from white with rufous barring to blackish with white edges. Uppertail is gray with narrow dusky subterminal band.

[h] BASIC I. Head, neck, and upperparts are black. Note *rufous patches on coverts;* scapulars lack rufous wash. Black rump shows some white markings. *Uppertail coverts are white.* Uppertail is gray with narrow dusky subterminal band and usually five or more fine dark bands or dark marbling. Note the retained faded juvenile outer primaries and two secondaries on each wing.

[i] BASIC I. Some Basic I hawks have a dark breast with *juvenile-like white slash* in center, but head lacks pale patches of juvenile.

[j] BASIC I. Head and neck are black, breast is white, and flanks and belly appear dark with pale mottling. *Underwings are two-toned:* dark coverts, usually including rufous lesser coverts, contrast with pale gray flight feathers, which show a wide dark subterminal band and paler bases on outer two or three primaries. Pale underside of tail shows narrow dusky subterminal band. Note the retained faded juvenile outer primaries and two secondaries on each wing.

PLATE 22

1 . WHITE-TAILED HAWK *Buteo albicaudatus*   **P. 205**

Large, long-winged buteo. *Wings narrow at body on trailing edges.* Juveniles have longer tails and narrower wings compared to adults and older immatures. *Wingtips project somewhat beyond tail tip.*

[a] JUVENILE. Typical juvenile. *Dark head shows pale spots.* Underparts consist of whitish breast and dark belly, latter with narrow whitish feather edges. Dark brown upperparts and upperwing coverts are mottled rufous-buff, with a hint of rufous-buff shoulder patch. *Pale gray uppertail shows numerous narrow dark bands.* Whitish leg feathers and undertail coverts show dark mottling.

[b] JUVENILE. Paler variant with *large pale patch* on head, whitish underparts with a Red-tailed Hawk–like dark belly band, and less dark mottling on leg feathers and undertail coverts.

[c] JUVENILE. Darker variant with reduced pale spots on head, fewer rufous-buff markings on upperparts and upperwing coverts, and a narrow white vertical slash on midbreast.

[d] JUVENILE. Typical juvenile. *Dark head shows pale spots.* Underparts consists of white breast, dark belly with narrow white barring, and whitish undertail coverts. Undersides of long, pointed-tip wings show gray flight feathers that lack a wide dark terminal band and dark coverts with some white mottling and two white lines. Note pale bases on outer two primaries. Pale undertail has numerous, somewhat faint narrow dark bands.

[e] JUVENILE. Darker variant with dark underparts with only a *pale vertical slash in midbreast,* heavily barred undertail coverts, and mostly dark underwing coverts.

2 . ZONE-TAILED HAWK *Buteo albonotatus*   **P. 210**

Large blackish buteo. Silhouette, underwing pattern, and flight habits are like those of Turkey Vultures. Face skin is light gray.

[a] ADULT. Head, body, and wing and tail coverts are black with a grayish bloom. *Black uppertail has one wide and one to two narrow gray bands. Wingtips extend beyond tail tip. Beak is all dark.*

[b] JUVENILE. Similar to adult but lacking grayish bloom and with *white spotting on body.* Wingtips reach tail tip. Cere is dull yellow.

[c] ADULT. Body is entirely black, and underwings are two-toned. Gray flight feathers have *narrow black banding on the outer primaries* and wide black terminal band. Black undertail shows one wide white band and, when spread, one or more narrower white bands.

[d] TAIL CUTOUT. Folded undertail shows only one white band.

[e] TAIL CUTOUT. Spread undertail can show up to four or five narrow bands (female only).

[f] JUVENILE. Similar in silhouette and pattern to adults, but body and coverts show a *variable number of white spots,* paler flight feathers lack wide dark terminal band, and undertail is pale with narrow dusky bands, subterminal wider.

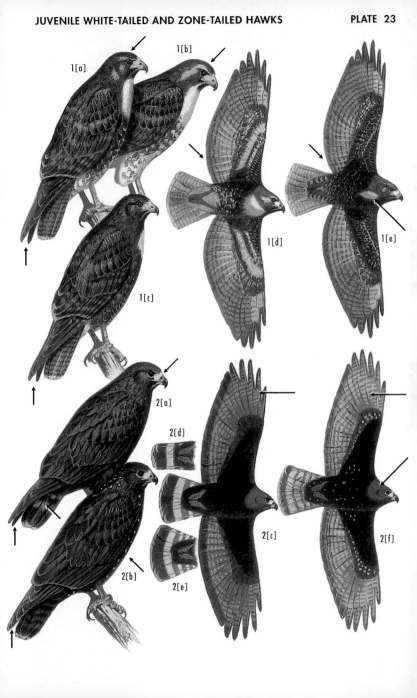

1 . RED-TAILED HAWK *Buteo jamaicensis* **P. 213**

Large widespread buteo. Light-morph adults have *rufous tails,* pale scapular markings forming a V on backs, and *dark patagial marks* on underwings. Wingtips reach or almost reach tail tips on perched Western, Alaskan, and most Florida and Fuertes' adults, but fall somewhat short on perched Eastern and Krider's.

[a] EASTERN ADULT. Typical Eastern adult. Throat is usually white, and belly band is sometimes absent.

[b] KRIDER'S ADULT. Similar to Eastern adult but overall whiter, with *white head,* more white mottling on upperparts, and *white tail with rufous on tip.* Never shows belly band.

[c] EASTERN ADULT. Eastern adults have pale underparts with lightly marked, incomplete belly band (sometimes lacking) and dark patagial marks. Throats are usually white, sometimes offset by a dark collar as shown here but can be streaked or completely dark.

[d] KRIDER'S ADULT. Similar to Eastern adult but with *white head and tail,* smaller faint rufous patagial marks, and no belly band or rufous wash on underparts. Note faint dark semicollar on neck.

[e] FLORIDA ADULT. Somewhat similar to Eastern adult but overall darker, with dark throat, heavier belly band, barring on flanks, and numerous narrow tail bands. Dark streaks on underparts are distinctive. Pale V on scapulars is reduced or absent.

[f] FUERTES' ADULT. Similar to Eastern but with longer wings and lacking dark belly band, sometimes lacking the dark subterminal tail band.

[g] WESTERN LIGHT-MORPH ADULT. Similar to Eastern adult but overall darker, with rufous wash on undersides, barred leg feathers, and usually heavier belly band and dark throat. Pale V on back can be whitish, buffy, or tawny.

[h] ALASKAN LIGHT-MORPH ADULT. Similar to darker Western adults, but with a stronger rufous wash on undersides.

[i] WESTERN LIGHT-MORPH ADULT. Similar to Eastern adult but with dark throat, rufous wash on undersides, heavier belly band, barring on flanks and axillaries, and often numerous narrow tail bands, subterminal wider.

2 . HARLAN'S HAWK *Buteo j. harlani* **P. 222**

Adults are similar in shape and size to Red-tail adults but have *whitish to gray tails* and lack rufous coloration on white underparts. Wingtips fall somewhat short of tail tips.

[a]. HARLAN'S LIGHT-MORPH ADULT. Head show strong face pattern. Blackish brown upperparts lack the warm brown tones of other Red-tails.

[b] HARLAN'S LIGHT-MORPH ADULT. Similar to Krider's adult but has stronger face pattern, *wider and darker patagial marks,* incomplete dark belly band, and gray tail with a variable amount of dusky mottling and a wide dark subterminal band. Undersides of secondaries can be mottled, banded, unmarked, or a mix of them as shown.

1[a]

1[b]

1[c]

1[d]

1[e]

1[f]

1[i]

1[g]

2[a]

1[h]

2[b]

1 . RED-TAILED HAWK *Buteo jamaicensis* **P. 213**

Large widespread buteo. Dark adults have *rufous tails* and usually lack pale V's on their backs. Wingtips reach or almost reach tail tips.

[a] RUFOUS-MORPH ADULT. Head is tawny with dark malar stripes. Dark upperparts lack the pale V of light-morph adults. Breast is rufous, and belly is uniformly dark, often with white spots. *Rufous tail* usually shows multiple bands, subterminal much wider. Rufous leg feathers have narrow dark brown barring.

[b] DARK-MORPH ADULT. Overall dark brown, except for rufous tail, which usually shows multiple dark bands, subterminal much wider. Some dark adults show incomplete multiple tail banding.

[c] DARK INTERMEDIATE ADULT. Similar to rufous-morph adult but with dark head, smaller rufous breast patch, often with dark streaking, and dark leg feathers with rufous edgings.

[d] DARK-MORPH ADULT. Overall dark brown, except for *rufous tail,* which usually shows multiple dark bands, subterminal much wider, and rufous barring on dark brown undertail coverts.

[e] CUTOUT OF TAIL OF HARLAN'S/RED-TAIL INTERGRADE. Some adults show some Harlan's ancestry by pale gray areas on tail base.

[f] RUFOUS-MORPH ADULT. Head is tawny with dark malar stripes. Breast is rufous, and dark belly often shows white spots. *Dark patagial marks* are noticeable. Note heavily barred axillaries.

2 . HARLAN'S HAWK *Buteo j. harlani* **P. 222**

Adults are similar to Red-tail adults but have *gray tails* and *lack rufous coloration* in plumage, except that many show rufous on their uppertail coverts. Wingtips fall somewhat short of tail tips. Tips of outer primaries can be barred or uniformly dark.

[a] INTERMEDIATE-MORPH ADULT. Dark head shows white superciliaries and throat. Breast is streaked dark and white, dark belly shows white spotting, and dark leg feathers have white edges. This variant has a *whitish tail* with some dark mottling and a dusky tip.

[b] DARK-MORPH ADULT. Overall blackish brown. This individual has a *dark gray tail.*

[c] INTERMEDIATE ADULT. Dark head shows white superciliaries and throat. Breast is streaked dark and white, dark belly and underwing coverts show white spotting, and dark undertail coverts have white edges. Undersides of flight feathers can be mottled, banded, or unmarked. Dark patagial marks are obscured by heavy markings on coverts.

[d] DARK INTERMEDIATE ADULT. Overall dark except for some white streaks on breast, a few white spots on dark underwing coverts, and often a white throat. Undersides of flight feathers can be mottled, completely banded, or unmarked.

[e]–[h] TAIL CUTOUTS SHOWING VARIATION. Tails vary from pale to dark gray, with dark mottling or barring or both.

1 . RED-TAILED HAWK *Buteo jamaicensis* P. 213
   Large widespread buteo. Light-morph juveniles have brown tails
   with narrow equal-width dark brown bands, subterminal sometimes wider, and pale scapular markings forming a V on upperparts. Juveniles always show *two-toned upperwings:* paler outer
   half of wing (primaries and primary coverts) contrasts with darker
   inner half. Compared to adults, juveniles have narrower wings
   and longer tails. *Wingtips fall somewhat short of tail tips.*

[a] EASTERN JUVENILE. Typical juvenile with strong face pattern, belly band
   of short dark streaks, unmarked breast, and brown tail with many
   narrow equal-width dark bands, subterminal sometimes wider.
   Note pale V on back. Eastern juveniles show white throat.

[b] TAIL CUTOUT SHOWING ALTERNATE PATTERN. On some juveniles, uppertails
   have a rufous cast and subterminal bands are narrow.

[c] EASTERN JUVENILE. Juveniles always show *two-toned upperwings:* paler
   outer half contrasts with darker inner half. Note white U on uppertail coverts and brown tail with many equal-width narrow dark
   bands.

[d] EASTERN JUVENILE. All Red-tailed Hawks show *dark patagial marks.* All
   juveniles show dark belly bands. Eastern juveniles usually have
   white throats, sometimes set off with a narrow dark collar.

[e] KRIDER'S JUVENILE. Similar to Eastern juvenile but with *white head,* uppertail, and uppertail coverts and more whitish spotting on upperwing coverts. Sparse belly band has few dark spots.

[f] KRIDER'S JUVENILE. *White head, uppertail,* and outer wings are distinctive. Crown or nape often shows dark streaks. Bands on base of
   tail are often lacking.

[g] KRIDER'S JUVENILE. Appears overall whitish, with *faint patagial marks*
   and sparse but noticeable belly band of dark spots. Note the *barring on tips of outer primaries.* (Not on juvenile Ferruginous
   Hawks.)

[h] WESTERN JUVENILE. Similar to Eastern juvenile but with darker head
   and upperparts, dark throat, wider, heavier belly band, and dark
   barring on leg feathers. Note pale V on back that can be buffy,
   tawny, or white.

[i] WESTERN JUVENILE. Similar to Eastern juvenile but with darker head and
   upperparts, dark throat, and wider, heavier belly band.

2 . HARLAN'S HAWK *Buteo j. harlani* P. 222
   Juveniles are similar to Red-tail juveniles but *lack warm brown
   tones,* having a colder, more blackish brown coloration, and usually show barred tips on outer primaries. Wingtips fall quite short
   of tail tips.

[a] LIGHT-MORPH JUVENILE. Similar to Krider's juvenile but has no white on
   base of uppertail and shows wide dark malar stripes and more
   blackish upperparts. Note *small dark spike on center of tips of tail
   feathers.*

1 . RED-TAILED HAWK *Buteo jamaicensis*   **P. 213**

Large widespread buteo. Dark juveniles have brown tails with equal-width dark brown bands, subterminal sometimes wider, and usually lack the pale scapular markings that form a V on backs and dark patagial marks on underwings of light morphs. Compared to adults, their wings are narrower and tails are longer. Tips of outer primaries are usually dark, lacking bars. *Wingtips fall a bit short of tail tips.*

[a] RUFOUS-MORPH JUVENILE. Head and upperparts are dark brown. Tawny to white breast is heavily streaked. Wide dark belly band is mottled white. Leg feathers are heavily barred.

[b] RUFOUS-MORPH JUVENILE. Rufous to white breast is heavily streaked, wide dark belly band is mottled white, and underwing coverts are heavily marked, obscuring dark patagial marks. Leg feathers and undertail coverts are heavily barred.

[c] DARK-MORPH JUVENILE. Juveniles always show *two-toned upperwings.* Dark juveniles lack the pale uppertail coverts of light-morph hawks. Dark tail bands are wider than those of light-morph juveniles.

[d] DARK-MORPH JUVENILE. Overall dark brown, with some subtle rufous markings and the row of white spots on the wing coverts. Dark tail bands are wider than those of light-morph juveniles.

[e] DARK INTERMEDIATE JUVENILE. Similar to dark-morph juvenile but with tawny-rufous breast patch that is sometimes streaked and more rufous markings on body and coverts.

[f] DARK-MORPH JUVENILE. Overall dark brown, sometimes with some rufous streaking on underparts and underwing coverts. Tail has equal-width dark bands and patagial marks are obscured.

2 . HARLAN'S HAWK *Buteo j. harlani*   **P. 222**

Juveniles are similar to Red-tail juveniles but have heads and upperparts that *lack warm brown tones* and usually show barred tips on outer primaries. Juveniles always show *two-toned upperwings.* Dark banding on tails is often wavy. *Wingtips fall quite short of tail tips.*

[a] INTERMEDIATE-MORPH JUVENILE. Head shows strong face pattern, with white throat. Breast is streaked. Dark upperparts show whitish spotting, including a pale V on back. Dark tail bands are wide and *wavy.*

[b] DARK INTERMEDIATE JUVENILE. Overall dark except for white superciliaries and throat and a few white streaks on breast.

[c] DARK-MORPH JUVENILE. Overall dark. Dark tail bands are wider. Note *dark spikes on tips of tail feathers.*

[d] INTERMEDIATE-MORPH JUVENILE. Dark, with strong face pattern and streaking on breast. Note barred tips on outer primaries. Note *dark spikes on tips of tail feathers* and secondaries.

1[a]

1[b]

1[c]

1[d]

1[e]

1[f]

2[a]

2[b]

2[c]

2[d]

Large long- and narrow-winged buteo. Ferruginous Hawks have long, tapered wings, large heads, wide gapes, robust chests, and legs feathered down to toes. *Outer primaries have narrow dark tips.* Pale whitish primary panel on upperwings does not include primary coverts (see juvenile Red-tailed Hawk, Pls. 26, 27). *Gape is huge, with yellow extending well below eyes.* Wingtips fall just short of tail tip.

[a] LIGHT-MORPH ADULT. Lightly marked adult with pale head, unmarked underparts, and *whitish leg feathers with narrow rufous barring.* Adults have *rufous upperparts* and white tails with a variable amount of rufous and light gray, often with some narrow dark mottling. Note *dark eye line, large gape, lack of wide dark malar stripe,* and *gray on outer primaries.*

[b] LIGHT-MORPH ADULT. Adult with some markings on head and belly and *rufous leg feathers with narrow dark brown barring.*

[c] LIGHT-MORPH ADULT. Darker adult with dark head and a rufous wash on heavily streaked breast and barred belly. Note *large gape.*

[d] LIGHT-MORPH ADULT. Adults show *rufous upperparts, gray uppersides of flight feathers, unmarked rufous and white tails,* and white upper-tail coverts. Pale panel is restricted to primaries; primary coverts are dark.

[e] LIGHT-MORPH ADULT. Adults show *dark V on belly, unbanded pale rufous undertail, narrow black tips on outer primaries,* and narrow dusky subterminal band on trailing edge of wings. Black comma is shared with many species.

[f] DARK-MORPH ADULT. Overall blackish brown, with gray uppertail and uppersides of primaries. Dark hawks show completely pale lores. Note *gray on outer primaries.*

[g] RUFOUS-MORPH ADULT. Head is blackish brown to dark gray, often with narrow white throat streaks. Back and upperwing coverts are dark brown, with wide dark rufous feather edges, but greater coverts are blackish brown with some rufous feather edges. Underparts are dark brown and dark rufous, often with some white streaks on the breast. *Uppertail is gray.* Note feathered legs and *gray on outer primaries.*

[h] RUFOUS-MORPH ADULT. Head is dark gray and back is blackish brown. Upperwing coverts are blackish brown with wide dark rufous feather edges, but greater coverts are blackish brown with narrow rufous feather edges. Uppertail coverts are rufous with dark centers, and *uppertail is gray,* usually with dark spots near the tips of outer feathers. Note pale primary panels and dark primary coverts. *Gray outer primaries are distinctive.*

[i] RUFOUS-MORPH ADULT. Head is dark gray, body and underwing coverts are dark rufous and dark brown. Note *white crescents at wrist, narrow dark tips of outer primaries,* and *unbanded whitish undertail.*

[j] HEAD-ON SILHOUETTE. Soars with wings in a strong dihedral.

PLATE 28

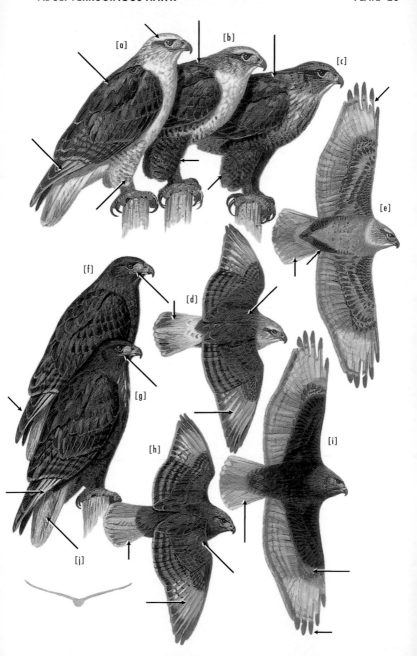

Large buteo. Ferruginous Hawks have long, tapered wings, large heads, *wide gapes*, robust chests, and legs feathered down to toes. Undersides of *outer primaries show narrow dark tips*. Light-morph juveniles in flight show a *dark line on their flanks*. Pale whitish primary panel on upperwings does not include primary coverts (see juvenile Red-tailed Hawk, Pls. 26, 27). Wingtips fall quite a bit short of tail tip.

[a] LIGHT-MORPH JUVENILE. Head shows dark crown and nape, pale superciliaries, dark eye lines, and *white cheeks lacking wide dark malar stripes*. White underparts show a sparse belly band of dark spots. Tail above is white on basal third, with the rest grayish brown with several indistinct dark bands. *White leg feathers have black spots.* White uppertail coverts show large dark spots. Note *gray on outer primaries*.

[b] LIGHT-MORPH JUVENILE. Recently fledged juveniles have rufous wash on breast that fades by fall. Belly band is heavier and more noticeable on this hawk. Note large gape.

[c] LIGHT-MORPH JUVENILE. Head shows dark eye lines and white superciliaries and cheeks. Back and upperwings are dark brown except for pale primary panels, with primary coverts dark. Uppertail is basal third white and the rest grayish brown with three or four indistinct dark bands. White uppertail coverts show large dark spots. *Gray outer primaries are distinctive.* Wingtips are pointed on gliding hawks.

[d] LIGHT-MORPH JUVENILE. Juveniles appear very white from below, with dark wrist commas, *dark line on flanks, narrow dark tips on outer primaries,* and whitish undertail with dusky tip. Note *white cheeks lacking dark malar stripes*.

[e] RUFOUS-MORPH JUVENILE. Overall dark brown except for rufous cast to head and breast, with sharp line between breast and dark brown belly. Dark uppertail shows two or three indistinct darker bands. Note *completely pale lores of dark hawks*.

[f] DARK-MORPH JUVENILE. (Rare.) Like rufous-morph juvenile except that head and breast are dark brown, lacking the rufous cast. Note the large gape and *gray on outer primaries*.

[g] RUFOUS-MORPH JUVENILE. Head is dark brown with a rufous cast. Back and upperwings are dark brown, except for pale primary panels, with primary coverts dark. Uppertail is brown with several indistinct darker bands. Wingtips are pointed on gliding hawks.

[h] RUFOUS-MORPH JUVENILE. Head and breast are dark brown with a rufous cast, belly is dark brown, with a sharp line of contrast between them. Underwings show *white commas at wrist*, narrow dusky band on trailing edge of wings, and *narrow dark tips on outer primaries*. Whitish undertail shows dusky tip.

[i] HEAD-ON SILHOUETTE. Soars with wings in a strong dihedral; glides with wings in a modified dihedral (not shown).

PLATE 29

Large long-winged buteo. They have small beaks and legs feathered to toes. Light-morph hawks have *black carpal patches* on underwings. Many individuals show pale nape patch with dark spot in center. *Wingtips extend just beyond tail tip.*

[a] LIGHT-MORPH ADULT MALE. Adult males have wide dark malar stripes, heavily marked breasts, and dark barring on flanks. This variant shows an unmarked belly, emphasizing the dark bib. *A few males have only one wide dark tail band.* Note white forehead and outer lores.

[b] LIGHT-MORPH ADULT MALE. More heavily marked male with barred belly and unmarked U between breast and belly. *Undertail shows another narrower dark band above the wide dark band.* Adult males show black, gray, and rufous-tawny markings on backs.

[c] LIGHT-MORPH ADULT MALE. More heavily marked male with barred belly and flanks, with unmarked white U between breast and belly. Note the *dark carpal patches.* Wings are long and narrow.

[d] HEAD-ON SILHOUETTES. Soars with wings in a dihedral; glides with wings in a modified dihedral, with wrists up and tips level.

[e] LIGHT-MORPH ADULT FEMALE. Females have buffy heads with dark eye lines, dark brown backs with buffy and white streaking, *solid blackish brown flanks,* and *one wide dark band in tail;* they usually lack wide dark malar stripes. Some females show pale bellies.

[f] LIGHT-MORPH ADULT FEMALE. More heavily marked female with blackish brown flanks and belly with a pale area down center, barred leg feathers, and unmarked U between breast and belly. *Some females have 1 or 2 narrower dark tail bands above the wide dark band.*

[g] LIGHT-MORPH ADULT FEMALE. Some adult females have *uniformly blackish brown flanks* and bellies and dark streaks in the breast, usually with a whitish unmarked U between the two. Note the *dark carpal patches* and unmarked buffy lines on underwing coverts. Some females have *1 to 3 narrower dark tail bands above the wide one.*

[h] DARK-MORPH ADULT MALE. Overall jet black with *3 narrow white bands on uppertail.* Note the *white forehead and outer lores.*

[i] DARK-MORPH ADULT. Both males and females can be overall dark brown with 3 narrow grayish bands on uppertails. Head usually shows rufous-buff superciliaries and cheek patches and dark eye lines.

[j], [m] CUTOUTS OF ADULT UNDERTAILS. Both dark-morph adult males and females can have *dark undertails with 3 narrow white bands* or whitish undertail with no narrow dark bands.

[k] DARK-MORPH ADULT. Dark brown adults show *blackish carpal patches* and narrow dark bands in undertails. Some adults have paler heads and some whitish streaking on upper breast.

[l] CUTOUT OF ADULT FEMALE UPPERTAIL. Dark-morph adult females can have uniformly dark uppertails.

[a] [b] [c] [d] [e] [f] [g] [h] [i] [j] [k] [l] [m]

Large long-winged buteo. Rough-legged Hawks have long wings, small beaks, and legs feathered to toes. Light-morph hawks have *black carpal patches* on underwings. Eyes of juveniles are pale gray to pale brown. All show white spot on forehead and outer lores, especially noticeable on dark hawks. Juveniles have wide dark tips on outer primaries. Many individuals show pale nape patch with dark spot in center. Pale square or trapezoidal primary patch on backlit wings is shared by many buteonines. *Wingtips just reach tail tip on perched juveniles.*

[a] LIGHT-MORPH JUVENILE. Juveniles have buffy heads with narrow dark eye lines and malar stripes, dark brown backs with buffy and white streaking, solid dark brown belly bands, and a *wide dusky band on tip of tail.* Leg feathers are lightly marked. *Belly bands* lack the blackish tones of those of adult females.

[b] LIGHT-MORPH JUVENILE. Juveniles have pale heads, brownish upperparts with noticeable whitish primary panels, dark primary coverts, and white base of tail. White uppertail coverts usually have dark centers.

[c] LIGHT-MORPH JUVENILE. Juveniles appear much like adult females, but they always have *solid dark brown belly bands,* relatively unmarked underwing coverts, narrow dusky trailing edge of wings, and *dusky tip to pale undertail,* lacking a wide dark band. Note pale primary panel on backlit wings.

[d] DARK-MORPH JUVENILE. Darker juvenile with dark head and pale bands on uppertail. Most are males, but some are females. Note pale primary patches and dark primary coverts of juveniles.

[e] DARK-MORPH JUVENILE. Darker juvenile with uniformly dark underwing coverts and dark bands on undertail. Most are males, but some are females. Juvenile underwings show *wide dark tips on outer primaries,* and a narrow dusky band on trailing edge. Note pale primary panel on backlit wings and *lack of white wrist commas.*

[f] DARK-MORPH JUVENILE. Darker juvenile with dark head and narrow bands on darkish undertails can be either sex. Note *whitish forehead and outer lores* and pale eyes.

[g] DARK-MORPH JUVENILE. Paler dark juveniles with paler heads, dark eye lines, and rufous streaking in the breast can be either sex. Pale undertails show only a wide dusky tip.

[h] DARK-MORPH JUVENILE. Paler juveniles that show *black carpal patches* that contrast with rufous to brown secondary coverts and pale undertail lacking dark bands but with dusky tip can be either sex. Juvenile underwings show *wide dark tips on outer primaries* and a narrow dusky band on trailing edge.

[i] HEAD-ON SILHOUETTES. Soars with wings in a dihedral; glides with wings in a modified dihedral, with wrists up and tips level.

Large dark eagle. *Golden crown and nape* vary from straw yellow to deep orange-brown among individuals but do not vary with age. *Bill and cere are tricolored:* beak tips are dark, bases are horn-colored, and ceres are yellow. *Legs are feathered to the toes.* Wingtips fall somewhat short of tail tip on perched adult and even shorter on subadults and juveniles. Adult plumage is acquired in four or five years.

[a] ADULT. Overall dark brown except for *golden crown and nape, tawny bar on folded wings,* buffy legs, and *grayish marbling on wing and tail.* Adult eyes vary from amber to brown. Wingtips fall somewhat short of tail tip on perched adult. Note mottled look due to mix of newer dark and older faded body feathers.

[b] ADULT. Overall dark brown except for *golden crown and nape, tawny bar on upperwings, and grayish marbling on wing and tail. Head and neck projection is less than half tail length.*

[c] SUBADULT. Some otherwise adult-appearing eagles (Basic III or IV) show a bit of white in their tails.

[d] BASIC I. Similar to juvenile, but with mottled body feathers, new fresh tertials, and *grayish marbling on central tail feathers.*

[e] BASIC I. Differs from juvenile by *tawny bar on upperwings,* ragged border between white and dark areas of tail, and ragged trailing edges of wings. Older immatures would show more new secondaries and would not show as many as 4 old faded outer primaries.

[f] SUBADULT TAIL CUTOUT. Basic III and IV eagles can show some white in the tail.

[g] JUVENILE. Similar to adult but is overall uniformly darker, has *white base on tail that extends to the edges,* and lacks tawny bar on folded wing. Eyes are dark brown. Wingtips barely reach the dark band on tail tip of perched juveniles.

[h] JUVENILE. Somewhat similar to adult but shows *white base that extends to the edges* and distinct border between light and dark on tail, and (sometimes) small white patches on upperwings and lacks grayish markings on upperwings and tail and tawny bars on upperwings, showing at most faint bars.

PLATE 32

Large dark eagle. Eagles have proportionally longer wings than most other raptors. All ages show *golden nape, buffy legs,* and *rufous undertail coverts.* On flying eagles, *head and neck projection is less than half the tail length.* Most show small rufous patches at wrists; some show rufous bars on underwing coverts. Adult plumage is acquired in four or five years.

[a] ADULT. Overall dark brown except for *golden crown and nape, grayish marbling on undersides of flight and tail feathers,* buffy legs, and rufous undertail coverts. Note the wide dark band on the trailing edge of wings and the tip of tail. *Head and neck projection is less than half the tail length.*

[b] ADULT TAIL CUTOUT. Some adult tails, usually those of males, show narrow gray bands.

[c] HEAD-ON SILHOUETTE. Soars and glides with wings in a dihedral.

[d] SUBADULT. Some eagles appear adultlike but show a bit of white in their tails. These are either Basic III or IV.

[e] OLDER IMMATURE. Individual that has almost completed molt of flight feathers, but shows retained outer primaries and one retained secondary on each wing. This eagle is Basic II because of the retained juvenile outer primaries. Note irregular white streaks on undersides of flight and tail feathers.

[f] BASIC I. Differs from juvenile by new inner primaries, ragged border between white and dark areas of tail, and ragged trailing edges of wings. Older immatures would show more new secondaries and would not show as many as 4 old faded outer primaries.

[g] JUVENILE. Somewhat similar to adult but lacking grayish markings on undersides of flight and tail feathers and often showing instead *variably sized usually oval white patches* at bases of inner primaries and outer secondaries and *white base that extends to outer edges of longer tail,* with a more-or-less even border with dark tip. Wings appear broader and fuller and trailing edge somewhat serrated, as juveniles' secondaries are longer and have pointed tips. Underparts and underwing coverts appear more uniformly colored.

[h] JUVENILE TAIL CUTOUT. Variant showing extensive white on base of tail.

[i] JUVENILE WING CUTOUT. Variant showing no white patch on underwing.

[j] JUVENILE WING CUTOUT. Variant showing extensive white patch on underwing.

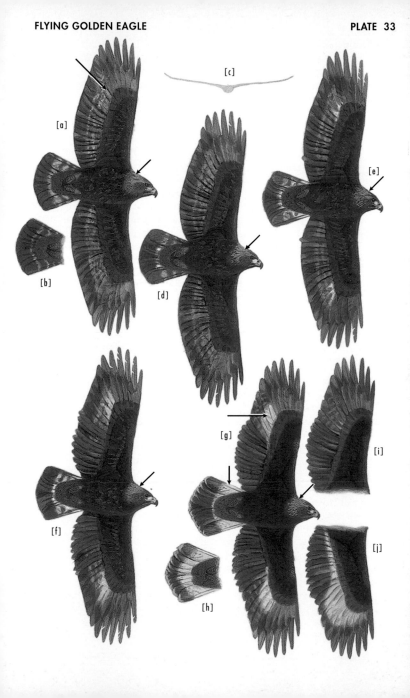

1 . CRESTED CARACARA *Caracara cheriway*   P. 248
Unusual large headed, long-legged falconid. *Bold black-and-white plumage, colorful face skin, large horn-colored beak, large crested head,* and *long neck in flight* are distinctive.

[a] HEAD-ON SILHOUETTE. Caracaras glide on cupped wings.

[b] ADULT. Adults appear overall black and white, with *orange face skin* and bright yellow legs. Adults' eyes are amber.

[c] ADULT. Adults appear overall black and white. In flight, their *large white primary panels* and *long head and neck* are distinctive.

[d] ADULT. Adults appear overall black and white. In flight their *long head and neck* and *large white primary panels* are distinctive.

[e] BASIC I. Similar to adult but overall more brownish black, with less defined barring on upper breast and back, more pinkish face, and duller yellow leg color. Dark crown shows fine rufous streaking.

[f] JUVENILE. Somewhat similar to adult but overall more brownish, with streaking on neck and upper breast. Facial skin is gray to pink, legs are pale yellowish gray, and eyes are dark brown.

2 . CRANE HAWK *Geranospiza caerulescens*   P. 295
Vagrant. Slender, long-legged, small-headed, Neotropical raptor. They have double-jointed legs.

[a] JUVENILE. Similar to adult but with a brownish cast to upperparts, pale face pattern, amber eyes, and buffy barring on underparts and leg feathers (not shown).

[b] ADULT. Overall slate gray, with red eyes and *long, orangish legs.* Leg feathers and undertail coverts show narrow whitish barring. *Long dark tail shows two white bands.*

[c] ADULT. Overall slate gray, with red eyes and long, orangish legs. *Wings show a curved row of white spots* near tips, and underwing coverts and base of flight feathers show narrow white barring.

3 . COLLARED FOREST-FALCON   P. 302
Micrastur semitorquatus
Vagrant. Slender, long-legged, secretive Neotropical raptor. They have white and buffy morphs as well as a rare dark morph.

[a] WHITE-MORPH ADULT. Crown, half-collar, and upperparts are black; *collar,* cheeks, and underparts are white. *Long black tail shows three narrow white bands.* Note head shape, white collar, dark half-collar, and dull greenish yellow face skin and cere.

[b] JUVENILE. Similar in pattern to adult, but upperparts are brown with narrow buffy feather edges; collar, cheeks, and underparts are washed with cinnamon; these last are barred dark brown. Note long dull yellow legs.

[c] TAWNY-MORPH ADULT. Like white-morph adult but with buffy to tawny underparts and collar. *Long black tail shows three narrow white bands.*

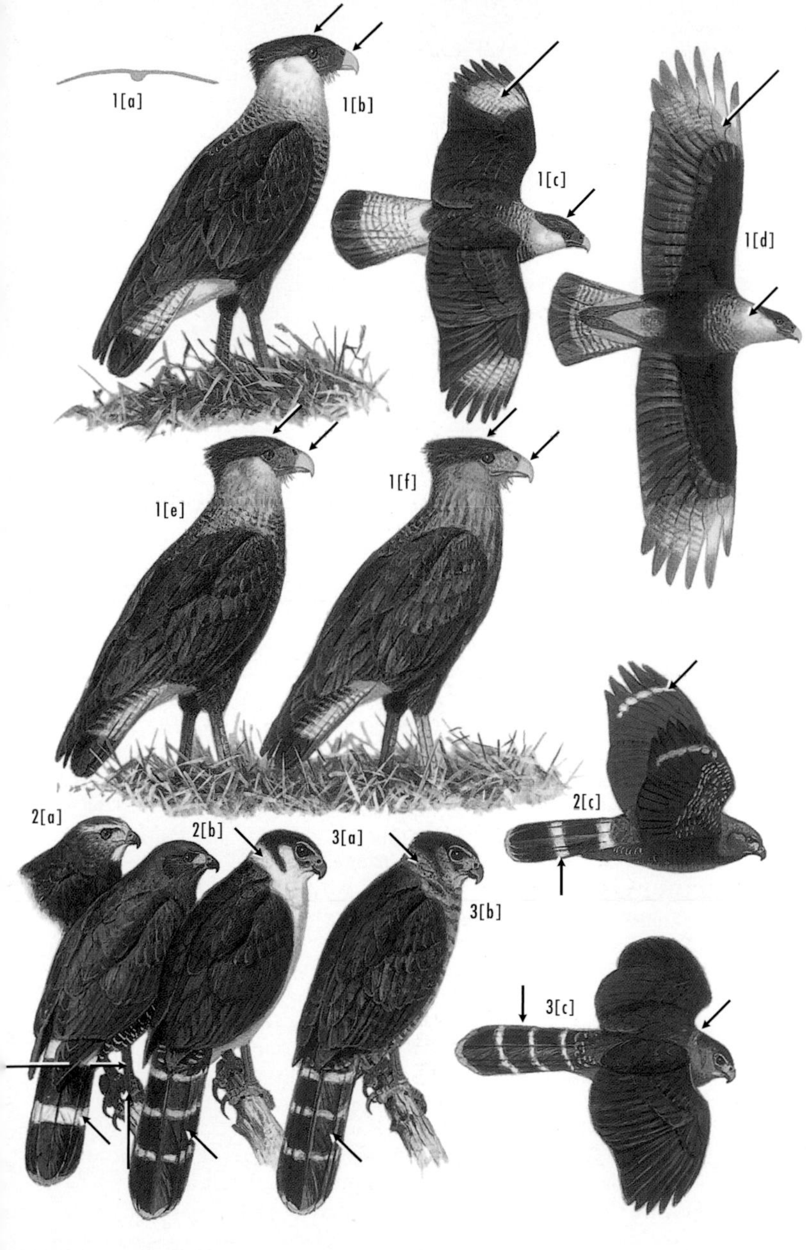
1[a]
1[b]
1[c]
1[d]
1[e]
1[f]
2[a]
2[b]
2[c]
3[a]
3[b]
3[c]

1 . COMMON KESTREL *Falco tinnunculus*   **P. 304**

Vagrant. Medium-sized, long-tailed falcon with a single narrow dark mustache mark. *Two-toned pattern on upperwings in flight is diagnostic.* Long tail has wedge-shaped tip when folded.

[a] ADULT MALE. Blue-gray head shows *narrow dark mustache marks* and short dark eye lines. *Tail is blue-gray* and wing coverts are rufous — the opposite of those of adult male American Kestrel. Rufous back has diamond-shaped dark markings.

[b] ADULT FEMALE. Similar to female American Kestrel, but larger and lacking bold face pattern. Adult females have dark triangular back markings and often a grayish wash on their uppertails.

[c] JUVENILE. Similar to adult females but with back more densely marked with dark even-width barring.

[d] JUVENILE FEMALE. Similar to adult females, but back is more densely marked with dark even-width barring. Juvenile females (and some males) lack grayish cast to uppertails. Note *two-toned upperwings.*

---

2 . AMERICAN KESTREL *Falco sparverius*   **P. 252**

Small colorful falcon. Head pattern of *two mustache marks on either side of white cheeks* and *dark ocelli on nape* are distinctive. Kestrels are the only North American falcon with *reddish on tail and back.* Rufous crown patch is variable in size.

[a] ADULT MALE, *PAULUS*. Similar to nominate race, but back is usually unmarked.

[b] ADULT MALE, *SPARVERIUS*. Adult male has rufous back barred on lower half, rufous to whitish breast usually unmarked, *blue-gray upperwing coverts* with dark spots, rufous tail with black subterminal band, and paler belly and flanks with black spots.

[c] JUVENILE MALE. Similar to adult male, but back is barred up to nape, pale breast is covered with narrow dark streaking.

[d] ADULT MALE. Male has *gray upperwing coverts* and *rufous tail* with black subterminal band. Note *row of white spots on primaries.* Adult male has unbarred area on upper back.

[e] ADULT MALE. Adult male has rufous to whitish breast, usually unmarked, and paler belly and flanks with dark spots. *Backlit underwings show row of white spots.* Tail appears rufous.

[f] [g] TAIL CUTOUTS SHOWING VARIATION. Tails of males often have black, white, and gray banding or gray areas or some combination of these.

[h] ADULT FEMALE. Head is like that of adult male. *Reddish brown back, tail,* and upperwing coverts are barred with dark brown.

[i] JUVENILE FEMALE. Almost identical to adult female, but some have narrow dark subterminal tail band, barely wider than the others. Napes of juveniles are often whitish or buffy.

[j] FEMALE. Females have creamy bodies with rufous streaking. Pale underwings when backlit show buffy spots that are not as noticeable as the white ones of males. *Tail appears reddish brown.*

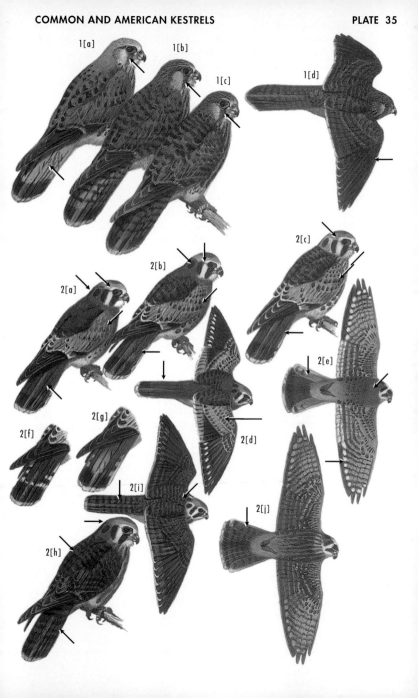

Small, compact falcon, with at most *faint mustache marks.* Wingtips fall somewhat short of tail tip.

[a] ADULT MALE *COLUMBARIUS*. Adult male Taiga Merlins have slate-blue crown, nape, and upperparts. Underparts are heavily streaked, with a rufous wash on breast and *stronger rufous coloring on leg feathers. Black tail has three narrow slate blue bands.* Cere, eyering, and leg colors are orange-yellow (nonbreeding) to bright orange (breeding).

[b] ADULT OR JUVENILE FEMALE *COLUMBARIUS*. Adult female and juvenile Taigas have head pattern like that of adult males but have dark brown upperparts and tails and lack rufous wash on legs and sides of breast. Adult females show a gray wash on uppertail coverts. *Dark brown uppertails of juvenile females have three narrow buffy bands; bands of adult females are buffy or gray.* Note the white throat.

[c] JUVENILE MALE *COLUMBARIUS*. Adult female and juvenile Taigas appear dark brown on uppersides. Juvenile males have whitish to *pale gray bands on uppertails;* juvenile females have *buffy bands.*

[d] ADULT OR JUVENILE FEMALE *COLUMBARIUS*. Taigas have *dark underwings* and underparts, with heavily streaked bodies. Note the white throat.

[e] UNDERWING CUTOUT OF ADULT MALE *COLUMBARIUS*. *Underwings of Taigas appear overall dark.* Adult males show whitish spotting.

[f] ADULT FEMALE OR JUVENILE *RICHARDSONII*. Prairie Merlins appear paler compared to the other races, with narrower streaking on underparts and leg feathers, pale underwings, and wide buffy tail bands.

[g] ADULT MALE *RICHARDSONII*. Similar to adult male Taiga but overall paler, with pale blue-gray upperparts, rufous-buff collar, and more lightly streaked underparts. Mustache marks are faint or absent. *Wider tail bands are usually whitish or pale blue-gray.*

[h] ADULT FEMALE OR JUVENILE *RICHARDSONII*. Similar to adult female Taiga but overall paler, with paler brown upperparts, pale collar, and more lightly streaked underparts. *Buffy tail bands are wider.*

[i] ADULT FEMALE OR JUVENILE *RICHARDSONII*. Similar to adult female and juvenile Taigas but overall a paler brown, with *wider buffy tail bands.*

[j] ADULT MALE *SUCKLEYI*. Similar to adult male Taiga but overall darker, with dark head, *slaty black upperparts* with a grayish cast, and dark underparts with some rufous streaking. *Tail bands are faint or absent.* Undertail coverts have dark barring.

[k] ADULT FEMALE OR JUVENILE *SUCKLEYI*. Similar to adult female Taiga but overall darker, with dark head, blackish brown upperparts, and dark underparts with rufous streaking. *Tail bands are faint or absent.* Undertail coverts have dark barring. Leg feathers are heavily streaked.

[l] ADULT FEMALE OR JUVENILE *SUCKLEYI*. Black Merlins appear very dark in flight, with dark head, some rufous streaking on underparts, and *few pale markings on dark underwings. Tail bands are faint or absent,* and undertail coverts are barred. Note large white throat patch.

PLATE 36

1 . A P L O M A D O   F A L C O N *Falco femoralis* **P. 262**

Colorful narrow-winged, long-tailed falcon. *Bold head pattern and dark belly band are distinctive.* Wingtips extend three-quarters down tail.

[a] ADULT FEMALE. Adults have lead gray back and upperwing coverts. Note *narrow white band on tips of secondaries.* Females show narrow streaking on creamy breast. Adults have fine white barring on *dark belly band.* Rufous legs are somewhat duller on females. *Long black tail has numerous narrow white bands.*

[b] ADULT MALE. Adults have lead gray upperparts. Males show no breast streaking. Rufous legs are somewhat brighter on males. Adults have bright yellow ceres, eye-rings, and legs.

[c] ADULT MALE. Bold head pattern noticeable on flying falcons. White breast, *hourglass-shaped dark belly band,* and rufous lower belly and undertail coverts are distinctive. Underwings appear uniformly dark with *narrow white band on trailing edge. Long black tail has numerous narrow white bands.*

[d] JUVENILE. Similar to adults, but back and upperwing coverts are dark brown, breast is buffy and has more and wider streaks, *dark belly band* lacks white barring, and leg feathers and undertail coverts are rufous-buff to buff. This is a falcon in worn plumage with pale yellow cere and eye-rings.

[e] JUVENILE. In fresh plumage, pale areas of head and breast are more rufous-buff. Cere and eye-rings are initially pale blue-gray.

[f] JUVENILE. *Bold head pattern* noticeable on flying falcons. Uppersides of long narrow wings are uniformly dark brown, lacking gray cast of adults. Note *narrow white band on tips of secondaries. Long black tail has numerous narrow white bands.*

2 . E U R A S I A N   H O B B Y *Falco subbuteo* **P. 308**

Vagrant. Long- and narrow-winged falcon. Always shows strong face pattern of white cheeks with 2 *narrow black mustache marks* and pale sides of nape. *Wingtips extend just beyond tail tip.*

[a] ADULT. Upperparts of adults are dark blue-gray. White underparts show wide black streaking. Leg feathers and undertail coverts are rufous. Upperside of folded tail is unbanded. Note distinctive head pattern. Cere and eye-rings are yellow.

[b] ADULT. White underparts have wide black streaking, with *many streaks extending from throat to lower belly.* Long, narrow underwings appear uniformly dark. Distinctive head pattern and *rufous leg feathers and undertail coverts* are usually noticeable.

[c] JUVENILE. Similar to adults, but back and upperwing coverts are dark brown, cheeks and underparts are creamy, and leg feathers and undertail coverts are buffy.

[d] JUVENILE. Similar to adults in flight, but underparts are creamy, leg feathers and undertail coverts are buffy, and pale banding on undertail is more noticeable.

1[a]
1[b]
1[c]
1[d]
1[e]
1[f]

2[a]
2[b]
2[c]
2[d]

Large, dark, long-winged falcon. All have *wide dark mustache marks*. *Underwings appear uniformly dark* on flying falcons. Only North American falcon whose *wingtips extend to, or almost to, tail tip*.

[a] ADULT TUNDRA. Tundra adults have slate gray head with pale forehead, narrow mustache marks, and white cheeks. Females average darker and are more heavily marked.

[b] ADULT ANATUM. Anatum adults have blackish heads with cheek patches small or absent and rufous wash on underparts. Adult males have orange-yellow eye-rings and ceres and orangish legs; females have yellower eye-rings and ceres.

[c] ADULT PEALE'S (ALEUTIAN). Peale's adults are overall darker, having heavily streaked breasts, heavily barred bellies, streaking in cheek patches, and lacking a rufous wash on underparts. Adults in the Aleutian Islands have more heavily streaked breasts.

[d] ADULT PEALE'S (QUEEN CHARLOTTE). Peale's adults are overall darker, having more heavily streaked breasts, heavily barred bellies, streaking in cheek patches, and lacking a rufous wash on underparts. Adults in southeast Alaska and the Queen Charlotte Islands have less heavily streaked breasts.

[e] ADULT TUNDRA. Adult Peregrines in flight show *dark underwings* and white breasts. Tundra adults show narrow mustache marks and larger white cheek patches.

[f] ADULT. Adult Peregrines have slate gray uppersides and uppertails, with *contrastingly paler blue-gray rump and uppertail coverts*.

[g] JUVENILE TUNDRA. Tundra juveniles have a distinctive head pattern: buffy forehead, dark brown crown, buffy superciliary lines, dark eye lines, buffy cheeks and throat, and *dark mustache marks*. Creamy underparts and leg feathers are narrowly streaked dark brown.

[h] JUVENILE ANATUM. Anatum juveniles have mostly dark heads with small rufous-buff cheek patches, upperparts with fewer and narrower tawny edges, and streaking on rufous-buff underparts that is wider and heavier. Dark markings on leg feathers are usually chevron-shaped.

[i] JUVENILE PEALE'S. Peale's juveniles are overall darker, with narrow dark streaking in pale cheek patches, little or no pale edges on backs and upperwing coverts, dark underparts with narrow pale streaking, barred undertail coverts, and pale tail bands that are narrower or absent. Dark leg feathers have narrow pale edges.

[j] JUVENILE TUNDRA. Some have pale heads with narrow eye lines and mustache marks but are *dark behind the eyes* (see Prairie Falcon).

[k] JUVENILE PEALE'S. Peale's juveniles are overall darker, with *dark underwings*, dark underparts with narrow pale streaking, and pale tail bands narrower or absent.

[l] JUVENILE TUNDRA. Juvenile Peregrines have streaked underparts and *dark underwings*.

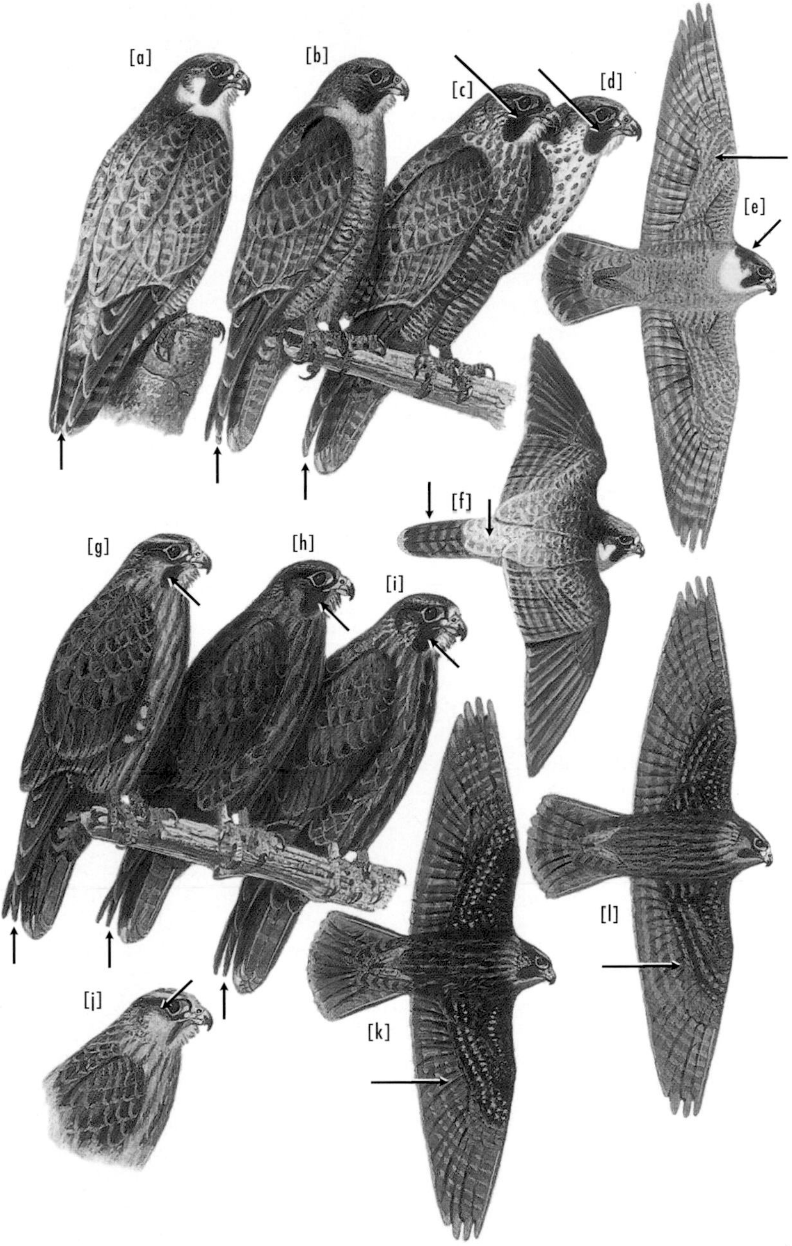
[a]
[b]
[c]
[d]
[e]
[f]
[g]
[h]
[i]
[j]
[k]
[l]

Largest falcon, primarily Arctic. They have three color morphs: white, gray, and dark. They are *heavier bodied, broader winged, and longer tailed* than other large falcons, with *wide, noticeably tapered tails*. Adult cere, eye-rings, and legs are yellow to orange. *Wingtips reach only about two-thirds down tail* on perched falcons.

[a] WHITE-MORPH ADULT. *Overall white*, with white head showing short narrow dark eye lines and lacking dark malar marks. Upperparts are marked with short brown to black barring. White tail sometimes shows narrow dark banding, either complete or partial. White underparts are usually unmarked.

[b] WHITE-MORPH ADULT. Overall white, with white head showing short narrow dark eye lines and lacking dark malar stripes. Underwings are white except for *narrow dark wingtips* and faint dusky narrow banding on secondaries. White tail sometimes shows narrow dark banding, either complete or partial. White underparts are usually unmarked.

[c] GRAY-MORPH ADULT. Head has narrow pale superciliary lines, pale forehead, and narrow dark mustache marks. Whitish underparts are heavily spotted, but barred on flanks. Underwings show *darker secondaries and paler primaries* and coverts. Tail has equal-width pale and dark bands.

[d] GRAY-MORPH ADULT. Head has narrow pale superciliary lines, pale forehead, and narrow dark mustache marks. Slate gray upperparts show pale gray barring. *Tail has equal-width pale and dark bands.*

[e] GRAY-MORPH ADULT. Head has narrow pale superciliary lines, pale forehead, and narrow dark mustache marks. Slate gray upperparts show pale gray barring. *Tail has equal-width pale and dark bands,* and *uppertail coverts are the same color as uppertail* (compare to adult Peregrines on Pl. 38). Note the *broad-based tapered tail.*

[f] DARK-MORPH ADULT. Head is completely slate gray. Slate gray upperparts can show faint gray markings. Some adults have characters intermediate between gray and dark morphs.

[g] DARK-MORPH ADULT. Head is completely slate gray. Slate gray upperparts show faint white spotting. Dark tail has narrow pale bands, and *uppertail coverts are the same color as uppertail.* Note the *tapered broad-based tail.*

[h] DARK-MORPH ADULT. Head is completely slate gray. *Underwing is two-toned;* dark coverts contrast with paler grayish unbarred flight feathers. Underparts are more heavily marked compared to those of gray-morph adults.

1 . GYRFALCON *Falco rusticolus*   P. 265

Largest falcon, primarily Arctic. Gyrs are *heavier bodied, broader winged, and longer tailed* than other large falcons, with *wide, noticeably tapered tails*. Wingtips reach only about two-thirds down tail.

[a] WHITE-MORPH JUVENILE. White head shows narrow dark eye lines and lacks dark malar marks. Upperparts are brown with white spotting and feather edges. Underparts have some fine brown streaking. *White tail has narrow brown bands.*

[b] WHITE-MORPH JUVENILE. Paler juvenile has brown on upperparts restricted to teardrop on center of feathers and usually has *faintly banded or unbanded tail* and few or no markings on underparts.

[c] GRAY-MORPH JUVENILE. Overall dark gray-brown, with head showing narrow pale superciliary lines, wider dark eye lines, and narrow dark mustache marks. *Brown tail has numerous narrow pale bands.* Some juveniles are intermediate between gray and dark morphs.

[d] GRAY-MORPH JUVENILE. Creamy underparts have heavy dark brown streaking. *Underwings are two-toned;* darker coverts contrast with paler flight feathers, but secondaries are usually somewhat darker than primaries. Brown tail has numerous narrow pale bands.

[e] DARK-MORPH JUVENILE. Head is dark brown except for whitish throat. Upperparts and *uppertail are uniformly dark brown.* Dark underparts have some whitish spots and streaks.

[f] DARK-MORPH JUVENILE. Head is dark brown except for whitish throat. Upperparts and *uppertail are uniformly dark brown.*

2 . PRAIRIE FALCON *Falco mexicanus*   P. 276

Large, pale, long-tailed falcon. *White area between eye* and dark ear patch and *dark axillaries* are distinctive. Large head appears blockish. Wingtips fall somewhat short of tail tip.

[a] ADULT. Head shows strong face pattern. Back and upperwing coverts are medium brown, with buffy bars and edges on most feathers. Males average paler than females. Adult's cere, eye-rings, and legs are yellow-orange, brighter on males. Adults show barring on flanks. Long tail often shows buffy banding. Note dark patch on sides of upper breast.

[b] JUVENILE. By spring, juvenile's cere and legs are pale yellow, underparts have faded to creamy or whitish, and upperparts appear darker as pale feather edges have worn off.

[c] JUVENILE. In fresh plumage, juvenile shows blue-gray cere and eye-rings; buffy, heavily streaked underparts; buff to rufous feather edges on dark brown upperparts; and pale gray legs.

[d] ADULT FEMALE WING CUTOUT. Adult females have dark median coverts, with little or no white spotting.

[e] ADULT MALE. Adult has white underparts with spots on belly and breast and bars on flanks. All Prairie Falcons have pale underwings with *dark axillaries,* but adult male has paler median coverts.

1[a] 1[b] 1[c] 1[d]

1[e] 1[f]

2[a] 2[b] 2[c] 2[e]

2[d]

SPECIES ACCOUNTS

NEW WORLD VULTURES
FAMILY CATHARTIDAE

The three species of New World vultures that occur in our area subsist almost exclusively on carrion, which they tear apart with their strong hooked beaks. Their heads are featherless, and their feet are relatively weak and not used for grasping prey. While perched in a tree, on the ground, or on a fencepost, all will often spread their wings and face toward or away from the sun. Various interpretations of this sunning behavior include gathering heat, drying feathers, or straightening feathers. Vultures are somewhat social and gregarious, roosting and eating together, but are solitary breeders. While they appear ungainly on the ground, in flight they are quite graceful.

New World vultures differ somewhat from Old World vultures and other raptors in Accipitridae and were thought to be more closely related to storks than to diurnal raptors. One difference is that our vultures often defecate on their legs for cooling or disease control or both, a behavior shared with storks. However, recent DNA work has shown that they are no closer to storks than they are to Accipitridae. We place the family in the group of diurnal raptors along with Accipitridae and Falconidae, which are not closely related either.

The misnomer "buzzard" was given to the two smaller American vultures by early European settlers, who thought these birds were related to the darkly colored European buteo called Common Buzzard. Unfortunately, this name is still in common use for our vultures.

Coragyps atratus

DESCRIPTION

The Black Vulture is a large, jet-black vulture. Eyes are dark brown. Short black tail and long, whitish legs are distinctive. Feathered nape can be extended onto crown in colder weather. Sexes are alike in plumage and size. Juvenile plumage is very similar to adult's. On perched vultures, wingtips reach tail tip and primaries barely extend beyond secondaries (short primary projection).

ADULT: Gray head skin is wrinkled and featherless. Beak is dusky with ivory tip. Body and wing and tail coverts are jet black, and back and upperwing coverts having a purplish iridescence. Upper- and underwings are black with large white primary patches, larger on underwings.

JUVENILE: Very similar to adult, but head and neck skin are black and smooth, not wrinkled, beak is completely dusky, and body plumage is somewhat less iridescent than that of adult. Feathered nape extends farther up hindneck than does that of adult. Older juveniles show ivory on tip of beak and begin to show wrinkling of skin on lower neck.

UNUSUAL PLUMAGES: Published sight records from Florida are of one fawn-colored (dilute plumage) and another mostly white (partial albino) individual. The reported hybrid between this

Black Vulture adult. All show whitish primary panels and legs and short, square-cornered tails. Florida, January (WSC)

Black Vulture adult. All show whitish primary panels on upperwings. Texas, February (BKW)

Black Vulture juvenile. Juveniles have smooth black heads; adults' heads are wrinkled and gray. Florida, January (WSC)

species and Turkey Vulture was a practical joke, apparent when the red paint wore off the head on a specimen of a normal Black Vulture.

SIMILAR SPECIES

(1) **TURKEY VULTURE** (Pl. 1) is brownish-black, not jet black, on the back; has longer, narrower wings and tail and silvery flight feathers on underwings; and flies with slower wingbeats and with wings held in a stronger dihedral. Flight of Blacks is more stable, with little or no "rocking." On perched Turkeys, primaries extend noticeably beyond secondaries. Adult Turkey Vultures have red heads. (2) **COMMON BLACK-HAWK** (Pl. 14) adult is also overall black. See under that species for differences.

FLIGHT

Active flight is distinctive: three to five shallow, rapid wingbeats of stiff wings, with wings thrust forward, followed by a short period of glide. Black Vultures soar with wings held level or in a slight dihedral and glide with wings level. Their wing loading is higher than that of Turkey Vultures, so they require stronger thermals for soaring and therefore do not begin flying in the morning until an hour or so after Turkey Vultures. Black Vultures usually soar higher than Turkey Vultures and, like that species, often bow their wings downward in a flex until the tips almost meet, then pull back up to a gliding position. They occasionally soar or glide with legs dangling.

Molt

Annual molt of adults is apparently complete, beginning in spring and finished by autumn. First prebasic (post-juvenile) molt begins when about one year old and is completed before winter. Molt sequence of flight and tail feathers is almost like that of accipitrid raptors.

Behavior

Black Vultures are more gregarious than Turkey Vultures and subsist on larger carcasses; they are dominant over Turkeys at carcasses mainly because of their greater numbers. They are reported to fish; to attack live prey, especially newborn pigs, other livestock, and even skunks; and to eat oil palm fruit. They locate prey not by smell, as do Turkey Vultures, but by watching other scavengers and by frequenting abundant food sources, such as dumps and slaughterhouses. Black Vultures form communal night roosts, often with Turkey Vultures. Breeding is solitary. Vocalizations reported are restricted to hisses and grunts.

Status and Distribution

Black Vultures are common, formerly abundant residents in the Southeast. They are uncommon to rare elsewhere, occurring

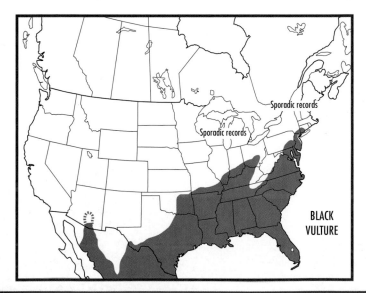

north to New Jersey, Pennsylvania, and Indiana and west to n. Texas, with a small population in s. Arizona. Range is extending northeasterly into s. New England. They are nonmigratory (except in the northeast) and have occurred as vagrants in California, Wisconsin, Quebec, New Brunswick, and Ontario.

FINE POINTS

The down of Black Vulture chicks is buffy; down of Turkey Vulture chicks is white.

SUBSPECIES

The range of the North American race (*C. a. atratus*) extends south into n. Mexico.

ETYMOLOGY

"Vulture" comes from the Latin *vulturus,* "tearer," a reference to its manner of eating carrion. *Coragyps* comes from the Greek *korax,* "raven," and *gyps,* "vulture." The Latin *atratus* means "clothed in black, as for mourning."

MEASUREMENTS

LENGTH:	59–74 cm (65);	23–28 in. (25)
WINGSPREAD:	141–160 cm (151);	55–63 in. (59)
WEIGHT:	1.7–2.3 kg (2.0);	3.8–5.1 lb. (4.4)

TURKEY VULTURE   PL. 1

Cathartes aura

DESCRIPTION

The widespread Turkey Vulture, a large, brownish black vulture, soars and glides with its *wings in a strong dihedral.* Eyes are gray-brown. Underwings are two-toned: silvery flight feathers contrast with blackish coverts. Feathered nape can be pulled down to expose long featherless neck when feeding or extended onto crown in colder weather. Sexes are alike in plumage and size. On perched vultures, wingtips reach tail tip, and primaries extend quite far beyond secondaries (primary projection is long).
    ADULT: *Red head* is featherless, with whitish warts in front of and below eyes, fewer on western vultures; reddish neck is wrinkled. Beak is whitish. Entire body is brownish black, blackish on under-

Turkey Vulture adult. Adults have red heads. All vultures "sun" themselves with wings outstretched. Florida, January (WSC)

Turkey Vulture young adult. First plumage adults have dusky tips on beaks. Florida, December (BKW)

parts, with upperwing coverts and back somewhat browner. Neck and back have a purplish iridescence. Uppersides of primaries are brown and contrast somewhat with the rest of the darker upperwings. *Underwings are two-toned:* silvery flight feathers contrast with black wing coverts. Underside of *long tail* is silvery but darker than flight feathers. Legs are pinkish to pale reddish but are often whitened by defecation.

JUVENILE: Similar to adult, but head is dusky, lacks wrinkles and warts, and is covered with brown fuzzy down on crown and hindneck. Face gradually turns pink with time. Beak is dusky, with a

Turkey Vulture juvenile. Juveniles have dark heads and mostly dark beaks. Florida, January (WSC)

Turkey Vulture adult. All show pale uppersides of outer primaries. Arizona, April (BKW)

pale base that gradually enlarges toward tip. Neck and back lack iridescence. Upperwing coverts have buffy feather edges. Silvery undersides of flight feathers are slightly darker than those of adults in fresh plumage, but underwings still show two-toned pattern.

BASIC I: Almost like adult, but with fewer warts on face and dusky tip on beak.

UNUSUAL PLUMAGES: Albinos reported are completely white. Partial albinos with some white feathers, including some with only the outer primaries white, have also been reported. Dilute plumage specimens are overall pale gray.

SIMILAR SPECIES

(1) **BLACK VULTURE** (Pl. 1) is somewhat similar; see under that species for distinctions. (2) **ZONE-TAILED HAWK** (Pl. 23) in flight appears much like a Turkey Vulture; see under that species for distinctions. (3) **NORTHERN HARRIER** (Pl. 10) also flies with wings in a strong dihedral. See under that species for differences. (4) **DARK-MORPH BUTEOS** also have two-toned underwings and dark bodies but have different tail patterns.

FLIGHT

Active flight is with slow, deep, deliberate wingbeats on flexible wings. Soars and glides with wings in a strong dihedral, often rocking or teetering from side to side. When the bird is gliding in strong winds, wings are pulled back and are held in a slight dihedral. Turkey Vultures often, especially when beginning to glide after soaring, bow their wings downward in a "flex" until the tips almost meet, then return them to the gliding position.

MOLT

Annual molt of adults, beginning in spring and continuing until late autumn, is almost complete, but not all primaries or secondaries may be replaced every year. First prebasic (post-juvenile) molt begins when about a year old and is completed before winter. Molt sequence of flight and tail feathers is almost like that of accipitrid raptors.

BEHAVIOR

Turkey Vultures spend much of the day soaring and gliding at low to moderate heights, searching for carrion. While carrion is its usual fare, there are isolated reports of Turkey Vultures catching live fish and attacking live animals, usually ones that are sick or in some way incapacitated. Turkey Vultures are able to locate carrion by smell as well as sight. Studies have shown that Turkey Vultures eat smaller prey than Black Vultures and that Blacks dominate at carcasses because of their numbers. Communal night roosts of up to several hundred birds, sometimes including Black Vultures, form in large trees and on radio towers. Vocalizations reported are limited to grunts and hisses. Breeding is solitary.

STATUS AND DISTRIBUTION

Turkey Vultures are fairly common, breeding over most of the United States and expanding recently into se. Canada, with records as far north as Nova Scotia. A few have wandered north as far as Alaska. Northern and western birds are migratory, some traveling as far as South America in winter.

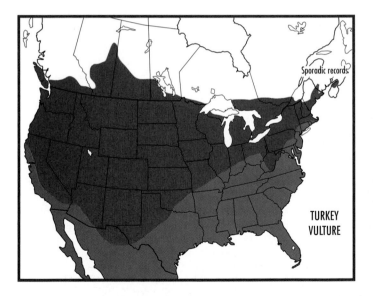

Sporadic records

TURKEY
VULTURE

FINE POINTS

One-year-old Turkey Vultures can be aged by their two-toned beaks, which are whitish with a dusky tip. Turkey Vultures have shorter, thicker beaks than do Black Vultures. Nestling's down is whitish; Black Vulture nestling's down is buffy.

The three subspecies that occur in North America cannot be distinguished in the field. They are: *C. a. septentrional* in the East, *C. a. meridionalis* in most of the West, and *C. a. aura* from the Southwest down into Mexico.

ETYMOLOGY

The Turkey Vulture is named for its resemblance (red head) to the Turkey. "Vulture" comes from the Latin *vulturus*, "tearer," a reference to its manner of eating carrion. *Cathartes* is from the Greek *kathartes*, meaning "a purifier"; *aura* possibly derives from Latin *aurum*, "gold," because of the head color of museum specimens, but it could be from a Latinized version of a native South American word for "vulture."

MEASUREMENTS

LENGTH:	62–72 cm (67);	24–28 in. (26)
WINGSPREAD:	160–181 cm (171);	63–71 in. (67)
WEIGHT:	1.6–2.4 kg (1.8);	3.5–5.3 lb. (4)

CALIFORNIA CONDOR   PL. 2

Gymnogyps californianus

DESCRIPTION

The endangered California Condor, our largest raptor, is *much larger than any eagle*. They are overall black, except for head and *bold white triangular patches* on underwings and narrow white bars on upperwings. Tail is relatively short, with a square tip. Long, broad wings show seven deeply slotted primaries on tips. Long spikelike black feathers at base of neck form a ruff, which can be raised to cover the long neck and base of head in colder weather. Sexes are alike in size and plumage. Legs are whitish, with red around upper joint of tarsi. Adult plumage is attained in six to seven years.

ADULT: *Reddish orange to yellow head* is unfeathered except for an unusual patch of short black feathers on the forehead between and below the eyes. Neck is blue-gray washed with pink, with a large red spot at base of foreneck and variably sized yellow stripe on hindneck; intensity of color varies with mood. Head and neck often appear swollen. Eyes and ring around eyes (scleral ring) are

California Condor subadult (five years old). Head is orange, and underwings show white patches on coverts and axillars. Note the bare red areas on throat and midbreast. California, March (WSC)

scarlet, and beak is horn colored. Body, tail coverts, tail, and upperwing coverts are black, somewhat brownish above. Crop skin is usually visible on perched and flying birds as a vertical red stripe in center of breast. White tips of inner greater secondary upperwing coverts form a narrow bar on upperwings of flying condors and on folded wings of perched condors. Flight feathers are black, but innermost secondaries show a whitish wash on upper surface. White underwing coverts form a large triangular patch on underwing.

JUVENILE: Somewhat similar to adult, but dusky head and neck are covered with short dusky down and lack the puffy appearance of adults. Beak is black, eyes are gray-brown, and scleral ring is pale pink. Whitish underwing coverts are mottled dusky; axillaries appear mostly dusky. An inconspicuous, narrow, dull whitish bar (tips of greater secondary upperwing coverts) runs through center of inner upperwings, and uppersides of inner secondaries lack whitish wash of adult's.

BASIC I: Second-plumage condors differ little from juveniles, except for worn and faded plumage. Five or six inner primaries and a few secondaries have been replaced.

BASIC II: Third-plumage condors are similar to younger condors but show more white in underwing coverts, but axillaries are still dusky. Head is still dusky, but lower neck is turning pinkish, producing a noticeable ring around neck. Whitish on uppersides of secondaries is beginning to be noticeable. Eyes are orange-brown, and scleral ring is red.

BASIC III–V: Older immatures gradually change into adult plumage and appear more like adults than juveniles. Scarlet eyes are attained after four years. Head and beak color, puffy head and neck, white underwing coverts and axillaries, and white bars on

California Condor Basic I (two years old). Much like juvenile with dark head. Arizona, July (WSC)

upperwings are attained after five or six years. **NOTE:** All condors in the wild now have numbered patagial markers.

UNUSUAL PLUMAGES: No unusual plumages have been described.

SIMILAR SPECIES

(1) BALD EAGLE (Pls. 7, 8) juveniles can appear somewhat similar — dark with whitish underwing coverts — but are noticeably smaller, have tawny bellies and long tails, and show long head and neck projection in flight. **(2) BLACK VULTURE** (Pl. 1) does not occur in the range of the California Condor.

FLIGHT

Active flight is with slow, stiff wingbeats. Soars and glides very steadily, appearing much like an airplane or glider, with wings held slightly upraised. When beginning a glide after gaining altitude in a soar, condors take a powerful wingbeat, bending their wings below the body until wingtips almost touch (called a "flex").

MOLT

Annual molt usually begins in February or March and continues until October or November. It is not complete; most flight and tail feathers are replaced every two years. First prebasic (post-juvenile) molt begins the next spring (March–April) after fledging.

BEHAVIOR

California Condors are large vultures that subsist entirely on carrion. They prefer large carcasses, such as deer, cattle, and beached large marine mammals but will readily feed on smaller carrion. They leave night roosts to begin foraging late in the morning, after strong thermals form, often returning to a known carcass. Condors spend much time perched and, when thermals are available, begin soaring, both singly and in small groups. Sunning behavior, common among vultures, has been frequently noted; perched birds spread their wings out and face away from the sun. Condors are usually dominant over other scavengers at carcasses. After feeding, they have a curious habit of rubbing their heads on branches, rocks, or the ground. They bathe frequently, usually at favored sites and often with other condors. They can inflate their cheeks, throats, and necks at will, which then appear quite bloated. Adult's head color varies, depending on mood.

STATUS AND DISTRIBUTION

Dozens of Condors have recently been reintroduced into the wild, at first in their limited range in s. California and later near the Grand Canyon in Arizona. After decades of steadily declining populations, the entire wild population was captured in the mid-1980s for captive breeding.

FINE POINTS

Soaring condors show seven long, narrow, deeply slotted primaries; these are bent upward and appear more brushlike and noticeable than those of other large, soaring raptors. Condors take from 13 to 17 seconds to complete a circle when soaring, longer than other raptors. Tails of flying condors, especially juveniles, sometimes appear to have wedge-shaped tips.

SUBSPECIES

Monotypic.

ETYMOLOGY

"California" and *californianus* refer to this species' range. "Condor" is Spanish and probably came from the Inca word *cuntur,* the name for the Andean Condor. *Gymnos* is Greek for "naked," a reference to the featherless head; *gyps* is Greek for "vulture."

MEASUREMENTS

LENGTH:	109–127 cm (117);	43–50 in. (46)
WINGSPREAD:	249–300 cm (278);	98–118 in. (109)
WEIGHT:	8.2–14.1 kg (10.5);	18–31 lb. (23)

OSPREYS
SUBFAMILY PANDIONINAE

The Osprey, the only species in this subfamily of Accipitridae, occurs throughout our area. Ospreys are large, long-winged, long-legged, eaglelike, fish-eating raptors. They are widespread throughout the N. Hemisphere and Australia. Their outer toes, like those of owls, are reversible; this character and the sharp spicules on the lower surface of the toes allow them to grasp slippery fish.

They are anatomically different from other raptors in Accipitridae, Cathartidae, and Falconidae, primarily in their specialized adaptations for catching fish. Ospreys are thought to be most closely related to the kites in Accipitridae and are often included in a separate family (Pandionidae) in some taxonomic arrangements.

OSPREY

Pandion haliaeetus

DESCRIPTION

The Osprey, a large, long-winged and long-legged raptor, is usually found near water. In flight, their *gull-like crooked wings and white head with wide black eye-stripe* are distinctive. Uppertails on distant flying birds can appear orangish. Sexes are almost alike in plumage, but females are somewhat larger than males on average. Juvenile plumage is similar to that of adults. Cere and legs are dull blue-gray. Perched birds appear long-legged and often show a *narrow white stripe between shoulders and body;* their wingtips extend just beyond tail tip.

ADULT: White head has dark brown central crown and nape patches and *wide dark brown eye-lines* that extend down the sides of the neck to the shoulders. Eyes are bright yellow. Back and upperwing and uppertail coverts are dark brown. Underparts are

Osprey adult male. Males usually have unmarked breasts. Note the striking underwing pattern. Idaho, May (WSC)

Osprey juvenile. Juveniles have orangish eyes and streaking on sides of crown and nape. Pale feather edges on upperparts have worn off. California, August (WSC)

white, usually with a more or less distinct band of short dark streaks forming a necklace across upper breast; females usually have more streaking, but there is some overlap; however, rarely do males show a noticeable necklace and females not show one. Underwings show gray flight feathers, with secondaries a bit darker,

Osprey juvenile. Juveniles show faint rufous wash on underwing coverts and white tips to flight and tail feathers. All show pale primaries and darker secondaries. New Jersey, October (BKW)

Osprey melanistic adult. Overall dark brown except for paler flight feathers and tail as in normal Ospreys. Melanism is rare in raptors. Florida, March (WSC)

black carpal patches, and white secondary underwing coverts; darker greater coverts form a blackish line on each underwing. Short tail appears dark with light bands from above, but light with dark bands from below.

JUVENILE: Similar to adult, but upperparts appear scaly due to pale tips on most upperwing coverts and back feathers. Head is like that of adult except that it has narrow dark streaking in white areas of crown and nape. Eyes are initially red but gradually fade to orange. Recently fledged birds show a rufous wash on napes, breasts, and underwing coverts, but this fades quickly and these areas are usually white by autumn migration. Flight feathers have wide pale tips. Undersides of secondaries are paler than those of adults; greater secondary underwing coverts have white tips, so black lines on underwings are not as distinctive as those of adults. Tail has a wider white terminal band than adult's.

UNUSUAL PLUMAGES: Birds with a few white feathers in place of normally dark ones have been reported. Melanistic individuals have been reported from Florida and France.

SIMILAR SPECIES

(1) **BALD EAGLES** (Pls. 7, 8) are larger, usually have dark bodies, fly with wings level, and lack black carpal patches on underwings (see Basic III Bald Eagle with eye-stripe). (2) **LARGE GULLS** can appear very Osprey-like but are smaller and have shorter, pointed wings, longer necks, and unbanded tails, and they lack the black carpal patches on the underwings.

FLIGHT

Active flight is with slow, steady, shallow wingbeats on somewhat flexible wings. *Soars and glides with wings crooked in a gull-winged shape*, with wrists cocked forward and held above body level and wingtips pointed down and back. Soars sometimes on flat wings. Hovers frequently while hunting over water.

MOLT

Ospreys molt both on the breeding and wintering grounds but they suspend molt during migrations. Molt is typical of large raptors, with primaries showing wave molt and with all rectrices replaced annually. Secondaries are usually replaced every other year; juvenile and later secondaries are the same length. Molt of flight and tail feathers is often asymmetrical and apparently random in older individuals. Juveniles begin the first prebasic (post-juvenile) molt on the winter grounds at an age of five to seven months old and replace all of their primaries and rectrices within 12 months there.

BEHAVIOR

Ospreys are superb fishermen, catching prey with their feet after a spectacular feet-first dive, usually from a hover but sometimes from a glide. They usually enter the water completely. They are able to take off from the surface and, after becoming airborne, shake vigorously to remove water. Ospreys always carry captured fish head forward. Although they are almost exclusively fish eaters, their diet has been reported to include a few other prey items such as birds, turtles, and small mammals. They are usually found near water and leave it only during migration.

Nest sites are usually near water and in the tops of dead trees, but nests are also placed on man-made structures such as duck blinds, channel markers, and navigation aids, and even on telephone poles and small wooden docks. Ground nests have been reported, most frequently on islands. Adults vigorously defend their nests but seldom strike humans. The high, clear, whistled alarm call, repeated continuously, is distinctive.

Courtship flights by males are a series of undulating dives and climbs, usually performed while the bird is carrying a fish and calling constantly. Flying Ospreys sometimes swoop down and drag their feet through the water, a practice that is thought to cool or clean their feet but may also be a displacement behavior.

STATUS AND DISTRIBUTION

Ospreys are common in the main breeding areas of Florida; along the Atlantic Coast, especially the Chesapeake Bay; and in the Great Lakes. They are uncommon inland in w. Montana and Wyoming, n. Idaho, and along the Pacific Coast south to Mexico, common on rivers in n. California, and fairly common from cen. Alaska to Newfoundland on lakes in the Boreal forest. They can be occasionally encountered on migration almost anywhere in the United States. Scattered nestings have occurred elsewhere (e.g., in e. Texas, Tennessee, n. Mississippi, w. Kentucky, s. Indiana, and Illinois). The entire North American population winters in the Caribbean, Central America, and n. South America, except for a few remaining along the Gulf Coast and in s. California. South Florida birds are year-round residents. All one-year-olds remain south on the winter grounds during their second summer. Two-year-olds return north, some to natal areas, but do not breed.

OSPREY

Local breeding

sparse migrant inland

A good number of three-year-olds join the breeding population. Occasionally Ospreys are found at sea far from land. Their distribution is worldwide.

FINE POINTS

Ospreys' lack of a supraorbital ridge makes them look pigeon-headed. In mated pairs, females almost always have the more distinct breast band, but there is overlap in this character. Clear-breasted, unmarked adult birds are usually, but not always, males.

SUBSPECIES

The North American race is *P. h. carolinensis*.

ETYMOLOGY

"Osprey" comes from the Latin *ossifragus,* meaning "bone breaker," but this name probably referred originally to another species. *Pandion* was the name of two mythical kings of Athens; *haliaeetus* is from the Greek *hals* and *aetos,* meaning "sea" and "eagle."

Measurements

LENGTH:	53–66 cm (58);	21–26 in. (23)
WINGSPREAD:	149–171 cm (160);	59–67 in. (63)
WEIGHT:	1.0–1.8 kg (1.6);	2.2–3.9 lb. (3.5)

KITES
FAMILY ACCIPITRIDAE

The five species of kites that occur in our area belong in one of three taxonomic subgroups: the first is characterized by the lack of supraorbital ridges (bony projections above the eyes) and includes the Hook-billed Kite and the Swallow-tailed Kite; the second, characterized by the fusion of the basal joint of the middle toe with the joint next to it, includes the Mississippi Kite and the Snail Kite; and the third, characterized by talons that are flat or rounded below, is represented by the White-tailed Kite.

For field identification purposes, however, it is better to separate the species into two types by wing shape: pointed-winged kites and paddle-winged kites. The more widespread species, the Swallow-tailed, White-tailed, and Mississippi Kites, all have pointed wings. The limited-range species, the Snail and Hook-billed Kites, have paddle-shaped wings.

The name "kite" comes from *cyta,* the Old English name of the two raptors in the genus *Milvus,* the Black and Red Kites. The New World kites were so named because of their light, buoyant flight, which was similar to that of *Milvus* kites. The kite made of wood and paper was also named after the *Milvus* kites.

HOOK-BILLED KITE   PL. 3

Chondrohierax uncinatus

DESCRIPTION

The Hook-billed Kite of the Rio Grande Valley of Texas has a *large hooked beak and broad paddle-shaped wings that pinch into the body on the trailing edges. Lores are greenish below and yellow above.* Sexes are similar in size but have different adult plumages.

Hook-billed Kite adult male. Males are overall dark gray. Note paddle-shaped wings that pinch in at the body. Texas, May (BKW)

Hook-billed Kite adult female. All show distinctive face markings and large hooked beak. Females have wide rufous collar. Texas, May (BKW)

Juvenile plumage is similar to that of adult female. Dark-morph kites occur in other parts of the range but one has been reported recently from Texas. Legs are yellow-orange. Eyes of adults are whitish, and ceres appear dull greenish yellow. Wingtips fall quite short of tail tip on perched kites.

ADULT MALE: Head, back, and upperwing coverts are slate gray (lacking pale collar). Underparts are slate gray, with white barring, more noticeable on the belly. Dark gray underwings show bold white barring on primaries. Slate gray tail has two wide bands, which appear paler gray above and white below.

ADULT FEMALE: Head has dark grayish brown crown and nape, distinctive wide *buffy-rufous collar on hindneck,* rufous cheeks, and creamy throat finely barred rufous. Back and upperwing coverts are gray-brown. Rufous underparts show coarse whitish barring. Pale underwings show rufous coverts and heavily barred primaries and outer secondaries; inner primaries have a rufous wash. Dark brown tail has two wide bands, which appear pale gray-brown above and white below.

JUVENILE: Similar to adult female, but crown and nape are blackish, eyes are medium brown, cere is yellowish, collar on hindneck is white, and whitish underparts have a variable amount of narrow dark brown barring, from almost none to lots. Dark brown back and upperwing covert feathers have buffy to rufous edgings. Pale underwings show creamy coverts and heavily barred primaries and outer secondaries and lack any rufous wash. Tail shows three sets of equal-width dark and light bands.

Hook-billed Kite juvenile. Juveniles have white underwing coverts and narrow tail bands. Texas, February (WSC)

DARK-MORPH ADULT: Entire body and coverts are blackish. Flight feathers are black. Black tail has one wide white band (some females can show a second partial white band). Females have subtly darker crowns. **NOTE:** A dark-morph adult male was recently seen and photographed in Bentsen-Rio Grande Valley State Park in Texas.

DARK-MORPH JUVENILE: Entire body and coverts are brownish black, with subtly darker crown. Outer primaries are barred black and white. Dark tail has two wide pale bands.

UNUSUAL PLUMAGES: No unusual plumages have been reported.

SIMILAR SPECIES

(1) GRAY HAWK (Pl. 15) adult is more finely barred below than adult male Hook-bill and has dark eyes, more pointed wingtips, smaller beak, and its underwings appear paler and lack boldly barred primaries. **(2) RED-SHOULDERED HAWK** (Pls. 16, 17) adults appear somewhat similar in flight to adult female Hook-bills, but its wings are narrower and have crescent-shaped wing panels and its beak is smaller. **(3) ROADSIDE HAWK** (Pl. 16) also has pale eyes and barred underparts but lacks large hooked beak and collar on hindneck and has solid or streaked breast. N. Mexican Roadside Hawks lack the rufous in primaries of adult female Hook-bills.

FLIGHT

Active flight is with slow, languid wingbeats of bowed wings, with wrists slightly cocked up and wingtips down. Soars and glides with wings slightly bowed, usually not soaring high, often just above treetops, but can soar up to heights.

Molt

Not well known. Apparently annual molt is complete for adults, beginning in spring and continuing through autumn. First prebasic (post-juvenile) molt of flight and tail feathers most likely begins in late spring of their second year, although body molt for many (all?) begins late in their first autumn with the head and then the underparts.

Behavior

Hook-billed Kites eat tree snails, which they locate by hunting from a perch in thick forest. Their favorite places for snail extraction are marked by piles of snail shells on the ground below. They soar for a while on early morning thermals and have been reported soaring in flocks. Call is a distinctive rattling, uttered when the bird is disturbed near its nest and during courtship. Courtship flight is with exaggerated slow, deep wingbeats and is performed by both sexes and often a third kite, presumably last year's young.

Status and Distribution

Hook-billed Kites are found in the United States only in the Rio Grande Valley of s. Texas between Falcon Dam and Brownsville. The 10 to 20 resident pairs breed in mesquite woodlands, especially at Santa Ana NWR and Bentsen-Rio Grande Valley State Park, and in riparian woodlands downstream from Falcon Dam. They are apparently not migratory.

Fine Points

In parts of its range outside the United States, this species occurs in two distinct forms that have different-sized beaks: individuals of one form have huge beaks. The difference is thought to be because they eat different-sized snails. Texas birds all have relatively small beaks. Hook-bills lack bony projections above the eye (supraorbital ridge), and thus have a pigeon-headed look.

Subspecies

Texas birds belong to the Mexican race *C. u. acquilonsis*.

Chondrohierax is from the Greek, *chondros*, meaning "composed of cartilage," and *hierakos*, "a falcon or hawk"; *uncinatus* is Latin for "hooked."

MEASUREMENTS

LENGTH:	43–51 cm (46);	16–20 in. (18)
WINGSPREAD:	87–98 cm (92);	34–38 in. (36)
WEIGHT:	215–353 g (277);	8–12 oz. (10)

SWALLOW-TAILED KITE   PL. 4

Elanoides forficatus

DESCRIPTION

The Swallow-tailed Kite is unmistakable in shape and coloration: *bold black-and-white plumage*; long, pointed wings; and *long, deeply forked black tail*. Sexes are alike in plumage, but females average slightly larger. Plumage of juvenile is similar to that of adult. Eyes are dark brown, not scarlet. Cere is dull blue-gray. Legs are blue-gray.

ADULT: Head, underparts, underwing coverts, undertail coverts, and a small area, usually covered, on lower back above rump are pure white. Undertail coverts and belly sometimes appear soiled. Back, rump, upperwing coverts, flight

Swallow-tailed Kite adult. Bold black-and-white plumage and deeply forked tails are distinctive. Texas, May (BKW)

Swallow-tailed Kite adult. Back and upperwings are two-toned. Florida, April (WSC)

Swallow-tailed Kite adult. Note white patches on lower back and pigeon-headed appearance. Texas, May (BKW)

feathers, uppertail coverts, and tail are blue-black and show a purplish to bronze iridescence in good light. In flight, upperwings and back show a silvery sheen (apparently because of a film of powder down on feathers), except for lesser coverts and upper back, which appear as a darker area. Some scapulars are mostly white; this is visible as white patches on back of perched birds but are usually not visible on flying kites.

JUVENILE: Similar to adult, but black areas have more greenish, less purplish iridescence, and flight and tail feathers have narrow white tips, which usually wear off by winter. Forked tail is shorter than that of adult. Fine black shaft streaks on head, nape, and breast feathers are usually not noticeable in the field. Fledglings have rufous bloom on upper breast that disappears soon after fledging.

UNUSUAL PLUMAGES: No unusual plumages have been reported for this species.

SIMILAR SPECIES

No other North American raptor is similar.

FLIGHT

Swallow-tailed Kites spend much time in flight hunting, riding air currents on steady wings with hardly a wingbeat, using their tails as a rudder. Active flight is with slow, flexible wingbeats. Soars and usually glides on flat wings but sometimes glides with wrists below body and wingtips up.

Molt

Not well studied. Many adults begin annual molt in summer while breeding, but apparently complete their molt on winter grounds in South America. Juveniles returning in the spring have usually undergone no molt; they most likely begin the first prebasic (post-juvenile) molt later that summer and complete it on the winter grounds.

Behavior

Swallow-tailed Kites hunt on the wing for a variety of prey: flying insects, tree frogs, hymenopteran nests, bats, lizards, and snakes, all of which are deftly plucked from the ground, air, or tree branches. They also snatch bird nests, from which the nestlings are extracted. They have also been reported to eat fruit. Kites often eat in flight, bending their head down to bite off a morsel from prey held with their feet, and drink on the wing in a swallow-like manner.

During courtship flights, pairs fly in close formation, calling *kee, klee, klee*. Swallow-tailed Kites are especially social and are often seen in groups of up to 50 individuals and form communal night roosts. A roost in Florida in late July contained over 1,500 kites.

Status and Distribution

The Swallow-tailed Kite's breeding range is now restricted to se. Texas, the Gulf Coast of Louisiana, Mississippi, and Alabama; most of Florida; and along the s. Atlantic Coast as far north as South Carolina. Individuals are regularly seen on the Outer Banks of North Carolina and along the Texas coast during migration. Swallow-tailed Kites prefer to breed near water, marshes, swamps, and along river courses or lakes.

During spring migration and after the breeding season in early fall, the birds wander far afield, ranging west to Colorado and north to Minnesota, New York, and s. Canada, and have been recorded casually in the Southwest. Most sightings are of single birds between April and September. The entire population leaves the United States by early September to winter in South America, returning to breeding areas as early as mid- to late February in South Florida and by mid-March farther north.

Prior to 1900 this species bred over a much larger area of the cen. United States as far north as Minnesota.

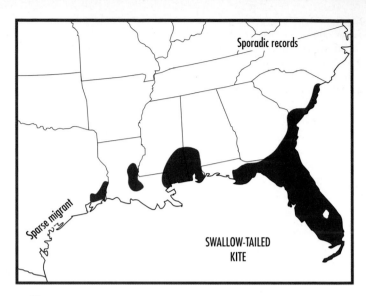

Sporadic records

Sparse migrant

SWALLOW-TAILED KITE

FINE POINTS

Swallow-tailed Kites lack bony projections above the eyes (supraorbital ridge) and so have a pigeon-headed appearance. All kites in the U.S. have dark brown eyes, except for two in captivity, which had orange eyes. Red eyes are erroneously reported in many references.

SUBSPECIES

The North American race is *E. f. forficatus.*

ETYMOLOGY

Elanoides is from the Greek *elanos,* "a kite," and *oideos* meaning "resembling"; *forficatus* in Latin means "deeply forked." The AOU changed the name from "American Swallow-tailed Kite" to "Swallow-tailed Kite" in 1996.

MEASUREMENTS

LENGTH:	52–62 cm (58);	20–25 in. (22)
WINGSPREAD:	119–136 cm (130);	47–54 in. (51)
WEIGHT:	325–500 g (430);	11–18 oz. (15)

Elanus leucurus

DESCRIPTION

The White-tailed Kite is a *whitish falcon-shaped kite* that is *gull-like in color and flight*. Central and outer tail feathers are noticeably shorter than the others. Charcoal black upperwing coverts form *black shoulders on perched birds and black patches on upperwings of flying birds*. Sexes are almost alike in plumage and size. Juvenile plumage is similar to that of adults. On perched birds, wingtips almost reach tail tip. Cere and legs are yellow.

ADULT: White head has narrow black circles around and small black areas in front of eyes. Eyes are orange-red to scarlet. Crown, nape, back, primary and greater secondary upperwing coverts, and uppersides of secondaries are medium gray (males average paler), and uppersides of primaries are a bit darker gray. Lesser and median upperwing coverts are charcoal black. Underparts are white. Underwings show blackish primaries, off-white to whitish secondaries, and white coverts, with *a black carpal patch. Tail is white*, except for gray central feathers.

JUVENILE: Somewhat similar to adult, but crown and nape are gray-brown with buff-tawny streaks. Eyes are brown, lightening to orange with age. Gray-brown back feathers have buffy edgings. Black upperwing coverts also show buffy edgings. Underparts are white, with a rufous wash across breast that fades or is molted

White-tailed Kite adult. Black shoulders and white tail are distinctive. Texas, January (WSC)

White-tailed Kite juvenile. Recently fledged juveniles show a strong rufous wash on breast. Texas, May (BKW)

White-tailed Kite juvenile. All hover for hunting. Small dark carpal patches are distinctive. Note falconlike pointed wings. California, August (WSC)

White-tailed Kite juvenile. All stoop on prey with wings held in a strong V. California, August (WSC)

soon after fledging. Gray flight feathers and greater upperwing coverts have white tips. Undersides of secondaries are pale grey and contrast somewhat with white wing linings. White tail feathers have dusky subterminal bands. Juveniles undergo a more or less complete post-juvenile molt of body feathers (and sometimes a few tail feathers) within months after fledging.

BASIC I : Older immatures in their first winter after undergoing post-juvenile molt appear much more adultlike but are distinguished by white tips to greater upperwing coverts and flight feathers and narrow dusky subterminal tail band. Eyes are pale orangish to orange.

UNUSUAL PLUMAGES: No unusual plumages have been described.

SIMILAR SPECIES

(1) MISSISSIPPI KITE (Pl. 6) has dark body and tail in all plumages. **(2) NORTHERN HARRIER** (Pl. 10) adult male appears somewhat similar. See under that species for differences. **(3) FALCONS** lack white unbarred tail and black carpal patches. **(4) ADULT GULLS** have longer necks and shorter tails and lack black carpal patches on underwings.

FLIGHT

Active flight is with light, steady wingbeats of cupped wings. Soars with wings in a medium dihedral with tips somewhat rounded. Glides with wings in a modified dihedral. Hovers regularly, sometimes dangling their legs. Stoop is distinctive, lowering slowly on wings held in a deep V high above the back and legs dangling, then finishing with a rush to the ground.

Molt

Annual molt of adults is complete, beginning in spring and completed by autumn, but may be suspended during parts of the breeding cycle, especially by the male. First prebasic (post-juvenile) molt begins approximately three months after fledging, continues for another 3 or more months, and is a more or less complete molt of body feathers; it sometimes includes a few tail feathers. Flight and the remaining tail feathers are not replaced until the next spring and summer. Basic I kites have adult body and tail coverts but retain juvenile flight feathers and wing coverts, with white tips of the coverts usually visible as narrow pale lines on both flying and perched kites. Tail molt precedes wing molt. Molt varies with fledging date; kites from early broods show more molt.

Behavior

White-tailed Kites behave somewhat like large Kestrels. Prey is almost exclusively rodents, which they always hunt by hovering. As they plunge after prey, they hold their wings fully stretched upward. Display flight of adult male is with fluttering wings held in a deep V above the body and is accompanied by raspy, creaking calls. Adults have been observed cartwheeling. Tail-cocking behavior, with the tail being raised over the back repeatedly, is distinctive; no other North American raptor does this. At times they are more active just after sunrise and before sundown. Communal night roosts of a few to several hundred kites are formed in fall and winter.

Status and Distribution

White-tailed Kites are fairly common residents west of the Sierra Nevada and deserts of California and in s. Texas; rare in peninsular Florida. They are becoming more numerous and are expanding their breeding range into s. Oregon, s. Arizona, and along the Gulf Coast of Louisiana and Mississippi. Single nest records in e. Oklahoma and Kansas are interesting. This species is nonmigratory, but individuals can wander far afield and have been recorded in New Mexico, Nevada, Georgia, and the Carolinas and as far north as Wisconsin, Minnesota, Nebraska, Washington, and British Columbia. They prefer grassland, savanna, marsh, and riparian habitats.

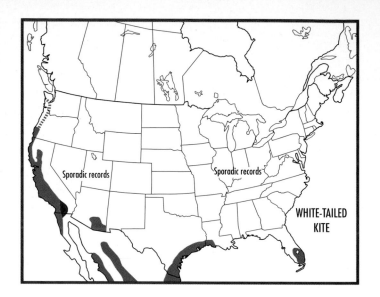

Sporadic records

Sporadic records

WHITE-TAILED
KITE

FINE POINTS

Adults and juveniles have light gray central tail feathers, and
folded uppertails appear this color on perched birds; from below,
their tails appear white. A few kites lack black carpal patches.

SUBSPECIES

The race in North America is *E. l. majusculus*.

ETYMOLOGY

Formerly considered a race of the Black-shouldered Kite (*Elanus
caeruleus*), but is now regarded by the AOU as a separate species
(see Clark and Banks 1992). *Elanus* is Latin for "kite"; *leucurus* is
Greek for "white-tailed."

MEASUREMENTS

LENGTH:	36–41 cm (38);	14–16 in. (15)
WINGSPREAD:	99–102 cm (101);	37–40 in. (39)
WEIGHT:	305–361 g (330);	10–13 oz. (11.6)

Rostrhamus sociabilis

DESCRIPTION

The Snail Kite of south and central Florida is a medium-sized, paddle-winged kite with a *thin, deeply hooked beak*. Sexes are similar in size but have different adult plumages. Juvenile and Basic I plumages are similar to that of adult female. Basic II (subadult) male plumage is similar to that of adult males. On perched kites, *wingtips extend beyond tail tip*.

ADULT MALE: Head, body, leg feathers, and wing coverts are slate gray. Eyes are scarlet, and *cere and face skin (sparsely feathered lores) are bright orange to reddish orange* (breeding). Flight feathers are unmarked slaty black above and below and contrast with paler upperwing coverts on upperwings. Blackish tail has square corners, narrow pale band on tip, and wide white base with a sharp line of contrast; tail coverts are white. *Legs are bright reddish orange.* Entire plumage is covered with a chalky bloom (lost on museum specimens). Adult male plumage is attained in four years.

ADULT FEMALE: Head is dark brown except for distinctive face pattern of narrow whitish superciliary lines and whitish cheek patches and throat. Cere and face skin (sparsely feathered lores) are yellow to orange (breeding). Eyes are a deeper red than those of adult male. Back and upperwing coverts are dark brown, with

Snail Kite adult male. Apple snails are primary prey. Florida, March (BKW)

Snail Kite adult male. Adult males are overall dark gray. Note the paddle-shaped wings. Florida, March (WSC)

Snail Kite adult female. Adult females are overall darker compared to immatures. Florida, July (WSC)

rufous feather edges in fresh plumage. Dark brown breast shows irregular whitish streaking; dark brown belly is mottled or streaked whitish and tawny. Undersides of wings show dark brown coverts mottled tawny and pale flight feathers that are narrowly banded, with subterminal band much wider, and usually with pale patches at base of outer primaries. Blackish brown tail has square corners, narrow pale band on tip, and wide white base with a sharp line of contrast; tail coverts are white. Leg feathers are dark brown with some pale mottling on younger kites. Legs are yellow to orange. Older females can appear somewhat like adult males, with dark gray heads that lack buffy superciliary lines and mostly dark underparts with some tawny mottling, but they retain an overall brown cast. Adult female plumage is attained in three or four years.

JUVENILE: (Sexes alike.) Similar to adult female, but superciliary lines and cheek patches are larger and buffy, eyes are dark brown, feathered lores are grayish, and cere is pale yellow to yellow. Dark brown upperparts have more and wider pale feather edges, and buffy underparts are streaked dark brown. Flight feathers and greater upperwing coverts have narrow pale tips, noticeable as pale lines on upperwings of flying kites. Undersides of wings show dark brown coverts mottled tawny and pale flight feathers that are narrowly banded, with subterminal band rather narrow. Dusky tail has ill-defined border with white base; tail coverts are white. Leg feathers are whitish with some dark streaking, and legs are yellow.

BASIC I: (Sexes alike.) Similar to juvenile, but replacement flight feathers have wider dark subterminal band, replacement tail is like that of adult female's, legs are orangish, and eyes have become reddish brown.

Snail Kite Basic I. Similar to juvenile. Note thin, deeply hooked beak. Florida, January (WSC)

BASIC II: (Sexes alike.) Similar to Basic I kites, but they are more heavily marked on undersides and eyes are scarlet on males and dark red on females. Whitish to tawny superciliaries and cheek patches are smaller; former does not reach forehead.

BASIC III (SUBADULT) MALE: After their third molt, subadult males are similar in plumage to adult males, with scarlet eyes, but they appear dark brown and slate gray; they also have a whitish throat patch, rufous-brown barring on belly and leg feathers, and bold white barring on the undersides of flight feathers. Their ceres, face skin, and legs are orange.

BASIC III FEMALE: Plumage is usually not distinguishable from adult female's.

UNUSUAL PLUMAGES: No unusual plumages have been reported.

SIMILAR SPECIES

NORTHERN HARRIER (Pl. 10) also shows white patch on uppertail coverts but has longer, narrower wings; flies in a more direct manner with wings held in a dihedral; and has no white on the base of longer, noticeably banded tail.

FLIGHT

Active flight is with *slow, floppy wingbeats on cupped wings.* Glides on cupped wings; soars with wings somewhat less cupped.

MOLT

Not well studied. Apparently adults undergo one more or less complete annual molt, beginning in February or March. Not all flight feathers are replaced annually. First prebasic (post-juvenile) molt begins as a partial body molt within two to four months after fledging. Subsequent immature molts are more or less complete and apparently begin at the same time as those of adults.

BEHAVIOR

Snail Kites are highly social and are often seen in large groups. They feed almost exclusively on snails of the genus *Pomacea,* which they capture from near the water's surface. They forage by slowly flying 2 to 5 meters above the water with more or less continuous slow flapping. When a snail is sighted, they brake, swoop down, and pluck it from the water deftly with a foot. The snail is transferred from foot to beak in the air. Kites also hunt from perches and perch to extract snails from shells using their specialized feet and beak. Hunting can take place at any time of day. Some prey items other than snails have been reported, especially turtles and crayfish.

Snail Kites form communal roosts at night, and nesting is often loosely colonial. During the middle of the day, they often soar, sometimes high enough to be out of sight from the ground. The vocalization most often heard is a harsh rattle.

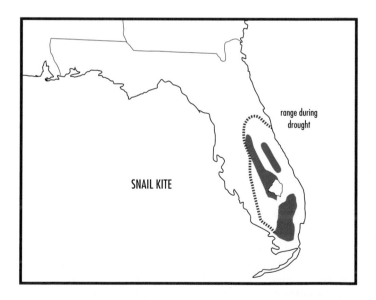

range during drought

SNAIL KITE

Status and Distribution

Snail Kites are fairly common but local, restricted to freshwater marshes and other wet areas in cen. and South Florida. During times of drought, however, they are found away from their usual haunts. Prior to 1900, the species was recorded from a much larger area of Florida, but draining of surface water has reduced its range. The species is common and widespread in marshlands from s. Mexico, Cuba, and Central America south to n. Argentina.

A recent photo record of a juvenile from s. Texas was accepted as the second state record.

Fine Points

The lores of adults are sparsely feathered, and this "face skin" is the same color as the cere. The lores of juveniles and Basic I kites are feathered and appear grayish.

Subspecies

The kites in Florida and Mexico belong to the race *R. s. plumbeus*.

Etymology

Called the "Snail Kite" because it preys almost exclusively on snails. *Rostrhamus* is from the Latin *rostrum*, "beak" and the Greek *hamus*, "hook"; *sociabilis* is Latin for "gregarious." The Florida race was formerly called the Everglade Kite.

Measurements

LENGTH:	36–40 cm (38);	14–16 in. (15)
WINGSPREAD:	106–116 cm (111);	43–46 in. (45)
WEIGHT:	340–570 g (420);	12–20 oz. (15)

MISSISSIPPI KITE

PL. 6

Ictinia mississippiensis

Description

The Mississippi Kite of the southern Great Plains, Mississippi valley, the Southeast, and recently the Southwest, is a dark falcon-shaped kite. *Outer primary is noticeably shorter than others.* Sexes are similar in plumage, but females are somewhat larger;

Mississippi Kite adult male. Adult males have black tails. Note short outer primary and flared tail tip. Colorado, June (WSC)

Mississippi Kite adult female. Adult females have pale shafts and undersides with dark tips on outer tail feathers. Wingtips extend beyond tail tip on all. Colorado, June (BKW)

juveniles have a different plumage. Kites in Basic I plumage returning in their first spring have adultlike gray bodies but have retained juvenile tail and flight feathers. *Wingtips of perched kites extend beyond tail tip.*

ADULT MALE: Head is whitish to pale gray, with a small area of black in front of and around eye. Eyes are scarlet. Cere is pale to dark gray, and beak is dark. Back and upperwing coverts are slate gray. Underparts, including undertail coverts, are medium gray. Whitish upperside of secondaries form a *whitish band on perched birds* and a *wide whitish band on inner trailing edge of upperwing* on flying birds. Underwing is slate gray with a short narrow white band on tips of secondaries. Males in flight often show rufous areas on inner primaries. *Flared tail* is overall black. Legs are orange-yellow, usually with a gray cast to upperside of toes and front of lower tarsi.

ADULT FEMALE: Similar to adult male but head is darker gray; tail is brownish black with pale feather shafts and usually pale undersides with dark terminal band on outer feathers; primaries usually show less rufous (but can have as much as shown by males); and undertail coverts vary from gray to gray with whitish barring to entirely white. Lower belly feathers are sometimes paler gray or white.

JUVENILE: Head is gray-brown with fine whitish streaks and *short, wide creamy to buffy superciliary lines.* Creamy throat is un-

Mississippi Kite juvenile. Juveniles are heavily streaked below with three narrow white tail bands. Virginia, August (WSC)

streaked. Eyes are dark brown, cere is yellow, and beak is dark. Back and upperwing coverts are dark brown with rufous to buffy feather edging. Dark brown scapulars show white spots. Underparts are creamy, with wide dark brown to rufous streaking. Dark flight feathers have white tips: they may be entirely dark; dark with a white spot on outer primary and pale area on inner two; or largely white on primaries, with or without white bases on secondaries. Secondaries show a grayish cast on uppersides and have narrow white tips. Underwings have mottled rufous-brown coverts. Dark brown tail has three or four incomplete narrow pale bands — sometimes not visible on folded uppertails — however, some show no pale bands on folded undersides of tails, and still others show pale undersides of outer tail feathers with wide dusky tips, as in adult females. Legs are orange-yellow to yellow, with a variable amount of gray wash on uppersides of toes.

BASIC I (SUBADULT): Kites returning their first spring have molted into adultlike gray bodies that often show small, oval white or buffy blotches both above and below, the result of retained juvenile feathers and whitish bases to first adult feathers. Eyes are scarlet. Cere and beak are as in adults. Flight and tail feathers and underwing coverts are retained from juvenile plumage. Subadults lack whitish band on trailing edge of wing. Sexes can often be determined by head color (whiter on males) and by undertail coverts (uniform gray on males and white or barred with white on females). Most individuals show noticeable molt of primaries throughout the summer. Underwing coverts are gradually replaced with gray adult feathers during the summer. The innermost or outermost or both secondaries are sometimes replaced by late summer. Juvenile outer primaries, most of the secondaries, and many tail feathers are not replaced until after migration to the winter grounds. Legs are orange-yellow, usually with a gray cast to uppersides of toes and front of tarsi. **EARLY STAGE:** After returning in the spring, until midsummer, subadults show no extensive molt in flight and tail feathers and have juvenile underwing coverts, but they soon show a gap as they drop the inner primaries in late May or early June. **LATE STAGE:** In midsummer subadults have begun replacing primaries and tail feathers and have new gray underwing coverts.

UNUSUAL PLUMAGES: No unusual plumages have been reported.

SIMILAR SPECIES

(1) PEREGRINE FALCON (Pl. 38) is similar in shape but has dark head, dark mustache marks, and straight sides to tail. Peregrine's flight is more powerful and purposeful, not as buoyant. **(2) WHITE-TAILED KITE** (Pl. 4) is similar in shape to Mississippi Kite. See under that species for differences.

FLIGHT

Active flight is light, buoyant, and graceful on flexible wings. Mississippi Kites spend considerable time soaring and gliding on flat wings, rarely flapping. Wingtips often curl up during soaring. Does not hover.

MOLT

Annual molt of adults is apparently complete, with most of the molt done on the winter grounds in South America. Molt is initiated after breeding but is suspended for migration. First prebasic (post-juvenile) molt begins approximately four to six months after fledging, soon after juveniles reach the winter grounds. It consists of an almost complete body molt, but no wing coverts or flight or tail feathers are replaced. After returning to the breeding grounds the next spring in Basic I plumage, they complete the body molt and initiate the molt of primaries in late May or early June, of underwing coverts in early summer, and of tail feathers beginning in late July or August or even later. The wing coverts are usually completely replaced, but only 5 to 7 inner primaries, the inner secondary, and usually only the central and outermost tail feathers are replaced. This molt is suspended for fall migration and completed on the winter grounds.

Mississippi Kites capture their prey, mainly insects, on the wing. Insects are often eaten in flight. But they hunt from perches as well, and nestlings are also fed frogs, toads, lizards, bats, snakes, and mice. They sometimes capture small birds in flight.

Kites are gregarious and often breed in small colonies of up to 20 pairs and hunt in small flocks. Groups of up to several hundred individuals are encountered in migrating flocks and night roosts. When not on the wing, birds perch inconspicuously for hours. Adults may be aggressive in their nest defense, and attacks on humans have been reported. Usually silent, around the nest they utter a double-syllable call, somewhat similar to the call of the Broad-winged Hawk.

STATUS AND DISTRIBUTION

The numbers and range of the Mississippi Kite are increasing. The main breeding range is on the s. Great Plains north to cen. Kansas and west to se. Colorado, along the s. Mississippi R. north to s. Illinois and Indiana, along the Gulf Coast into n. Florida, and along the s. Atlantic coast north to North Carolina and n. Vir-

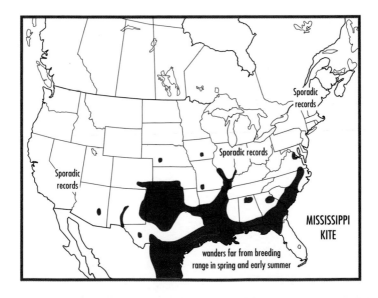

Sporadic records

Sporadic records

Sporadic records

MISSISSIPPI KITE

wanders far from breeding range in spring and early summer

ginia. Isolated breeding colonies exist in Arizona and New Mexico. On the Great Plains, Mississippi Kites prefer parks and shelterbelts; in the Southeast, Southwest, and along the Mississippi R., they prefer to nest in riparian forests.

The entire population is migratory, retiring to South America in the fall and not returning until spring. The birds are seen on migration in large numbers in s. Texas in late August and early September and again in early April. Individuals wander far outside the breeding area in late spring and late summer and are reported from New York, Maine, Wisconsin, Minnesota, Saskatchewan, Wyoming, and California.

FINE POINTS

The relatively short outer primary extends only four-fifths of the way to wingtip, a character that can be seen on a flying bird. A few juveniles have dark brown tails lacking pale bands.

SUBSPECIES

Monotypic.

ETYMOLOGY

"Mississippi" and *mississippiensis* refer to the state in which the type specimen was collected by Wilson. *Ictinia* is from the Greek *iktinos,* meaning "kite." Species name was originally spelled *misisippiensis,* a printer's error. This form was used until the AOU corrected it in 1976.

MEASUREMENTS

LENGTH:		33–37 cm (35);	13–15 in. (14)
WINGSPREAD:		75–83 cm (79);	29–33 in. (31)
WEIGHT:	Male	216–269 g (246);	8–10 oz. (9)
	Female	278–339 g (311);	10–12 oz. (11)

Sea and Fishing Eagles
Genus *Haliaeetus*

Only one species of sea or fishing eagle of the genus *Haliaeetus,* the Bald Eagle, occurs regularly throughout North America. Two others, the White-tailed Eagle and the Steller's Sea Eagle, occur as rare vagrants (see under Vagrants for those species accounts). They are large eagles usually found near water, where they can prey on their favorite food, fish. They also take a variety of other prey, including waterfowl, regularly eat carrion, and pirate prey from other raptors. They are characterized by large size, large beaks, pale heads in adult plumage, and unfeathered lower tarsi.

Eagles have proportionally longer wings than the smaller buteos, which they resemble in flight. Females are larger than males. All species have longer tails and wider wings in their first (juvenile) plumage than in older immature and adult plumages.

"Eagle" comes from the Middle English *egle* and the Old French *egle* or *aigle,* which in turn derived from the Latin word *aquila,* "eagle." *Haliaeetus* is from the Greek *halos* and *aetos* for "sea" and "eagle," respectively.

BALD EAGLE

PLS. 7, 8

Haliaeetus leucocephalus

DESCRIPTION

The Bald Eagle, one of two large, dark North American eagles, is widespread but local and usually found near water. In flight, *head and neck protrude more than half tail length.* Trailing edge of wings is nearly parallel to leading edge, except on juveniles and Basic I eagles. Sexes are alike in plumage; females are larger than males. Adult's *white head and tail* and dark brown body and wings

Bald Eagle adult. White head and bright yellow-orange beak are distinctive. Washington, February (WSC)

Bald Eagle Subadult (Basic IV). Some first-plumage adults show black on head and tip of tail. Washington, February (WSC)

are distinctive. Plumages of juveniles and older immatures are different from adult's. There are no plumage differences between northern and southern eagles. Unfeathered legs are orange-yellow. Wingtips almost reach tail tip on perched Balds, except for juveniles, on which they fall quite short of tip. Adult plumage is acquired in four or five years.

ADULT: *Head and neck are white,* sometimes with a few brown or black spots, even on older adults. *Beak and cere are bright orange-yellow;* eyes are pale lemon yellow. Body and wing coverts are dark brown with paler feather edging. Flight feathers are dark brown. Tail coverts and *tail are white.*

JUVENILE: Head is dark brown, with crown and superciliaries somewhat paler brown, more noticeable in winter and spring. Beak and cere are black, and eyes are dark brown. *Back and upperwing coverts are tawny brown and contrast with dark brown flight feathers,* which can show a whitish wash on undersides of some feathers, especially inner secondaries and inner primaries. Breast is dark brown and usually contrasts with dark tawny (fresh) to creamy (faded) belly. Some juveniles have white streaking on underparts, usually where breast and belly meet but sometimes sparsely elsewhere as well. The trailing edges of wings are relatively smooth as all of the secondaries are the same length, but they appear gently serrated, as each secondary has a pointed tip. Tail is noticeably longer than in subsequent plumages and is uniformly dark, dark with a pale oval patch on the upperside (usu-

Bald Eagle Basic I. Basic I and II eagles can show white triangles on their backs, but beak is all dark on Basic I eagles. Colorado, February (BKW)

Bald Eagle juvenile. Juveniles have two-toned upperwings. Washington, February (WSC)

ally not seen on later plumages), or pale mottled gray with dark terminal band and dark edges. Wingtips fall quite short of tail tip on perched juveniles. **NOTE:** All juveniles and Basic I and II eagles have pale lores and yellow gapes and most show *white axillaries and white lines on underwings* (but the latter may not be noticeable on birds that have mostly white underwing coverts). These characters are not useful for aging.

BASIC I: Dark brown head has wide *buffy (rarely whitish) crown and superciliaries* that contrast strongly with wide dark brown cheeks and pale throat. Eyes have lightened to light brown or amber (rarely whitish), and beak and cere have faded to a slate gray with a little yellow visible at the nostrils. Back and upperwing coverts are dark brown, usually showing a *white triangle on back* that has a variable amount of dark spotting. Upperwings are uniform dark brown, with a variable amount of white spotting on the coverts. Dark brown breast appears as *a dark bib*, contrasting with white belly, which usually has a variable amount of short dark streaks.

The most distinctive feature of Basic I eagles in flight is the ragged trailing edge of the wings, due to the mix of new shorter and retained longer secondaries. New secondaries are shorter and have blunt tips; retained juvenile ones are longer and have pointed tips. Most have replaced about half of their secondaries, however, some southern eagles, especially in Florida, have replaced more because of the longer molt season, and others, pre-

Bald Eagle dilute-plumage adult. Unusual plumage shows reduction in dark brown pigmentation in the plumage. Washington, February (WSC)

sumably northern eagles with a shorter molt season, have replaced fewer. Usually old secondaries S3–S4 and S7–S11 show as two groups of paler, longer feathers on trailing edge of wings. From 3 to 6 primaries (P1–P3 to P1–P6) are new and noticeably darker. Tail molt is usually complete; new shorter tail is dirty white to whitish, with dark band on tip and dark edges.

BASIC II: Similar to Basic I eagles, but *crown and superciliaries are whitish;* dark lines behind eyes are narrower; and cheeks and throat are usually whiter. Eyes are now pale brown to whitish yellow, beak has lightened to horn color with some dirty yellow spots, and cere is yellowish. White triangle on back and white belly are often, but not always, retained (See Note below). Juvenile secondaries have often been replaced by shorter feathers; wings now appear smooth on the trailing edge. However, sometimes a longer old secondary or two (S4 or S9 or both) is retained. Wings now appear narrower than those of juveniles or Basic I eagles. Molt of primaries continues where it left off in post-juvenile molt, but usually one (rarely two) outer juvenile primary (P10) is retained. One to three inner primaries (P1-P3) have been replaced again. **NOTE:** Some Basic I and II eagles have dark heads, backs, and bellies that show little or no white; they are best aged using characters on the beak and cere, and, in flight, the trailing edge of the wings.

BASIC III: Appears somewhat adultlike. Heads are now mostly white, sometimes with narrow Osprey-like dark eye lines and often with some brownish streaking on crown and nape. Yellow-orange beak shows some dusky smudges, cere is yellow-orange, and eyes are usually pale yellow. White on neck does not extend as far down as on adults. Some whitish feathers are retained on the body, wing coverts, and flight feathers; and tail coverts are white with dark mottling and dark tips. Tails are variable at this age; they are often white with dark mottling and tips but can be like those of younger immatures. Basic III eagles usually have new outer primaries (P10) but some retain juvenile P10 on one or both wings. New flight feathers are uniformly dark, lacking white, but can show some white mottling on inner secondaries. **NOTE:** It is not always possible to distinguish all Basic II and III eagles, as advanced Basic IIs and retarded Basic IIIs can be intermediate between the characters described for the age classes above.

BASIC IV: Some eagles attain full adult plumage at four years, but others (subadults) show white heads with brown or black streaking or narrow Osprey-like dark eye lines or both. Their body and wing coverts are usually dark brown with few, if any, of the white areas shown in the previous plumage. Tail coverts are usually all white. Their tails often show a dark terminal band on many or all feathers. **NOTE:** It is occasionally not possible to distinguish some Basic III and IV eagles, as advanced Basic IIIs and retarded Basic IVs can be intermediate between the characters described for the age classes above.

UNUSUAL PLUMAGES: Several dilute-plumage juveniles and adults have cream-colored bodies and wing coverts. Partial albino nestlings and immatures have been seen in the West.

SIMILAR SPECIES

GOLDEN EAGLE (Pls. 32, 33) in flight shows head and neck that protrude less than half tail length, whereas head and neck of Bald Eagle protrudes more than half the tail length. The trailing edges of wings are more curved on Goldens. Immature Goldens have white on underwings restricted to base of flight feathers; white on Balds is primarily on underwing coverts and axillaries. Axillaries of Goldens are always dark, but they are white on immature Balds. White in Golden's tail usually extends to the edges (except on some older immatures), whereas immature Balds always have dark edges on whitish tails, which can be otherwise similar to tails of Goldens. Tawny median upperwing coverts of adult and older immature Goldens form a tawny bar on upperwings, visible on flying and perched birds and lacking on all Balds. Perched Goldens show the golden nape, yellow cere, and bicolored beak; Balds usually have uniformly colored cere and beak. Bald's tarsi are bare; Golden's are completely covered with buffy feathers. Balds begin gliding after active flight with a downstroke of their wings; Golden Eagles begin gliding with an upstroke.

Flight

Active flight is with slow, powerful wingbeats. Soars usually on flat wings but sometimes with a small dihedral. Glides on flat wings with wrists cocked forward. They soar often, much of the time with other eagles. Bald Eagles have a noticeable, unusual flight behavior of banking and flapping their wings vigorously while vertical, apparently a danger signal to other eagles of human presence.

Molt

Annual molt of adults is not complete, beginning in spring, finishing in late autumn, and usually suspended for winter. Eagles in Florida most likely continue molt throughout the winter. Only about half of the flight and body feathers are replaced annually, but the tail is usually completely replaced. Post-juvenile molt begins in March or April and is not complete, with from 4 to 6 primaries (P_1–P_4 to P_1–P_6) and from 4 to 7 secondaries (S_1–S_2, S_4–S_5, and S_{12}–S_{14}) replaced.

Behavior

Bald Eagles are usually found near water, where they can find fish, their favorite food, but they also occur far from water, especially in winter and on migration. Breeding areas are almost always near water. In winter, when fish may be scarce, they also eat carrion and waterfowl. They regularly pirate food from other raptors, especially Ospreys, but also other Balds. They are superb fishermen and agile raptors but prefer to obtain food in the easiest possible way. Nevertheless, they will pursue with agility and perseverance other raptors with prey, sometimes for long chases.

Bald Eagles are social and form communal night roosts, most commonly in winter, of several up to occasionally several hundred eagles. Individuals often spend considerable time perching; some remain perched in night roosts for a day or two. They are vocal, particularly around other eagles.

Cartwheeling (talon-grappling), when two eagles lock talons and whirl with each other while in flight, is almost always a territorial defense.

Nests are almost always in a supercanopy tree, and some become huge after years of use. Occasional nests are placed on a cliff ledge, and even on the ground in the Aleutian Islands.

Bald Eagles are locally common during the breeding season in Florida; Chesapeake Bay; coastal Maine through the Maritime Provinces; Great Lakes; the Boreal lake region from w. Ontario through to coastal British Columbia; most of Alaska, where they are abundant on the se. coast; Washington south to n. California; and the greater Yellowstone areas of w. Wyoming, s.-cen. Montana, and e. Idaho. Smaller local breeding populations exist along the Gulf Coast of Texas and Louisiana, coastal South Carolina, along the Mississippi R., and in cen. Arizona. There is an increasing number of widely scattered pairs in many other states. Most individuals leave inland northern breeding areas in winter. Large winter concentrations have been noted along Chilkat R. in Alaska, in Klamath basin in Oregon, and along the upper Mississippi R. Some wintering and migrant Bald Eagles are found far away from water in areas of the West. Many nonbreeding birds from Florida and the Southeast disperse north and west throughout e. North America during summer.

BALD
EAGLE

Fine Points

Many nape feathers in juvenile and older immature eagles have buffy tips, but these are much less noticeable than the golden nape of Golden Eagles. Bald's wrists during glides are pushed forward more and primaries are folded more than are those of Goldens. Bald Eagles have unfeathered tarsi for about 1½ inches above the feet.

Subspecies

Best thought of as monotypic, as the two described races differ only in size, with northern eagles clinally larger.

Etymology

In Old English *balde* means "white"; thus "Bald-headed Eagle" for their white heads, later shortened to "Bald Eagle." *Haliaeetus* is from the Greek *halos*, "sea," and *aetos*, "eagle"; *leucocephalus* is from the Greek *leucos*, "white," and *kephalus*, "head."

Measurements

LENGTH:	70–90 cm (79);	27–35 in. (31)
WINGSPREAD:	180–243 cm (210);	71–96 in. (83)
WEIGHT:	2.5–6.6 kg (4.6);	5.5–14.5 lb. (9.5)

HARRIERS
GENUS *Circus*

Circus, a worldwide genus of 13 species, is represented in our area by a single species, the Northern Harrier. Harriers are slender, medium-sized raptors that have long legs, wings, and tails and occur mainly in open areas. They have owllike facial disks and, in most species, a conspicuous white patch on the uppertail coverts. Adult males and females have different plumages; males are usually gray, females brown. Juveniles are similar in plumage to adult females. Harriers hunt with a distinctive slow, quartering hunting flight low over the ground with wings held above the horizontal; they are active throughout the day, especially at dawn and dusk.

"Harrier" comes from the Old English *hergian,* meaning "to harass by hostile attacks."

NORTHERN HARRIER   PL. 10

Circus cyaneus

DESCRIPTION

The widespread Northern Harrier, a slim-bodied raptor, has a long tail, wings, and legs. In all plumages they show a *white patch on the uppertail coverts* and a *dark head that appears hooded.* Their slow, quartering flight, low over the ground with wings held in a strong dihedral, is distinctive. They all show an owllike facial disk when seen up close. Plumages of adult males and females are different, those of Basic I by sex are very similar to those of adult, and plumages of juveniles are similar to adult females'. Females are noticeably larger than males. Cere is greenish yellow to yellow. Legs are orange-yellow. Wingtips fall somewhat short of tail tip on perched harriers.

Northern Harrier adult male. Harriers hunt low over the ground with wings held above the horizontal. All show white uppertail coverts. Oregon, February (WSC)

Northern Harrier adult female. Adult females have barred flanks and heavily streaked underparts. Oregon, February (WSC)

ADULT MALE: *Gray head, neck, and upper breast form a dark hood,* with a small brownish or pale area on nape sometimes noticeable. Eyes are lemon yellow, usually with an orangish cast. Back is darker sooty gray, and upperwing coverts are gray to sooty gray. Uppersides of flight feathers are gray with black tips. *White uppertail covert patch is distinctive.* White underparts show small rufous spots, heavier on breast. Underwings are mainly white, sometimes with indistinct dark markings on coverts, and with wide black tips on outer primaries, narrow gray tips on inner primaries, and dark band formed by narrow black tips of secondaries. Leg feathers and undertail coverts are white, often covered with small rufous spots. Tail appears medium gray above and whitish below, with narrow dark bands, subterminal widest; bands are rufous on basal half of outer feathers.

ADULT FEMALE: Head, back, and upperwing coverts are dark brown, with tawny-buff streaking on neck and tawny-buff mottling on median upperwing coverts. Eyes are yellow flecked with brown to yellow (taking two or three years to become completely yellow). Uppersides of flight feathers are dark brown with indistinct paler brown bands; older females usually show a gray cast on them and the pale bands on the uppertail. *White uppertail covert patch is distinctive.* Primaries below are white with narrow dark brown banding; secondaries are white with wider dark brown bands and appear a bit darker than primaries. Axillaries and greater underwing coverts are dark brown, forming a small dark patch on underwings; other wing coverts are buffy with dark brown markings.

Northern Harrier Basic I male. Head, breast, and upperparts are browner than those of adult males. Colorado, January (BKW)

Northern Harrier juvenile male (winter/spring). Rufous color of lightly streaked underparts usually fades to creamy by winter. Colorado, February (BKW)

Buffy (fresh) to creamy (faded) underparts are completely streaked dark brown, with dark brown barring noticeable on flanks of flying harriers. Buffy to creamy leg feathers and undertail coverts are marked with large rufous-brown spots. Central pairs of tail feathers show even-width light and dark brown bands; outer ones show even-width rufous-buffy and dark brown bands.

JUVENILE: Similar to adult female but appears overall darker, with much less tawny-buff streaking on neck and less tawny-buff mottling on upperwing coverts. Eyes of females are chocolate brown; eyes of males vary from light gray to light gray-brown to greenish yellow (rarely brown). By spring, eyes of females are pale brown and those of males are yellowish. Underparts in fresh plumage are dark rufous but fade to pale buff or creamy by spring, and if they have dark streaking, it is restricted to upper breast and flanks. They lack the flank barring of adult females. Underwing pattern is similar to that of adult female, but pale bands through secondaries are dusky; these and dark axillaries and greater coverts form a *dark secondary patch* on each underwing. Rufous leg feathers and undertail coverts are unmarked. Tail is like that of adult female.

BASIC I (SUBADULT) MALE: Almost like adult males but show a brownish cast to crown, face, nape patch, breast, back, and upperwing coverts; more and browner markings on underparts and underwing coverts; more or less noticeable black banding on undersides of flight feathers; and wider dark bands in the tail. Facial ring is often more distinct, and eyes usually lack orangish cast.

BASIC I (SUBADULT) FEMALE: Like adult females, except that some have more rufous-buff underparts and fewer pale markings on head and upperparts. Their eyes are pale brown to yellow with brown flecks.

UNUSUAL PLUMAGES: A dilute plumage harrier was seen repeatedly in Rhode Island. Albinism has been reported for the Eurasian race. A melanistic harrier seen in California was an overall dark sooty charcoal gray, had yellow irides and cere, orange-yellow legs, and black tips to outer primaries and lacked white uppertail coverts. It was thought to be an adult male. Another melanistic harrier, seen in Montana, was overall dark brown and judged to be an adult female by relative size, eye color, and markings on tail and undersides of primaries. Both lacked white uppertail coverts.

SIMILAR SPECIES

(1) ROUGH-LEGGED HAWK (Pls. 30, 31) light morph has white at base of tail, not on uppertail coverts, and a dark carpal patch on underwing. **(2) TURKEY VULTURE** (Pl. 1) also flies with wings in a dihedral but is larger, has a dark body, red head, and lacks white uppertail coverts. **(3) WHITE-TAILED KITE** (Pl. 4) appears gray, black, and white like adult male harriers but has black shoulder patch, small black carpal marks on underwings, and white tail; it lacks gray hood, black trailing edge of underwings, and white uppertail coverts. **(4) RED-SHOULDERED HAWK** (Pl. 17) adult can appear similar to rufous-colored juvenile harriers when soaring or gliding at height but has crescent-shaped wing panel and lacks dark secondary patches. **(5) SWAINSON'S HAWK** (Pls. 20, 21) also flies with wings in a strong dihedral and can show pale uppertail coverts but has pointed wingtips and two-toned underwings.

FLIGHT

Harrier's slow, quartering flight low over the ground, with wings held in a strong dihedral, is distinctive. Active flight is with soft, slow wingbeats of flexible wings. Harriers usually soar with wings in a slight dihedral but also on flat wings and appear somewhat buteo-like when soaring and gliding at high altitudes. They glide at altitude with wings in a modified dihedral, but when hunting close to the ground, they glide with wings in a strong dihedral.

MOLT

Annual molt of adults is usually complete. Adult females begin molt in late spring, prior to egg laying, but can suspend it while breeding until young are independent. Males begin molt later than females but complete it earlier. Juveniles molt directly into Basic I plumage in their second summer, beginning in late spring. They usually retain a few juvenile upperwing or uppertail coverts in Basic I plumage, and sometimes a juvenile secondary or two.

BEHAVIOR

Northern Harriers hunt using a distinctive quartering flight, flying low over the ground and pouncing quickly when prey is spotted. They occur mainly in open fields, meadows, grasslands, prairies, and marshes but usually breed only in moister habitats. Males prey more on birds; females more on mammals. They have been seen drowning waterfowl. Studies have shown that Northern Harriers can locate prey by sound almost as well as owls can, an explanation for their owllike facial disk.

When soaring and quartering in strong winds, harriers rock somewhat like a Turkey Vulture. Courtship flights of males are spectacular, with steep dives and climbs and a series of rapid loops with the bird upside down at the top of each loop.

The Northern Harrier is the only North American raptor that is regularly polygynous; one male may mate with as many as three females. Nests are placed on the ground. Harriers usually perch on the ground but will use fence posts or other low perches and occasionally trees and phone lines. In winter, they form communal night roosts on the ground in grassy areas composed of a few to hundreds of birds, sometimes in company with Short-eared Owls.

STATUS AND DISTRIBUTION

Northern Harriers are fairly common as breeding birds in the north, less common farther south, breeding throughout most of the w. United States and mid-latitudes of e. United States (with scattered breeding records farther south, including the Gulf Coast of Texas) north to the Boreal forests of Canada and Alaska. Northern populations are migratory, and in winter harriers are found throughout most of the United States.

FINE POINTS

Juvenile's eye color is dimorphic: chocolate to medium brown in females and gray to gray-brown to greenish yellow in males.

NORTHERN HARRIER

Subspecies

The North American race is *C. c. hudsonius*. The Eurasian race, *C. c. cyaneus* differs enough from ours that they could be considered separate species.

Etymology

Circus is from the Greek *kirkos*, "circle," from its habit of flying in circles; *cyaneus* comes from Greek *kyaneous*, "dark blue," for the male's back color. It was formerly called the "Marsh Hawk."

Measurements

LENGTH:	Male	41–45 cm (43);	16–18 in. (17)
	Female	45–50 cm (48);	18–20 in. (19)
WINGSPREAD:	Male	97–109 cm (103);	38–43 in. (41)
	Female	111–122 cm (116);	43–48 in. (46)
WEIGHT:	Male	290–390 g (346);	10–14 oz. (12)
	Female	390–600 g (496);	14–21 oz. (18)

ACCIPITERS
GENUS *Accipiter*

Accipiters are forest raptors. Three species occur in North America: Northern Goshawk, Cooper's Hawk, and Sharp-shinned Hawk, in order by decreasing size. They are all characterized by strongly barred flight feathers and long tails with three or four pairs of even-width dark and pale brown bands. There is no size overlap between species, nor even between sexes within species. Sexual dimorphism, with females much larger than males, is pronounced in this genus. However, as size is difficult to judge in the field, plumage and shape similarities make field identification a challenge, particularly that of separating Cooper's and Sharp-shinned Hawks.

Accipiters are aggressive, capable of rapid acceleration, and agile and reckless when in pursuit of their prey. They are less noticeable than other raptors because they are denizens of forests. During migration they may be conspicuous, however, especially at raptor concentration locations such as Cape May Point, New Jersey; Duluth, Minnesota; Holiday Beach, Ontario; Golden Gate, California; Goshute Mountains, Utah; and Hawk Mountain, Pennsylvania. All three species soar regularly, usually for a short while on many days. They also frequent bird feeders to try to capture songbirds.

Accipiter is Latin for "bird of prey." It probably derived from *accipere*, "to take," but also possibly from the Greek *aci*, "swift" and *petrum*, "wing." The word "hawk" properly refers only to raptors in this genus but in common usage is applied to all diurnal raptors except eagles, vultures, falcons, and kites. It comes from the old Teutonic root *haf* or *hab*, meaning "to seize."

Accipiter striatus

DESCRIPTION

The Sharp-shinned Hawk, our smallest accipiter, occurs commonly in northern and mountain forests but is widespread and local in forests throughout much of the United States and Canada. It is more common in the South in winter. On gliding birds, *head does not project much beyond wrists.* Outer tail feathers are same length, or almost so, as central pair. *Corners of tail appear squarish on males and slightly rounded on females, and tip shows a narrow white terminal band and often appears notched.* Sexes are almost alike in plumage, with females separably larger than males. Juvenile plumage differs from that of adults. Cere is yellow-green to yellow. Sticklike legs are yellow. On perched birds, head almost always appears rounded as hackles are never raised, and wingtips reach less than halfway to tail tip. Widespread race *velox* is described below.

ADULT: Head shows rufous cheeks and blue-gray crown and nape, with *crown the same color or slightly darker than blue-gray back* and lacking line of contrast with nape. Skin of supraorbital ridge, if visible, is yellow. Eyes are orange to red. Back and upper-

Sharp-shinned Hawk adult male. Crown and nape are the same color on small rounded head. Note the narrow white tip on relatively short tail. Minnesota, September (BKW)

Sharp-shinned Hawk adult female. Adult females have a slight brownish cast to upperparts. Note the sticklike legs. Minnesota, September (BKW)

Sharp-shinned Hawk juvenile female. Many juvenile females lack crisp dark band on trailing edge of wings. Note the short, square-cornered tail. Michigan, May (WSC)

wing coverts are blue-gray, brighter on males and, by spring and summer, browner on females. White underwing coverts and undersides, including leg feathers, are finely barred rufous. Undersides of flight feathers show bold dark barring; some birds, more commonly females, have dusky, rather than dark, tips of flight feathers. Tail has narrow white band on tip in fresh plumage, and upperside shows equal-width bands of black and blue-gray (males) or gray-brown (females), except for outer pair of feathers, which have more and narrower black bands. Undertail coverts are white.

JUVENILE: Dark brown head shows long narrow pale superciliary lines and pale throat; cheeks are somewhat paler on some individuals, usually those with narrow dark streaks on underparts. Eyes are yellow, becoming orangish by spring. Back and upperwing coverts are dark brown with narrow rufous feather edging, usually with little or no mottling from white feather bases showing. Whitish to creamy underparts of most females have *thick rufous streaking, becoming thicker and more barred on flanks and belly,* but streaking is a narrower dark brown to rufous-brown on most males and some females. Undersides of flight feathers show bold dark barring; some birds, more commonly females, have dusky rather than dark tips of flight feathers. Buffy underwing coverts have narrow dark streaking or small spotting. Upperside of tail has equal-width bands of dark brown and and paler gray-brown, except for outer feathers, which have more and narrower dark bands; all show a narrow pale terminal band in fresh plumage. Undertail coverts are white.

RACIAL VARIATION: Adults of *perobscurus* average darker than *velox* and show uniform rufous areas on breasts, rufous leg feathers with pale barring, and rufous spots on undertail coverts. Juveniles, especially females, are much darker, with heavier markings on underparts, reduced or absent pale superciliaries, streaks on undertail coverts on many, and reduced white bases on feathers of back and upperwing coverts. However, many juvenile males are not separable from those of *velox*. Adults and juveniles of *suttoni* show uniform rufous markings on thighs. See Pl. 11 for differences.

UNUSUAL PLUMAGES: A partial albino with white wings has been reported, and dilute-plumage specimens have creamy or café-au-lait color instead of dark brown upperparts and only rufous markings on underparts.

SIMILAR SPECIES

(1) COOPER'S HAWK (Pl. 12) in spite of size difference appears very similar but is more robust; has thicker legs; has longer, more rounded tail, usually with a wide white terminal band; and often raises hackles on rear-crown. Head projects far beyond wrists on gliding birds, and they often soar with leading edge of wings straight out from body and with wings in a dihedral. Adult's crown is darker than nape and back, with a noticeable line of contrast. Juveniles' underparts are more finely streaked, with fewer belly markings; their backs have more whitish mottling and cheeks may be tawny (brown on immature Sharpies). Juvenile Cooper's show a wide dark brown subterminal band on the trailing edge of underwings; this is usually a less obvious dusky band on juvenile female Sharpies. Some Cooper's in flight show a "stair step" at the corners of the tail; white band is noticeably shorter on tips of outer two feathers. **(2) MERLIN** (Pl. 36) is also a small dark raptor but has larger, squarish head; dark eyes; pointed wings; and dark tail with thin light bands.

FLIGHT

Active flight is light and buoyant, with rapid, light wingbeats. Soars and glides on level wings with wrists pushed forward. They occasionally use a rapid undulating flight to attack birds.

MOLT

Annual molt of adults is complete, except for northernmost breeders. Adult females begin molt prior to egg laying but usually suspend it while breeding until young are independent. Males wait until young are well on the wing to begin molting. Juveniles molt directly into adult plumage in their second summer. Often they retain a few juvenile upperwing or uppertail coverts in the first adult plumage.

BEHAVIOR

Sharp-shinned Hawks are shy and retiring. They usually hunt from inconspicuous perches in wooded areas for small birds, their primary prey, which are captured after a brief, rapid chase. They are fond of catching birds at feeders and often collide with picture windows. They also hunt by coursing over or through the woods, hoping to surprise their prey.

Sharp-shinned Hawks soar on most sunny days, usually for a while in the morning. On migration they move by active flight until thermals form, thereafter soaring, often up to an altitude of thousands of feet. They almost never raise their hackles, and so their heads appear rounded.

STATUS AND DISTRIBUTION

Sharp-shinned Hawks are common in forests throughout most of North America, leaving northern areas in winter. The main breeding areas are western mountains and northern forests, but Sharp-

SHARP-SHINNED
HAWK

shins breed in low densities in most areas except the Florida peninsula, the Gulf Coast, the Great Plains, and deserts. They are seen in greatest numbers during migration. Northern birds move as far south as Central America and Cuba during winter.

FINE POINTS

Cooper's and Sharp-shinned Hawks do not overlap in size, but western Cooper's Hawks are smaller than eastern ones. In the Southwest there is a slight overlap in the wing chord measurements between small male Cooper's and large female Sharpies, but there is no overlap in weight or overall length.

SUBSPECIES

Three races occur north of Mexico: *A. s. velox* is widespread, *A. s. perobscurus* breeds on the Queen Charlotte Islands and occurs farther south into California in winter, and *A. s. suttoni* is resident in very southeastern Arizona and southwestern New Mexico.

ETYMOLOGY

"Sharp-shinned" refers to the raised ridge on the inside front of the tarsus (not actually a shin); *striatus* is Latin for "striped," a reference to the underparts of the juvenile, which was described prior to the adult.

MEASUREMENTS

LENGTH:	Male	24–27 cm (26);	9–11 in. (10)
	Female	29–34 cm (31);	11–13 in. (12)
WINGSPREAD:	Male	53–56 cm (54);	20–22 in. (21)
	Female	58–65 cm (62);	23–26 in. (25)
WEIGHT:	Male	87–114 g (101);	3-4 oz. (3.6)
	Female	150–218 g (177);	5-8 oz. (6)

COOPER'S HAWK   PL. 12

Accipiter cooperii

DESCRIPTION

The robust Cooper's Hawk, our medium-sized accipiter, occurs in woodlands from southern Canada southward. On gliding birds, *head projects far beyond wrists. They usually soar with the leading edges of the wings held perpendicular to the body and forming a*

Cooper's Hawk subadult male.
Basic I adult males have rufous
cheeks and orange eyes. Dark
crown contrasts with paler nape.
New Jersey, October (BKW)

Cooper's Hawk juvenile. Many
juveniles have rufous head and
neck. Note wide white tip on rela-
tively long tail. Minnesota,
September (BKW)

straight line, and with wings held in slight to medium dihedral.
Outer tail feathers are progressively shorter than central pair.
Corners of tail tip appear rounded, and tip usually shows a broad
white terminal band. Sexes are almost alike in plumage, with females separably larger than males. Juveniles have different
plumage from that of adults. Cere is yellow-green to yellow. Stout
legs are yellow. On perched birds, *head often appears squarish be-*
cause of raised hackles but rounded when not raised, and wingtips
reach less than halfway to tail tip.

ADULT: Head has *dark blue-gray crown that contrasts with pale*
gray nape and blue-gray back. Crown color of some females and
younger males is not much darker than their back colors, but they
always contrast with their paler napes. Cheeks are rufous on females, sometimes with a grayish cast (older females?), and gray
on older males. Skin of supraorbital ridge, if visible, is grayish.
Eyes are orange to red. Back and upperwing coverts are blue-gray
on males and brownish gray on females, becoming more brownish
by spring and summer. White underwing coverts and underparts,
including leg feathers, are barred rufous. Flight feathers are heavily barred below, but band on tip is usually dusky, paler than the
other dark bands. Many males show less obvious barring on secondaries. Upperside of long tail has equal-width bands of blackish
brown and blue-gray (males) or gray-brown (females), except for
outer pair of feathers, which have more and narrower dark bands;
all show a broad white terminal band in fresh plumage. Undertail
coverts are white.

JUVENILE: Brown head usually lacks pale superciliary lines; many

Cooper's Hawk juvenile female. Juveniles show a crisp dark band on the trailing edge of wings. Note the noticeably shorter outer feathers on the relatively long tail. Arizona, July (WSC)

individuals have a tawny wash on cheeks. Eyes are light greenish gray to dull greenish yellow, becoming a brighter yellow by spring. Back and upperwing coverts are dark brown but appear paler due to whitish mottling and wide rufous feather edging. Underparts are white with narrow dark brown streaking, usually but not always *becoming sparse or absent on the belly,* sometimes with dark barring on the flanks. Flight feathers are heavily barred below; all show a crisp, narrow, dark band on the trailing edge of underwings. Creamy underwing coverts have narrow dark streaks and spots. Upperside of long tail has equal-width bands of dark brown and paler gray-brown, except for outer pair of feathers, which have more and narrower dark bands; most show a broad white terminal band in fresh plumage, but a few have a paler gray-brown subterminal band with a narrow white terminal band, like that of juvenile Sharpies. White tips of shorter outer two tail feathers often noticeable on flying hawks as two white "stair steps" on corners of tail. White undertail coverts are usually unmarked, but a few western hawks show narrow dark shaft streaks here.

BASIC I (SUBADULT): First-plumage adults look like older adults except that males have rufous cheeks, rufous or gray napes, and orange to orange-red eyes, females have rufous napes and cheeks and bright yellow, occasionally orangish, eyes. Both can show brown retained juvenile feathers on upperwing or uppertail coverts or both.

UNUSUAL PLUMAGES: Dilute-plumage specimens have creamy or café-au-lait color instead of dark brown upperparts and only rufous markings on underparts.

SIMILAR SPECIES

(1) **SHARP-SHINNED HAWK** (Pl. 11) in spite of size difference appears very similar in all plumages to Cooper's Hawks. See under that species for distinctions. (2) **NORTHERN GOSHAWK** (Pl. 13) juvenile is similar but is larger and has relatively longer and more tapered wings, more heavily streaked underparts, wide pale superciliary lines, markings on undertail coverts, paler, more mottled back, and irregular, wavy tail bands. Adult Goshawk has pale blue-gray breast and black head with wide white superciliaries. (3) **BROAD-WINGED HAWK** (Pl. 18) juveniles are similar to juvenile Cooper's Hawks. See under that species for differences.

FLIGHT

Active flight is with stiff, strong wingbeats. Glides with wings level, wrists cocked a bit forward. Soars occasionally with wings level, but usually held in a slight to medium dihedral, with leading edge of the wing straighter and more perpendicular to the body than those of other accipiters.

MOLT

Annual molt of adults is complete. Adult females begin molt prior to egg laying but usually suspend it while breeding until young are independent. Males wait until young are well on the wing to begin. Juveniles molt directly into subadult plumage in their second summer. Often they retain a few juvenile upperwing or uppertail coverts in first adult plumage.

BEHAVIOR

Cooper's Hawks are mainly still hunters, perching inconspicuously in woods, waiting to attack their prey at an opportune moment. In the West, they occur in more open habitats. They hunt, on occasion, by flying through or over woodlands or along fencerows to surprise potential prey and pursue prey into dense cover, sometimes on foot. The preferred prey of Cooper's Hawks is birds, but many small mammals are taken, and, in the West, lizards. Usually secretive, some birds, particularly in the West, will vigorously and vociferously defend their nests. Display flight is with slow, deep, exaggerated wingbeats, tail tightly closed, and white undertail coverts fluffed out on both sides.

Recently, Cooper's nesting in urban and suburban areas have become quite tame and confiding. As with most accipiters, this species will soar for a short period on sunny days; migration is mostly by soaring and gliding. When perched, the birds often raise their hackles, making the head appear larger and squarish.

Status and Distribution

Cooper's Hawks are fairly common to uncommon in open woodland over most of their breeding range, which covers most of the United States and s. Canada, except for South Florida and much of the n. Great Plains. Northern birds are migratory, moving as far south as Mexico and South Florida. In the West they occur at lower elevations than other accipiters and are fairly common in riparian areas.

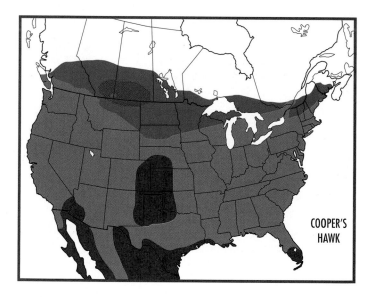

COOPER'S
HAWK

Fine Points

Western Cooper's Hawks average smaller than eastern ones, thus closer in size to Sharp-shinned Hawks. But there is still no overlap in overall length or weight.

Monotypic.

ETYMOLOGY

"Cooper's" and *cooperii* after William Cooper, a New York ornithologist.

MEASUREMENTS

LENGTH:	Male	37–41 cm (39);	14–16 in. (15)
	Female	42–47 cm (45);	16–19 in. (18)
WINGSPREAD:	Male	70–77 cm (73);	28–30 in. (29)
	Female	79–87 cm (84);	31–34 in. (33)
WEIGHT:	Male	302–402 g (341);	10–14 oz. (12)
	Female	479–678 g (528);	17–24 oz. (19)

NORTHERN GOSHAWK   PL. 13

Accipiter gentilis

DESCRIPTION

The Northern Goshawk, our largest accipiter, is a breeding resident in northern and western mountain forests. Wings are long for an accipiter, rather buteo-like. Tip of folded tail is wedge-shaped. Sexes are almost alike in plumage, with females separably larger than males. Juvenile plumage is different from that of adults. Cere is greenish yellow to yellow. Legs are yellow. On perched birds, wingtips extend halfway to tail tip. Widespread race *atricapillus* is described below.

ADULT: Head is black except for *wide white superciliary lines* and whitish throat. Eye color varies from orange to red to mahogany, darkening with age. Back and upperwing coverts are blue-gray and average darker on females; they contrast with blackish uppersides of flight feathers. Underwing coverts and *underparts are pale blue-gray* with fine black vermiculations and some vertical black streaking. Females usually have coarser, darker barring and more vertical black streaking. Primaries show dusky banding on undersides; secondaries show, at most, faint banding. Tail is blue-gray, with three or four incomplete blackish bands. Undertail coverts are white and fluffy.

JUVENILE: Brown head has noticeable wide pale superciliary lines. Eyes vary from pale green-yellow to yellow to orangish yellow,

Northern Goshawk subadult male. Adults show two-toned upperwings. Note retained juvenile secondaries. Minnesota, October (BKW)

Northern Goshawk juvenile. Note wide pale superciliary and wavy dark tail bands. New Jersey, October (WSC)

rarely light brown. Brown back and upperwing coverts have extensive tawny and white mottling (and appear paler than those of Cooper's Hawks); a pale bar is usually noticeable on the wing coverts of perched juveniles and on the upperwing coverts of flying ones. Undersides of flight feathers are boldly banded with dark brown. Buffy underparts are marked with wide blackish brown streaks. Undertail coverts are marked with wide dark blobs (a few individuals have unmarked undertail coverts). Tail has irregular, wavy, equal-width dark and light brown bands, with *thin whitish highlights* at many of the boundaries of these bands and a wide pale terminal band. Dark bands of outer pair of feathers are narrower than light ones. Undersides of folded tails show a zigzag pattern (however, some Cooper's and Sharp-shinned Hawks' undertails appear similar).

BASIC I (SUBADULT): Almost like that of adult but upperparts are darker, with heavier dark streaking and bolder barring on underparts. Eyes are yellow-orange to orange-red. Undersides of flight feathers show distinct dark banding. Some brown juvenile outer primaries (seldom), middle secondaries (often), or tail feathers (sometimes) can be retained, as well as a few uppertail or upperwing coverts (usually). Dark tail bands are usually more noticeable than those on adult.

RACIAL VARIATION: Adults and juveniles of the race *laingi* are overall darker, with narrower, less obvious, pale superciliary lines. Adults are overall darker, with black nape and more sooty-gray breast; juveniles are also overall darker, especially on head and

Northern Goshawk juvenile. Wings, especially primaries, are noticeably longer than those of other accipiters. Note dark markings on undertail coverts. Minnesota, October (BKW)

upperparts, with broader dark streaking on rich rufous underparts. See Pl. 13 for differences.

UNUSUAL PLUMAGES: Partial albinism, with some white feathers, has been reported, and dilute-plumage specimens have creamy or café-au-lait color instead of dark brown upperparts and only rufous markings on underparts.

SIMILAR SPECIES

(1) **COOPER'S HAWK** (Pl. 12) juveniles are similar to juvenile Goshawks. See under that species for distinctions. (2) **RED-SHOULDERED HAWK** (Pls. 16, 17) juveniles usually have pale superciliary lines like juvenile Goshawks but have tawny crescent-shaped wing panels, dark malar stripes, and unequal-width dark and light tail bands. (3) **GYRFALCON** (Pl. 39) adults are also gray and have pointed wingtips and a heavy flight but often have two-toned underwings and lack adult Goshawk's dark hood, two-toned upperwings, and pale superciliary lines. On perched Gyrs, wingtips extend more than halfway to tail tip. (4) **BUTEOS** have shorter tails and lack tapered wings and heavily barred undersides of flight feathers. On perched buzzards, wingtips extend almost to tail tip. **NOTE:** Many juvenile Red-shouldered, Broad-winged, and Cooper's Hawks can also show distinct pale superciliary lines, so this field mark is not diagnostic for juvenile Goshawk.

FLIGHT

Active flight is strong, with powerful, stiff wingbeats; wingtips often appear rather pointed in active flight. Soars on level wings, appearing much like a buteo. Glides with wings level and wrists cocked somewhat forward.

MOLT

Annual molt of adults is not complete; not all flight and tail feathers are changed every year. Adult females begin molt prior to egg laying, but usually suspend active molt while breeding until the young are independent. Males wait until young are well on the wing to begin. Juveniles molt into Basic I plumage in their second summer, beginning later than adults. Hawks in Basic I plumage usually retain a few juvenile outer primaries, middle secondaries, or a tail feather or two, as well as some juvenile upperwing or uppertail coverts.

BEHAVIOR

Goshawks are almost always found in forests, where they are usually quite inconspicuous. They prey on medium to large mammals and birds and hunt from a perch or while flying. They are quick, agile, and persistent in pursuit of prey. They also pursue prey on the ground. Goshawks courageously defend their nest areas and will even strike humans, usually on the head or back. Like most accipiters, they soar for a while on most sunny days, usually in the morning.

STATUS AND DISTRIBUTION

Goshawks are uncommon residents on their breeding grounds in the northern forests and in forested mountains. Many juveniles and some older birds migrate south of the breeding range every winter or, in the West, to a lower elevation as well. They can be seen on migration in good numbers around the Great Lakes (e.g., at Duluth, Minnesota, in the fall and at Whitefish Point, Michigan in spring). Every 9 to 11 years, due to low prey cycles, larger numbers of birds — including many adults — move southward, some as far as the Gulf of Mexico.

FINE POINTS

Juvenile Goshawks usually show a hint of a facial disk and sometimes a second shorter buffy bar on upperwings. Goshawk's short tarsus is feathered halfway to feet (only one-third feathered in Cooper's Hawk).

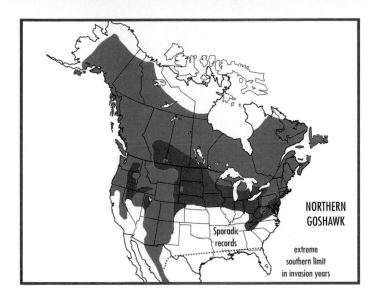

NORTHERN
GOSHAWK

Sporadic records

extreme
southern limit
in invasion years

SUBSPECIES

The two North American races are *A. g. laingi* on islands off British Columbia, and *A. g. atricapillus* throughout the rest of the continent.

ETYMOLOGY

"Goshawk" was derived from the Anglo-Saxon words *gos* for "goose" and *havoc* for "hawk" — hence, a hawk that captures geese. *Gentilis* is Latin for "noble." The Goshawk was named during the era when only the nobility could fly this bird in falconry.

MEASUREMENTS

LENGTH:	Male	46–51 cm (49);	18–20 in. (19)
	Female	53–62 cm (58);	21–24 in. (23)
WINGSPREAD:	Male	98–104 cm (101);	38–41 in. (39)
	Female	105–115 cm (108);	41–45 in. (43)
WEIGHT:	Male	615–1014 g (816);	24–36 oz. (29)
	Female	758–1,400 g (1,059);	26–43 oz. (37)

BUTEONINES
FAMILY ACCIPITRIDAE

Ten species of *Buteo* and two other buteonines (*Buteogallus, Parabuteo*) occur in our area. Six buteos are widespread throughout eastern or western North America or both; the other four and the two related species breed on our southern periphery. They are all characterized by robust bodies; long, broad wings; and short to medium-length tails. All soar regularly, and many hover and kite. Underwing and undertail patterns, wing shape, and sometimes behavior help in their field identification. Many species have, in addition to the normal or light morph, dark or rufous color morphs, or both, and some species only occur in the dark morph.

As in most raptor species, the tails of juvenile buzzards are noticeably longer than those of adults, but, unlike other species, juveniles' wings are narrower than those of adults in most *Buteo* species. Some individuals of all buteonines can show a pale nape patch that has a dark central spot; these are called "buteo spots" or "buzzard spots."

Buteo is Latin for "a kind of hawk or falcon." "Buzzard" is the proper name for these raptors; it comes from the same Latin root as *Buteo* through Old French and Old English. European settlers of this continent mistakenly applied the name to vultures, mistaking them for the darkish Common Buzzard, *Buteo buteo,* that inhabits northern Europe.

COMMON BLACK-HAWK
PL. 14

Buteogallus anthracinus

DESCRIPTION

The Common Black-Hawk of the Southwest, a large, dark buteonine, has *wide wings* and long legs. Sexes are nearly alike in

Common Black-Hawk adult. Wide wings make tail appear short. White commas at base of outer primaries are not always bold. New Mexico, April (BKW)

Common Black-Hawk adult. Uppersides of flight feathers show rufous-buff markings and dark band on trailing edge. Arizona, April (BKW)

plumage; females average larger than males, with some overlap in size. Juveniles' plumage appears quite different from adults', and they have longer tails and narrower wings. On perched adults, wingtips almost reach tail tip, but juvenile's wingtips fall somewhat short of tail tip.

ADULT: Head, body, and wing coverts are coal black, sometimes with a grayish cast. Eyes are dark brown. Adult females often show a white bar under each eye. Cere is bright orange-yellow, *with orange-yellow color extending onto the base of the otherwise dark beak.* Lores appear orange-yellow. Wings appear black except for *small white marks at the bases of outer two or three primaries on underwings* and faint to noticeable rufous to buffy markings on the flight feathers; this is visible under good light conditions on both under- and upperwings and contrasts somewhat with wide dark tips, which form a terminal band. Black tail has one wide white band and a thin white terminal band and appears short because of wide wings. Some females show a narrow white band on side of tail near the base. Legs are orange-yellow.

JUVENILE: Head shows dark brown crown and nape with buffy streaking and strong face pattern composed of buffy superciliary lines, dark eye lines, buffy cheeks, dark malar stripes, and buffy throat. Dark malar stripes extend down the neck onto the sides of upper breast. Eyes are medium brown. Cere is greenish yellow, and beak is dark with a pale base. Lores appear pale gray. Back and upperwing coverts are dark brown, with buffy to rufous mark-

Common Black-Hawk juvenile. Juveniles have heavily streaked underparts. Note strong face pattern and irregular white tail bands. Arizona, July (WSC)

ings and feather edging. Dark brown *upperwings show buffy primary patches* in flight. Underparts are rufous-buffy, with irregular dark brown streaking; flanks are dark brown. Underwings are buffy, with a black wrist comma, dark streaking on coverts, fine dark banding in the flight feathers, and pale primary patches. Leg feathers are whitish with fine dark brown barring. Buffy undertail coverts have wide dark brown barring. *Black tail shows many irregular white bands* and a narrow white terminal band. Legs are yellow.

UNUSUAL PLUMAGES: Partial albinism in this species has been reported from South America, in one case, a juvenile with some white, some pale brown, and some normal-colored feathers. Dilute plumage adult and juvenile specimens have been collected in Panama.

SIMILAR SPECIES

(1) ZONE-TAILED HAWK (Pl. 23) perched adults also show one white tail band on undertail, but band on uppertail is gray. They also have completely black beaks, narrow white foreheads, and pale gray lores, and show longer primary projection and white barring on fore-edge of folded wings. In flight, Zone-tailed Hawks' narrower wings appear more contrastingly two-toned below. **(2) BLACK VULTURE** (Pl. 1) is also black overall like adult Common Black-Hawk but has large white primary patches, shows whitish legs, and lacks white tail band. **(3) DARK-MORPH BUTEOS** have two-toned underwings: Pale flight feathers contrast strongly with dark coverts.

FLIGHT

Active flight is with strong, medium slow wingbeats. Soars on flat wings, with tail fanned. Glides on flat wings.

MOLT

Annual molt of adults is nearly complete (not all flight and body feathers are replaced annually). It begins in the spring soon after arrival on the breeding grounds and is completed before departure in the autumn. First prebasic (post-juvenile) molt begins the spring following fledging and is apparently complete. It too is completed before departure in the autumn.

BEHAVIOR

Common Black-Hawks are closely associated with aquatic habitats. They capture a wide variety of prey: fish, frogs, crabs, crayfish, insects, reptiles, and less often birds and mammals. They are still hunters, searching for prey while sitting quietly on a perch, often a low one, overlooking a stream or small river. They often wade into shallow water and chase after prey on foot. Calls of this vocal species are a series of staccato whistled notes, very different from calls of other buteonines.

The display flight of the male is a series of undulating climbs and dives, often performed while the bird is dangling its feet and calling. The pair often fly together, sometimes with exaggerated, deep wingbeats.

STATUS AND DISTRIBUTION

Black-Hawks are uncommon but local during the breeding season in riparian areas of e., cen., and s.-cen. Arizona, w. New Mexico, and w. Texas; and rare in s. Utah. There are reports of stragglers in Nevada and California and a vagrant from Minnesota. Most birds migrate south for winter, but winter records exist from s. Texas and Arizona.

FINE POINTS

White marks on underwings at the base of outer primaries are most visible when adults are flying away from the observer, though these can be faint or absent.

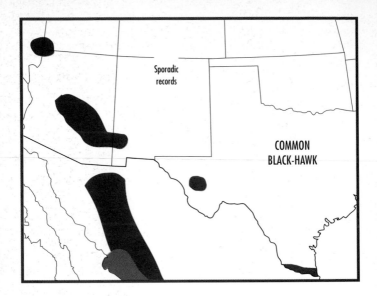

COMMON
BLACK-HAWK

SUBSPECIES

B. a. anthracinus is the race in the southwestern United States.

ETYMOLOGY

Buteogallus is from the Latin *buteo,* "a hawk or falcon," and *gallus,* "chicken" (literally, "chicken hawk"); *anthracinus* means "coal black" in Latin. Palmer (1988) calls this species "Lesser Black-Hawk."

MEASUREMENTS

LENGTH:	51–56 cm (54);	20–22 in. (21)
WINGSPREAD:	102–133 cm (117);	40–52 in. (46)
WEIGHT:	630–1,300 g (950);	1.4–2.9 lb. (2.1)

Parabuteo unicinctus

DESCRIPTION

The Harris's Hawk, a long-legged, long-tailed, dark buteonine, inhabits arid areas of the southwestern United States. Their wings appear somewhat paddle-shaped in flight. Their *rufous thighs and shoulder patches* and white tail coverts are distinctive. Sexes are alike in plumage, but females are noticeably larger. Juvenile's plumage is similar to that of adults. On perched birds, wingtips reach only halfway down the tail. Eyes are dark brown. Cere, lores, and legs are orange-yellow.

ADULT: Head, body, and greater upperwing coverts are dark brown. Rufous median and lesser upperwing coverts form a shoulder patch on perched birds. *Underwings with rufous coverts and dark gray flight feathers* are distinctive. Leg feathers are rufous. Greater uppertail and undertail coverts are white. *Black tail has wide white base and a fairly wide white terminal band.*

JUVENILE: Somewhat similar to adults; they show narrow pale streaking on head and neck and their dark underparts are streaked white, heavier on belly. Some have noticeably whiter bellies (due to narrow dark streaking), more often males. *Underwings with rufous coverts, finely barred gray secondaries, and whitish primaries with dark tips* are distinctive. Leg feathers are finely barred rufous and white to uniform rufous on dark-bellied individuals.

Harris's Hawk family group. Adult female, juvenile male, and adult male (left to right). *Texas, February (BKW)*

Harris's Hawk adult. Rufous upperwing coverts and wide white tip of tail are distinctive. Texas, February (BKW)

Harris's Hawk juvenile. Juveniles have streaked underparts, whitish primaries, and pale gray secondaries. Arizona, July (WSC)

Tail coverts are white. Tail appears dark brown with narrow white tip from above but appears light gray with fine dark bands from below, darker near the tip.

UNUSUAL PLUMAGES: No unusual plumages have been described.

SIMILAR SPECIES

(1) RED-SHOULDERED HAWK (Pls. 16, 17) juveniles are somewhat similar to paler juvenile Harris's Hawks, but their pale primary panels are crescent shaped, and they lack rufous underwing coverts. **(2) DARK-MORPH BUTEOS** lack rufous thighs and shoulder patches and white tail coverts.

FLIGHT

Active flight is more energetic than that of buteos, with quick, shallow wingbeats of cupped wings. Glides on cupped wings with wrists above body and wingtips pointed down. Soars on flat wings. Does not hover.

MOLT

Not well studied. Annual molt of adults is apparently complete. First prebasic (post-juvenile) molt presumably begins at about one year of age. A female in juvenile plumage with chicks began molt before the chicks fledged. Adult secondaries are a bit longer than those of juveniles.

Polyandry, the mating of two males with a single female, has been documented and is apparently more frequent in Arizona than in Texas. Harris's Hawks prey mainly on mammals and birds but also take lizards and insects. They hunt primarily from perches but also on the wing; however, hovering, a characteristic of some buteos, has not been reported. They perch more horizontally than other raptors and are often seen in cooperative hunting groups of up to a dozen individuals, especially in winter. Vocalization most often heard is an alarm call, rendered as a hoarse crowlike *krraah*.

STATUS AND DISTRIBUTION

Harris's Hawks are fairly common in coastal scrub prairies of s. Texas, mesquite deserts of sw. Texas and se. New Mexico, and mesquite and saguaro–palo verde deserts of s. and cen. Arizona. A few pairs breed periodically in se. California, apparently the result of range extensions every few decades, no doubt also the reason for breeding records in Louisiana and Kansas. They have been casually reported in Nevada, Utah, Oklahoma, and Louisiana.

Captive-bred Harris's Hawks are used widely in falconry; es-

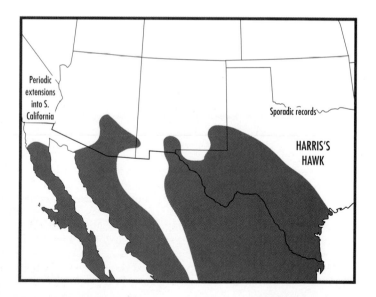

capees can be expected almost anywhere in our area. This is most likely the source for records in Iowa, Ohio, New York, New Jersey, and Florida.

FINE POINTS

The bellies of some juveniles in our area are mostly white with some dark streaking, but juveniles are almost always dark-breasted, usually with a sharp dividing line between dark breast and lighter belly.

SUBSPECIES

The race in Texas is *P. u. harrisi*; that in Arizona is *P. u. superior,* but racial distinctions are few, if any.

ETYMOLOGY

Named after Edward Harris, a friend of Audubon. *Parabuteo* is from the Greek *para*, "beside or near," hence, "similar to buteo." *Unicinctus* is from Latin *uni*, "once," and *cinctus*, "girdled," a reference to the white band at base of tail. This species is also called the Bay-winged Hawk (e.g., by Palmer 1988).

MEASUREMENTS

LENGTH:		46–59 cm (52);	18–23 in. (20)
WINGSPREAD:		103–119 cm (108);	40–47 in. (43)
WEIGHT:	Male	536–829 g (663);	1.2–1.8 lb. (1.5)
	Female	789–1,203 g (966);	1.7–2.6 lb. (2.1)

GRAY HAWK   PL. 15

Buteo nitidus (or *Asturina nitida*)

DESCRIPTION

The Gray Hawk of southeastern Arizona and southern Texas is a small, pale, long-tailed, accipiter-like buteo. *Greater uppertail coverts form a white U above base of tail*. Sexes are alike in plumage; females are noticeably larger. Juvenile plumage is quite different from that of adults. Wingtips reach halfway to tail tip on perched birds. Legs are orange-yellow.

ADULT: Head, back, and upperwing coverts are medium gray. Eyes are dark brown, cere is bright orange-yellow, and beak is

Gray Hawk adult. Narrow dark tips on outer primaries are distinctive. Spread tails often show a third white band. Arizona, July (WSC)

Gray Hawk adult. Overall gray, with orange cere and legs. Mexico, January (WSC)

dark. *Underparts, including leg feathers, are finely barred with white and medium gray.* Whitish underwing coverts are lightly barred with gray; whitish undersides of flight feathers show narrow dark bands. Outer primaries have narrow dark tips. Undertail coverts are white. Black tail has two white bands, one wide and a narrow one near the base.

JUVENILE: Crown, nape, back, and upperwing coverts are dark brown, with rufous edging on back and coverts. *Striking face pattern* consists of creamy superciliary lines, dark eye lines, pale lores and creamy cheeks, dark malar stripes, and buffy throat. Eyes are medium brown, cere is yellow, and beak is dark. Creamy to

Gray Hawk juvenile. Juveniles have strong face pattern and barred leg feathers. Mexico, January (WSC)

white underparts are heavily streaked with dark brown. Pale underwings show light markings. Faint but distinct crescent-shaped pale panels are often seen near wingtips of backlit wings, similar to those of juvenile Red-shouldered Hawks. Creamy leg feathers are narrowly barred with dark brown. *Long, medium-brown tail has six or more progressively wider, chevron-shaped dark brown bands.*

UNUSUAL PLUMAGES: No unusual plumages have been reported.

SIMILAR SPECIES

(1) BROAD-WINGED HAWK (Pl. 18) juvenile is similar but has more pointed wings; streaked, not barred, leg feathers; four or fewer dark bands in tail; and lacks strong face pattern and white U above base of tail. Adult Broad-wing has rufous-banded underparts. **(2) COOPER'S HAWK** (Pl. 12) juveniles appear very similar, especially in flight (see comment under Flight regarding wing attitude), but show more rounded corners to tips of tail, four or fewer equal-width dark and light tail bands, and more boldly marked flight feathers below and lack white U above tail base. They rarely show the bold head pattern and barring on leg feathers like those of juvenile Gray Hawks. **(3) HOOK-BILLED KITE** (Pl. 3) adult male is similar to Gray Hawk adult in appearing overall gray. See under that species for differences.

FLIGHT

Active flight is rapid and accipiter-like, with quick wingbeats followed by short glides on flat wings. Soars on flat wings, although usually at a lower altitude than do other buteos, with wings held such that leading edges are perpendicular to the body. Courtship flights are similar to those of other buteos.

MOLT

Annual molt of adults is complete and begins in spring before nesting. It is prolonged and most likely completed on the winter grounds. Males may suspend molt while food demands are high during the breeding cycle. First prebasic (post-juvenile) molt most likely begins in the second spring, later than that of adults.

BEHAVIOR

Gray Hawks are dashing raptors. Their relatively short wings and long tail allow them to maneuver in dense cover in pursuit of prey, mainly lizards and small birds but occasionally insects and small mammals. They usually hunt from perches but also from low glides, and with rapid stoops from soar.

Status and Distribution

Gray Hawks are uncommon and local in riparian areas of south-eastern Arizona, usually occurring where there is permanent running water. There are more than 60 known breeding pairs. A few pairs breed in Texas in Big Bend National Park and along the lower Rio Grande Valley. There are breeding records from w.-cen. New Mexico. The Arizona and w. Texas birds are migratory, leaving by October and returning in late March or early April. The Rio Grande Valley birds are sedentary.

GRAY HAWK

Fine Points

When soaring, Gray Hawk's wingtips appear more rounded and tail appears longer than those of the Broad-winged Hawk. In flight, their wings appear longer and corners of tail tip appear more square than those of Cooper's Hawks.

The race in the southwestern United States is *B. n. plagiata*. **NOTE:** The AOU (1998) and Palmer (1988) have followed Amadon and Bull (1988) in assigning this species to the genus *Asturina* (with resulting species name *nituda* or *plagiata*, respectively). However this has not been universally accepted (e.g., del Hoyo, 1994), most likely because the Red-shouldered and Roadside Hawks are closely related to the Gray Hawk and should also be included in *Asturina* (as done by Palmer [1988] but not AOU [1998]).

ETYMOLOGY

Nitidus in Latin means "bright, shining."

MEASUREMENTS

LENGTH:	36–46 cm (42);	14–18 in. (17)
WINGSPREAD:	82–98 cm (87);	32–38 in. (34)
WEIGHT:	378–660 g (524);	13–23 oz. (18)

RED-SHOULDERED HAWK   PLS. 16, 17

Buteo lineatus (or *Asturina lineata*)

DESCRIPTION

The Red-shouldered Hawk, a medium-sized, long-legged, long-tailed, slender buteo, is usually found in wet woodlands or savannas. It has four recognizably different plumage forms that correspond more or less with races: Eastern (*lineatus*), Southeastern (*alleni*) and Texas (*texanus*), which are not separable; South Florida (*extimus*); and California (*elegans*). All show *crescent-shaped primary panels* when flying. Sexes are alike in plumage; females are larger, but there is overlap in size and weight. Juvenile plumage is different from that of adults. Wingtips on perched birds extend three-quarters of the way down the tail. Legs and feet are pale yellow. Descriptions start with a full description of the nominate race (Eastern) birds, then describe how the other forms differ.

EASTERN ADULT: Head is medium brown with tawny streaking on crown and neck, tawny superciliaries and cheek patches, usually dark eye lines, dark brown malar areas, and white to darkly streaked throat. Eyes are dark brown; cere is bright yellow. Back is dark brown with rufous feather edges. Rufous lesser upperwing

Red-shouldered Hawk adult B. l. alleni. *Adults have rufous underparts and underwing coverts. Note white crescent-shaped primary panels. Texas, February (BKW)*

Red-shouldered Hawk adult B. l. lineatus. *Some adults, more often females, have pale rufous barring on underparts. Virginia, March (WSC)*

coverts form *red shoulders on perched birds*; rest of upperwing coverts are dark brownish gray with white markings. *Flight feathers are boldly barred above with black and white*, with a *white crescent-shaped panel* near the tips of the outer primaries. Underwing appears two-toned: rufous coverts contrast with paler flight feathers, which show narrow dark barring and *whitish crescent-shaped panels near the tips of the outer primaries on backlit wings*. Under-

Red-shouldered Hawk adult B. l. alleni. *All glide on cupped wings. Texas, February (BKW)*

Red-shouldered Hawk adult B. l. extimus. *South Florida adults have pale rufous barring on underparts and gray heads. Florida, March (WSC)*

Red-shouldered Hawk juvenile B. l. elegans. California juveniles are rather adultlike. California, August (WSC)

Red-shouldered Hawk juvenile B. l. lineatus. Juveniles have dark tails with narrow pale bands; juvenile lineatus often have wider dark band on tail tip. Note the tawny crescents on outer primaries. New Jersey, November (Jerry Liguori)

parts are rufous, with dark brown streaks and narrow creamy barring; occasional birds are more creamy than rufous, especially on the belly. Creamy leg feathers have fine rufous barring, and creamy undertail coverts are unmarked. *Black tail shows three or four narrow white bands.*

TEXAS AND SOUTHEASTERN hawks overlap completely in plumage characters and are described together. There is some intergradation in characters between Southeastern and both nominate and South Florida hawks. Sizes average 10% smaller than nominate.

TEXAS/SOUTHEASTERN ADULTS: Similar to Eastern adult but lacking dark streaking on underparts. Heads average paler and backs average grayer. Adults in the western part of range (*texanus*) have, on average, brighter rufous underparts.

SOUTH FLORIDA hawks are the smallest and palest. There is some intergradation in characters with *alleni* on hawks in central Florida.

SOUTH FLORIDA ADULT: Somewhat similar to Eastern adult but is noticeably smaller, head is pale gray, back is grayish, and rufous underparts appear paler (although they can look somewhat bright in fresh plumage), and lack dark streaking.

CALIFORNIA hawks are the most distinctive in plumage, as they are reproductively isolated from the other races.

CALIFORNIA ADULT: Somewhat similar to Eastern adult, but head is completely tawny, with somewhat darker malar areas; gray back and scapulars have more whitish markings; uniformly rufous breast lacks white barring; and white bands in tail are wider. Rufous of underparts and shoulders averages brighter than does those of other races.

EASTERN JUVENILE: Head is medium brown, with narrow buffy streaks on crown and nape and buffy superciliaries, cheeks, and throat and dark brown malar areas. Eyes are light to medium gray-brown. Cere is greenish yellow to yellow. Back and upperwing coverts are dark brown with some tawny mottling, often with a hint of the red shoulder. Uppersides of primaries are dark brown with a *crescent-shaped tawny patch* near the darker tips of the outer primaries. Secondaries above are dark brown with indistinct paler bands and with three paler spots on the outer web that usually form *three pale bands on folded wings of perched hawks.* Creamy underparts are marked with a variable amount of dark brown streaks and blobs. Creamy underwings have narrow dark bands on secondaries and inner primaries and dark tips on outer primaries and show *crescent-shaped pale panel when backlit;* coverts have some dark streaking. Creamy leg feathers and undertail coverts are lightly spotted dark brown. *Tail is dark brown with many narrow pale gray-brown bands;* banding does not extend to tip, resulting in a wider unbanded dark area at the tip. There is a variable amount of rufous wash on the base of the uppertail.

TEXAS AND SOUTHEASTERN JUVENILES: Similar to Eastern juvenile, but creamy underparts are variably marked with streaks and arrowhead-shaped barring, heavier on breast, leg feathers are narrowly barred dark rufous-brown. Tail has fewer pale bands with little or no rufous wash on base and lacks wider unbanded area on the tip. Pale spots on secondaries are larger; the three pale bands on folded wings are more noticeable.

SOUTH FLORIDA JUVENILE: Similar to Eastern juvenile, but underparts are marked with narrower dark streaking, often heavier on breast and forming a bib, and with some dark barring on the flanks. Leg feathers are barred with pale rufous. Primary panels are sometimes white. Pale spots on secondaries are larger; the three pale bands on folded wings are more noticeable. Tail has fewer pale bands with no rufous wash on base and lacks wider unbanded area on the tip.

CALIFORNIA JUVENILE: Somewhat different from juveniles of other races and more adultlike. However, head is similar to those of other juveniles but has tawny superciliaries and cheeks and dark throat. Back, upperparts, uppersides of flight feathers, and tail pattern are like those of nominate adult. Rufous shoulder is more noticeable than those of other juveniles. Buff to rufous-buff underparts are broadly streaked on breast, often also marked with arrowhead-shaped barring, spotted on belly, and barred on flanks.

Underwings appear adultlike, as underwing coverts are rufous-brown and contrast with pale undersides of flight feathers. Crescent-shaped wing panels are white. Adultlike tail is brownish-black with 3 or 4 narrow whitish bands, but outer band usually grayish. Dark brown uppertail coverts show some pale bands and spots.

UNUSUAL PLUMAGES: Albinism and partial albinism have been reported. One bird was all white with yellow eyes and faint tail banding.

SIMILAR SPECIES

(1) **BROAD-WINGED HAWK** (Pl. 18) juveniles when perched are difficult to distinguish from perched juvenile Red-shoulders. Juvenile Red-shoulders show 3 pale bands across the secondaries on folded wings that are not present on perched juvenile Broad-wings, which lack rufous on base of uppertails (see also Fine Points) and have longer legs. In flight, Broad-wings appear smaller and have more pointed wings with square, not crescent-shaped, pale primary panels on backlit wings. Adult Broad-wings' tails have only one wider white band (but may show another narrower white band near tail base), and their underwing coverts are usually creamy (as are the undersides of flight feathers) but are rarely rufous. (2) **NORTHERN GOSHAWK** (Pl. 13) juveniles can appear similar to juvenile Red-shoulders. See under that species for differences. (3) **NORTHERN HARRIER** (Pl. 10) juveniles soaring and gliding at height also show rufous underparts and underwing coverts. See under that species for differences.

FLIGHT

Active flight is accipiter-like, with three to five quick, stiff, shallow wingbeats, followed by a period of glide. Soars with wings held level and with wrists pressed forward. *Glides with wings bowed;* wrists up, tips down. While gliding at altitude, they occasionally flap, but they do not hover.

MOLT

Not well known. Annual molt is apparently complete. Adults begin molt in the spring—possibly slowing or suspending it while breeding until young are independent—and complete it in late summer or early autumn. Juveniles molt directly into adult plumage, presumably beginning and finishing at the same time as adults.

Behavior

Red-shouldered Hawks are vocal, and their distinctive call, especially evident during courtship, should be learned (however, Blue Jays are good at mimicking this call). Hunters of wet woodlands, they sit quietly on an inconspicuous perch, searching for their prey: mammals, birds, frogs and toads, snakes and lizards, and occasionally crustaceans, fish, and insects. In winter they are seen in more open areas, but they select lower and less open perches than those used by Red-tails. In Florida, along the Gulf Coast, in Texas, and in California, they occur in more open areas, using exposed perches, including telephone poles and wires. Red-shouldered Hawks are fond of soaring and often vocalize while in the air. They will sometimes join a group of crows mobbing large owls and have been observed eating suet at bird feeders. Recently they have nested in suburban neighborhoods.

Status and Distribution

Eastern form is fairly common east of the Great Plains in river bottom habitat, ranging from e. Kansas and South Carolina north into s. Canada. Northern birds are migratory, especially juveniles, moving as far south as Florida and Mexico in winter. Recorded casually in Colorado.

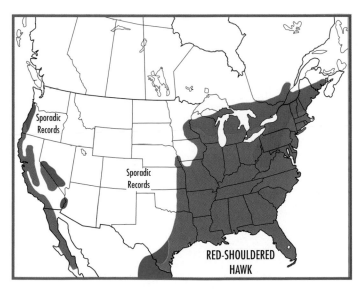

Texas/Southeastern form is a fairly common resident from South Carolina west to cen. Oklahoma, and south to cen. Florida and west to the Nueces River of Texas, regularly farther west in riparian areas, with a few pairs along the lower Rio Grande River. New Mexico records are most likely this form. Boundaries between nominate and South Florida forms and *alleni* are not clearly defined, most likely because of genetic flow.

South Florida form is a common to abundant resident in peninsular Florida from Lake Okeechobee south through the Keys.

California form is a fairly common resident in California west of the deserts and the Sierra Nevada in riparian, oak woodland, and suburban habitats, ranging into s. Oregon. Recorded regularly in Arizona, Nevada, and Washington, and casually in Idaho and Utah.

FINE POINTS

Juvenile Red-shouldered Hawk's uppertail is dark with light bands; juvenile Broad-wing's undertail is light with dark bands.

SUBSPECIES

The AOU in their 1957 *Check-list of North American Birds* (5th ed.) recognized five races: *B. l. lineatus, B. l. alleni, B. l. extimus, B. l. texanus,* and *B. l. elegans.* We believe that *alleni* and *texanus* represent a single taxa. Palmer (1988) placed this species, along with Gray and Roadside Hawks, in the genus *Asturina.* See comment under Subspecies in the account of Gray Hawk.

ETYMOLOGY

"Red-shouldered" refers to the rufous patch on upperwing coverts; *lineatus* is Latin for "striped," a reference to the tail.

MEASUREMENTS

LENGTH:	38-47 cm (42);	15-19 in. (17)
WINGSPREAD:	92-107 cm (100);	37-42 in. (40)
WEIGHT:	460-930 g (629);	1.1-1.9 lb. (1.4)

Buteo platypterus

DESCRIPTION

The Broad-winged Hawk, a crow-sized buteo, is found mainly in summer in eastern and northern forests or widespread on migration. Rare dark-morph birds breed only in western Canada. *Wingtips are relatively pointed for a* buteo. Sexes are alike in plumage; females are larger than males but with overlap in size. Juvenile plumage is different from that of adults. Cere is greenish yellow to yellow; legs are dull yellow. Wingtips of perched birds reach three-quarters of the way down tail.

LIGHT-MORPH ADULT: Head is dark brown with darker malar stripes and white throat. Eyes are medium brown. Back and upperwings are uniform dark brown, with blackish outer primaries forming dark wingtips. White underparts have a variable amount of wide rufous-brown barring; some adults have unbarred rufous-brown breasts that form a bib. Whitish leg feathers have narrow rufous-brown barring; whitish undertail coverts are unmarked or, at most, sparsely marked. Underwings have creamy coverts that are lightly marked and whitish flight feathers that have faint narrow dark banding; dark tips of primaries and secondaries form a wide dark band on tips and trailing edges of wings. *Dark blackish brown tail has one wide whitish to pale gray band*; most females

Broad-winged Hawk adult. All show pointed wingtips when gliding. Michigan, May (WSC

Broad-winged Hawk adult. Some adults, usually females, show a second narrower white band on uppertails. Minnesota, September (BKW)

Broad-winged Hawk juvenile. Juveniles show no pale spots on sides of folded secondaries. Note short legs. Florida, January (WSC)

Broad-winged Hawk. Kettle with one dark-morph adult. Michigan, May (WSC)

and some males have another narrower band, visible when the tail is fanned.

DARK-MORPH ADULT: Body and wing and tail coverts are uniform dark brown. Underwing is two-toned: whitish flight feathers contrast with uniformly dark brown coverts. *Tail is like that of light-morph adult.*

LIGHT-MORPH JUVENILE: Head is medium brown with narrow buffy streaks on crown and nape; buffy superciliaries, cheeks, and throat; and dark brown malar stripes. Eyes are pale gray-brown to pale brown. Upperparts are dark brown with some narrow pale feather edges on scapulars and wing coverts. Uppersides of flight feathers are brown with indistinct narrow darker bands. Creamy to buffy underparts are marked with a variable amount of dark brown streaking; some show an unmarked area in mid-breast and others no streaking at all. More heavily streaked individuals can also show dark barring on flanks or dark central throat streak or both. Underwings appear similar to those of adults, except dark band on tips and trailing edges is dusky and narrower. Some juveniles have dusky tips but others show narrow dark bands on tips of outer primaries. Creamy leg feathers are variably marked with dark brown streaks or, in some more heavily marked individuals, with dark brown barring. Tail above is brown and below is creamy, with dark brown bands, subterminal band widest; some individuals show an accipiter-like pattern of equal-width dark and light bands.

DARK-MORPH JUVENILE: Similar to dark-morph adult except that some hawks have rufous or whitish mottling or streaking on underparts and underwing coverts. Tail is like that of light-morph juvenile.

UNUSUAL PLUMAGES: There have been reliable sightings of completely white adults and of a juvenile with many white feathers on its back and wings.

SIMILAR SPECIES

(1) RED-SHOULDERED HAWK (Pl. 16) juveniles when perched are difficult to distinguish from perched juvenile Broad-wings; see under that species for distinctions. (2) COOPER'S HAWK (Pl. 12) juveniles are somewhat similar to juvenile Broad-wings but have equal-width dark and light tail bands and wider, more rounded wings that are heavily barred below. Cooper's also lack malar stripes. (3) DARK-MORPH BUTEOS of other species are larger, have different tail patterns, and, except for Short-tailed and Swainson's Hawks, do not have pointed wingtips.

FLIGHT

Active flight is with strong, stiff wingbeats. Soars and glides with wings held level or in a slight dihedral. Does not hover.

MOLT

Annual molt is apparently complete, however, not all flight and tail feathers may be replaced every year. Adults begin the molt soon after reaching the breeding grounds, females prior to males, and complete the molt before beginning the autumn migration. Juveniles in spring initiate the first prebasic (post-juvenile) molt prior to reaching the summer grounds; they are seen with missing inner primaries in May. Apparently the post-juvenile molt is completed prior to autumn migration, but adults with retained juvenile flight and tail feathers have been seen in the spring.

BEHAVIOR

Broad-winged Hawks are found in forests except during migration. They prey on small mammals, birds, frogs, toads, snakes, and insects. They are still hunters and search for prey from a perch along a forest edge. On migration, large numbers of Broad-winged Hawks are often seen soaring and gliding together in some locations.

They can be aggressive in their nest defense and have struck humans climbing to their nests. Vocalization is a two-noted, high-pitched whistle and is often given by hawks in flight over the forest.

STATUS AND DISTRIBUTION

Broad-winged Hawks are common to uncommon in forested areas east of the Great Plains and south to n. Florida and in the Boreal forest from Nova Scotia west to Alberta. They are local on the e. Great Plains, sometimes in urban areas. The entire population is migratory, with most going into Central and South America, some as far as Chile and Argentina. They are common to abundant locally on fall and spring migration in the East and along the s. Texas Gulf Coast; casual throughout the West. Hundreds of thousands have been counted during fall migration at hawk counts at Erie Metro Park south of Detroit and Hazel Bazemore Park near Corpus Christi, Texas.

A few linger in the East into December. Some birds winter in subtropical areas of Florida, the Gulf Coast, and s. California. Winter sightings outside these areas are more likely to be of juvenile Red-Shouldered Hawks; however, valid winter records exist for Arizona (two specimens), Georgia, and Nova Scotia.

Rare dark-morph hawks occur in the western portion of the breeding range in Canada, mainly Alberta, but are regularly en-

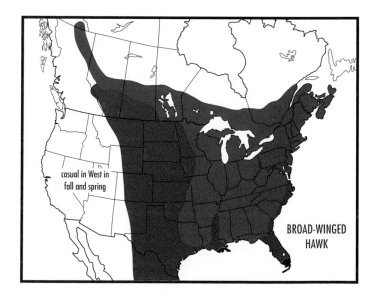

casual in West in fall and spring

BROAD-WINGED HAWK

countered on migration on the e. Great Plains, less frequently in the West and rarely in the East.

FINE POINTS

Broad-winged Hawks have only three notched outer primaries, versus four for Red-tailed and Red-shouldered Hawks. Their brown upperwings usually have noticeable black tips.

SUBSPECIES

The North American race is *B. p. platypterus*; the other races occur in the Caribbean.

ETYMOLOGY

Platypterus is from the Greek *platys*, "broad," and *pteron*, "wing."

MEASUREMENTS

LENGTH:	34–42 cm (37);	13–17 in. (15)
WINGSPREAD:	82–92 cm (86);	32–36 in. (34)
WEIGHT:	308–483 g (401);	11–17 oz. (14)

SHORT-TAILED HAWK   PL. 19

Buteo brachyurus

DESCRIPTION

The Short-tailed Hawk of Florida, a small long-winged buteo, is an aerial hunter of birds. They are most often seen in flight. *Wingtips are relatively pointed for a* buteo. Light and dark color morphs occur. Sexes are alike in plumage; females are larger. Juvenile plumages are similar to adult's. *Wingtips reach tail tip* on perched birds. Cere and legs are yellow.

LIGHT-MORPH ADULT: Head is uniformly dark brown, including cheeks, except for white throat and forehead. *Dark cheeks that contrast with white throat and white forehead* are noticeable on flying hawks. Eyes of adults are dark brown. Back and upperwings are dark brown. Whitish underparts are unmarked except for small rufous areas on sides of neck next to cheeks. Underwing is two-toned: *whitish coverts contrast with darker gray flight feathers, but primaries, especially outer ones, are paler than secondaries.* Tail above is brown and below whitish and shows a wide dark subter-

Short-tailed Hawk adult dark morph. Note white primary patches. Florida, November (BKW)

Short-tailed Hawk juvenile dark morph. Juveniles have white spotting on belly and underwing coverts. Mexico, November (WSC)

minal band and several other faint to bold narrow dark bands.

DARK-MORPH ADULT: Dark brown head shows white forehead. Body and wing and tail coverts are dark brown. Eyes of adults are dark brown. Flight feathers are grayish below with *a noticeable white oval patch on outer primaries*. Tail is like that of light-morph adult, except that dark bands are wider.

LIGHT-MORPH JUVENILE: Similar to light-morph adult, but head shows narrow pale superciliaries, dark eye lines and malar stripes, and pale cheeks, which sometimes have narrow pale streaking but are still noticeably pale. Back and upperwing coverts are paler brown and contrast with darker brown flight feathers, and underparts and underwing coverts are creamy, not white, and breast usually has a few fine streaks on each side. Eyes of juveniles are pale to medium brown. Undersides of secondaries are paler than those of adults, especially on their bases, and contrast less with coverts. Recently fledged birds have a rufous wash on breast. Tail is brown above and whitish below; pattern varies from many narrow, equal-width dark bands (more commonly seen on n. Mexican birds) to unbanded or with several faint, narrow, often incomplete bands, with a noticeably wider dark subterminal band.

DARK-MORPH JUVENILE: Similar to dark-morph adult, but head shows pale patches on cheeks and throat, belly varies from lightly spotted to heavily streaked with white to uniformly dark like adult's, dark underwing coverts are variably marked with white streaking but are uniformly dark on dark-bellied hawks, and (usually) unmottled breast forms *dark bib*. On underwings, gray sec-

Short-tailed Hawk juvenile light morph. Upperparts on light-morph hawks are two toned; paler brown secondary coverts contrast with rest of dark brown upper-wing. Mexico, October (WSC)

Short-tailed Hawk juvenile light morph. Florida juveniles show no streaking on underparts. Florida, November (BKW)

ondaries contrast somewhat with white primaries. Tail pattern is more distinct than that of light-morph juveniles and shows 5 to 7 equal-width dark bands, subterminal band sometimes wider.

UNUSUAL PLUMAGES: No unusual plumages have been reported.

SIMILAR SPECIES

(1) BROAD-WINGED HAWK (Pl. 18) juveniles are somewhat similar to light-morph Short-tails but are usually streaked on underparts, have flight feathers and coverts the same pale color, and lack dark cheeks. Broad-wings have relatively shorter wingspans. Wingtips do not reach tail tip on perched birds. Dark-morph Broad-wings are similar to dark-morph Short-tailed Hawks but show a uniform color on undersides of all flight feathers and have different tail patterns. Dark-morph Broad-wings have apparently not been recorded in Florida. **(2) SWAINSON'S HAWK** (Pls. 20, 21) light-morph hawks also show two-toned underwings, but their primaries and secondaries are uniformly dark gray. They fly with wings in a strong dihedral. Adults have dark breasts; juveniles usually have more heavily streaked underparts. Dark-morph Swainson's always have contrasting pale undertail coverts.

FLIGHT

Active flight is with stiff, strong wingbeats. Soars with wings held in a slight dihedral. Glides on flat wings, often with tips noticeably turned up. Short-tailed Hawks in flight are best identified by their characteristic hunting behavior, kiting or moving slowly upwind on stiff, flat wings with primaries upturned and head down, then plunging downward in a steep, spectacular, Peregrine-like stoop.

MOLT

Apparently not studied. Presumably annual molt is complete, and first prebasic (post-juvenile) molt is initiated when juveniles are nearly a year old.

BEHAVIOR

Short-tailed Hawks are specialized aerial hunters of small birds. They soar up to heights of 50 to 300 meters, sometimes higher, face into the wind, and hang stationary or move slowly upwind on outstretched wings and fanned tail, with their heads down, searching the forest canopy or field below. When prey is spotted, they fold their wings and stoop rapidly. Sometimes, to get a better look at potential prey, they lower themselves slowly on raised wings and then stoop. Often, after an unsuccessful stoop, they alternately flap and sail over the canopy, apparently hunting. They have been reported sitting under the canopy, near treetops, with only their heads visible, most often early in the morning or in inclement weather. Once airborne on thermals or the wind, they remain on the wing with few interruptions until an hour or so before sunset.

STATUS AND DISTRIBUTION

Short-tailed Hawks are uncommon to rare, but they are often overlooked, in peninsular Florida in summer. Their preferred habitat is mixed woodland savanna or wooded edge. The population retreats in winter to the southern third of the peninsula and the Florida Keys. Dark-morph birds are more common than light-morph ones in Florida. There are ten or so accepted recent sight records from s. Texas and two accepted records from se. Arizona, presumably of hawks from Mexico and not Florida.

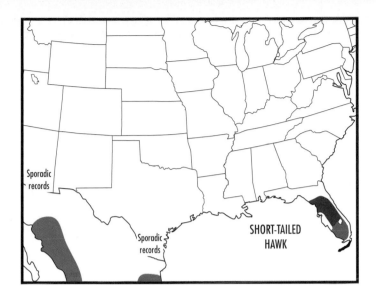

Fine Points

In flight, all forms show a distinctive small white spot on forehead and into lores. Light-morph juveniles in n. Mexico (presumably the source of hawks sighted in Texas and Arizona) show more distinct dark tail bands.

Subspecies

The race in Florida and n. Mexico is *B. b. fuliginosus.*

Etymology

Brachyurus is from the Greek *brachys,* "short," and *ours,* "tail."

Measurements

LENGTH:	39–44 cm (41);	15–17 in. (16)
WINGSPREAD:	83–103 cm (93);	32–41 in. (37)
WEIGHT:	342–560 g (426);	12–20 oz. (15)

Buteo swainsoni

Description

The Swainson's Hawk, a large, slender buteo with long, pointed wings, is polymorphic in plumage. This is the only adult buteo that has dark undersides of flight feathers, but with pale bases on outer primaries. *Two-toned underwing* pattern of all but darkest birds is distinctive. Three age classes are recognizable: adult, Basic I (one-year-old), and juvenile. Sexes are similar in plumage; females average larger than males. Wingtips reach or slightly exceed tail tip on perched adults, reach or almost reach tail tip on juveniles.

Adults vary in plumage in a continuous cline from light morph through rufous (intermediate) morph to dark morph. Base color of adult's underparts, leg feathers, and underwing coverts varies from whitish to rufous to dark brown to black; breast is usually contrastingly darker than belly. Back and upperwing coverts are dark brown, sometimes with grayish cast. Light gray-brown tail has numerous fine dark bands, with subterminal band much wider, and white tip. Eyes are dark brown. Cere and legs are yellow; beak is dark. Typical examples of each morph are described and depicted on the color plates, but many intermediates occur.

Swainson's Hawk adult male light morph. Adult males usually have gray faces and rufous breasts. Idaho, May (WSC)

Swainson's Hawk Basic I intermediate morph. All light and intermediate birds show two-toned underwings. Note incomplete molt of flight feathers. Colorado, September (BKW)

Swainson's Hawk Basic I intermediate morph. Just beginning molt into adult plumage at almost two years of age. All show wingtips that extend beyond tail tip. Idaho, May (WSC)

LIGHT-MORPH ADULT: Rufous to dark brown breast forms a bib that contrasts with lighter-colored belly; latter is often spotted or barred. Underwing is two-toned: creamy to white coverts contrast with gray flight feathers. Head and underparts are usually one of three types: 1. head rufous or dark with gray face, breast rufous, and white belly and leg feathers unmarked or lightly marked rufous (almost always male), 2. head dark brown with rufous-brown breast, white belly with dark spotting, and white leg feathers (usually female but also male), and 3. head and breast are both dark brown (usually only female). All show white forehead and throat. A few lightly colored adults have

Swainson's Hawk juvenile (Spring). Many juveniles returning in spring show white heads. Note whitish scapulars and wingtips reaching tail tip.Idaho, May (WSC)

Swainson's Hawk juvenile. Many juveniles show a white V on scapulars. Idaho, May (WSC)

Swainson's Hawk juvenile light morph. Juvenile in fresh plumage. Colorado, September (BKW)

incomplete bibs with a pale area in the center of breast. Adults with rufous or dark brown spotting or barring on their bellies usually show the same markings on their axillaries and, to a lesser extent, on their underwing coverts. Pale greater uppertail coverts form a light U above tail base.

LIGHT INTERMEDIATE ADULT: Similar to light-morph adult but with belly, underwing coverts, and leg feathers more heavily barred with dark brown or rufous.

RUFOUS-MORPH ADULT: Similar to light-morph adult but with belly and leg feathers overall rufous. Males usually have gray faces and completely rufous underparts lacking a contrastingly darker bib and dark barring; females have dark brown faces, breasts, and dark markings on rufous bellies. A few individuals have dark brown bellies and rufous breasts (appearing much like adult rufous-morph Red-tailed Hawks). *Underwing is two-toned:* rufous and creamy coverts contrast with dark flight feathers and are variably marked with dark, sometimes extensively. *Whitish undertail coverts contrast with rufous belly* and are sometimes lightly barred with rufous.

DARK INTERMEDIATE ADULT: Similar to dark-morph adult but with rufous barring on lower belly and rufous barring or all rufous leg feathers. Often they show small white areas on throat and forehead. Underwing coverts vary from dark rufous to dark brown with pale barring.

DARK-MORPH ADULT: Body and upperwing and uppertail coverts are overall dark brown, rarely jet black; almost all have *pale undertail coverts,* which are usually barred dark brown but are rarely uniformly dark. Underwing coverts are usually dark brown and rufous but are sometimes completely dark brown.

JUVENILE: (All morphs.) Head pattern of dark crown (often faded by spring), wide buffy superciliaries, narrow dark eye lines, and buffy throat and cheeks separated by wide dark malar stripes. Eyes are pale brown. Cere is yellow, occasionally greenish yellow; beak is dark. Back and upperwing coverts are brown, with broad buffy feather edgings (less prominent on darker birds), and pale markings on scapulars that form a pale V on back. Uppertail coverts form a pale U above tail base. Markings on buffy underparts and underwing coverts vary in a cline from lightly streaked, usually with malar stripes extending into *a dark patch on each side of upper breast* (light morph), to heavily streaked with dark brown (intermediate or rufous morph) to overall dark with some whitish streaking (dark morph). Undersides of flight feathers are pale gray with narrow dark barring, lacking the wide dark subterminal band of those of adults; outer primaries appear whitish. Flight feathers contrast somewhat with buffy underwing coverts, but with less contrast than shown on the underwings of adults. Some intermediate- and dark-morph individuals' underwings appear uniformly darkish due to heavily mottled coverts. Wings of juveniles are narrower than those of adults because their secondaries are shorter. Long gray-brown tail has many equal-width narrow dark bands and white tip. Legs are pale yellow.

BASIC I: Juveniles begin molt into their second plumage soon after returning from their winter grounds in the spring, when many, particularly paler birds, have noticeably pale heads. Basic I plumage is similar to that of juveniles in all morphs, but new flight and tail feathers are a darker gray with wider dark subterminal bands; new secondaries are longer, resulting in wider wings; and underwings show a mix of new and old flight feathers. Eyes are now medium brown. Three or four old outer primaries form a pale patch on underwings of fall migrants. Upperparts of Basic I light-morph hawks average darker than those of juveniles, usually lacking pale V on scapulars. Underparts and underwing coverts of some dark-morph birds have fewer pale markings than do those of juvenile plumage; they appear darker than juveniles. Molt of flight and tail feathers is only partially completed during the second summer; it is suspended for migration and completed on the winter grounds. Many Basic I birds returning in spring have already begun body molt into adult plumage.

UNUSUAL PLUMAGES: Individuals with some white feathers have been reported. A dilute plumage juvenile specimen had pale gray upperparts and tail and paler gray-brown markings on underparts but normal flight feathers.

(1) ROUGH-LEGGED HAWK (Pl. 30) some perched light-morph adult males also show dark bib and pale belly but have completely feathered tarsi. **(2) RED-TAILED HAWK** (Pls. 26, 27) juveniles appear similar to juvenile Swainson's but are separated by rounded wingtips, paler flight feathers, and dark patagial marks on underwings. Perched juvenile Red-tails appear similar, including having a pale V on scapulars, but their wingtips fall quite short of tail tips; their ceres are greenish, not yellow; they have white breasts and dark belly bands; and they lack bold dark eye lines. **(3) NORTHERN HARRIERS** (Pl. 10) also fly with their wings held in a dihedral and show pale uppertail coverts. See under that species for differences. **(4) PRAIRIE FALCON** (Pl. 40), perched, can appear similar to pale juvenile Swainson's but has dark eyes, white area between eye and dark ear patch, and wingtips that do not reach tail tip. **(5) DARK-MORPH BUTEOS** of other species have dark undertail coverts and silvery flight feathers, except for juvenile White-tailed Hawk. See under that species for distinctions.

Two species share light-morph Swainson's Hawk's underwing pattern of light coverts and dark flight feathers: the Short-tailed Hawk in Florida and the adult White-tailed Hawk in coastal Texas. Only Swainson's has all flight feathers uniformly dark gray. See under those species for other distinctions.

FLIGHT

Active flight is light and relatively buoyant, with somewhat kite-like wingbeats. Soars with wings in medium to strong dihedral; glides with wings in a modified dihedral. Hovers and kites often, especially in strong winds.

MOLT

Annual molt of adults is initiated after breeding, suspended during migration, and completed on the winter grounds, except for one to three outer primaries and some secondaries on many adults; these are replaced soon after arrival on the breeding grounds. First prebasic (post-juvenile) molt into Basic I plumage and second and subsequent prebasic molts are initiated in March to early May soon after arrival in the summering area and continue throughout the summer but are suspended during migration and completed on the winter grounds.

Swainson's Hawks hunt both from perches and on the wing. They prey in summer on small mammals and insects but also on snakes and other reptiles, and occasionally birds. During migration and on winter grounds, their main diet is insects, especially grasshoppers. They follow tractors and mowers, capturing disturbed rodents, insects, and even birds. Vocalization is a drawn-out *keerrr,* less wheezy than that of Red-tailed Hawk.

Swainson's Hawks are very kitelike in flight. They soar effortlessly for long periods and often hunt from a soar or glide. Adults are superior in flying agility to adult Red-tailed Hawks and, in areas where both breed, occasionally force flying Red-tails to the ground. On migration they are often seen in small to large flocks, flying or descending en masse to feed on grasshoppers.

They are sometimes aggressive in nest defense, especially if they have chicks, and have struck human intruders. However, they will sometimes abandon their nest if disturbed prior to eggs hatching.

STATUS AND DISTRIBUTION

Swainson's Hawks are fairly common and obvious during summer in most grassland and many agricultural areas of the West, from

SWAINSON'S
HAWK

casual in East
in fall and
spring

the Great Plains westward, but are absent on the Pacific Coastal plain; they occur east to nw. Illinois (and formerly sw. Wisconsin) and north rarely into e.-cen. Alaska and the Yukon Territory. Although California and Oregon populations have been reduced, other populations seem stable. The entire population is migratory, and most birds move into s. South America, mainly Argentina, in winter; annual migration counts at Veracruz, Mexico, average over half a million.

Dozens to hundreds of birds winter in South Florida, and winter specimen, photographic, and sight records exist for s. Texas and s. California. The only valid winter records (late December through February) from North American temperate areas are of a dozen or more birds in the Sacramento Delta of cen. California, however, valid early December records exist for Alaska and other northern areas.

Dark morph hawks are rare, usually from 1 percent to 10 percent of local populations, but can constitute as much as 35 percent in areas of n. California.

Swainson's Hawk is a rare but regular fall and spring visitor to e. North America. There are many sight, specimen, or banding records from almost all states and provinces.

Fine Points

Unlike most other buteos, Swainson's Hawks take two years to acquire adult plumage; juvenile plumage is replaced by the similar Basic I plumage after the post-juvenile molt. They have only three notched primaries, a character shared with Broad-winged and White-tailed Hawks; all other buteos have four notched primaries.

Subspecies

Monotypic.

Etymology

Common and scientific names after William Swainson, English naturalist.

Measurements

LENGTH:	43–55 cm (49);	17–22 in. (19)
WINGSPREAD:	120–137 cm (128);	47–54 in. (51)
WEIGHT:	595–1,240 g (900);	1.3–2.7 lb. (2.0)

Buteo albicaudatus

DESCRIPTION

The White-tailed Hawk, a large buteo with long, pointed wings, occurs only in southern Texas. Wings narrow noticeably at body on trailing edges in all plumages. Sexes are almost alike in plumage; females are darker and somewhat larger. Unusual for a buteo, they have three immature plumages: juvenile, Basic I, and Basic II. On perched birds, wingtips of adults and older immatures extend well beyond tail tip, but those of juveniles just surpass tail tip. Eyes are dark brown to dark amber. Long legs are yellow.

ADULT: Head and neck are medium gray, with white lores and usually white throat, but some adults (younger?) have grayish throats. Cere is pale yellow to pale yellowish green. Back is medium gray, and scapulars have a rufous wash. Lesser upperwing coverts form *rufous shoulder patches* on otherwise blackish brown upperwings, noticeable on flying and perched adults. Uppertail coverts and rump are white. Underwings are two-toned: dark primaries contrast with white coverts and whitish secondaries, with whitish bases on outer two or three primaries. Underparts are white, often with fine dark barring on flanks, belly, and

White-tailed Hawk adult. Typical adult. All show wingtips that extend far beyond tail tip. Texas, January (WSC)

White-tailed Hawk Basic II. Similar to adult, but with dark throat and dark barring on belly and underwing coverts. Texas, February (BKW)

White-tailed Hawk Basic I.
Darker variant with small white
breast patch that is similar to juve-
niles, but with wide dark band on
trailing edge of wings and tip of
tail. Texas, February (BKW)

White-tailed Hawk juvenile. Paler
variant with whitish underwing
coverts and Red-tailed Hawk–like
belly band. Texas, February
(BKW)

leg feathers. *White tail has wide black subterminal band* and five or more fine black bands.

JUVENILE: Head and neck are dark brown, with variably sized pale patches on cheek and behind eyes and dark throat. Cere is pale blue to pale yellow-green. Back and upperwings are dark brown; upperwing coverts have rufous-buff edgings, with a hint of the rufous-buff patches on lesser upperwing coverts. White greater uppertail coverts form a *white U* above tail base. Underwings appear somewhat two-toned; pale gray flight feathers that lack dark terminal bands contrast with dark axillaries and usually with dark brown coverts, which show a variable amount of white mottling and one or two white diagonal lines, but coverts can also be mostly white or mostly dark with no visible white lines. Outer two or three primaries usually have white bases. Underparts are usually dark brown with a variably sized creamy to white breast patch, often appearing as a vertical slash, and whitish edging on belly feathers, but underparts can be mostly white with a Red-tailed Hawk–like dark belly band. Undertail coverts are white with a variable amount of dark brown mottling. Leg feathers vary from creamy with dark brown mottling to dark brown with some whitish mottling. Long pale gray uppertail shows numerous closely spaced indistinct narrow bands, sometimes with the subterminal band somewhat wider. Juveniles' tails are longer and wings narrower than are those of adults and older immatures.

BASIC I: Head and neck are blackish, with dark throat (no pale

White-tailed Hawk juvenile. Variant with large pale area on face. Note wingtips extend beyond tail tip. Texas, February (BKW)

patches except faint ones sometimes). Back and scapulars are blackish, and lesser upperwing coverts form *rufous patches* that contrast with other blackish coverts. Rump is blackish with some white markings, and uppertail coverts are white. Underwings are two-toned: dark coverts, usually including rufous lesser coverts, contrast with pale gray flight feathers, which show a wide dark subterminal band and pale bases on outer two or three primaries. Breast is usually white but sometimes blackish with vertical white slash, and belly is heavily barred and mottled with black or dark reddish brown or both. White leg feathers have dark reddish brown barring. Undertail coverts are whitish, with some dark mottling. Uppertail is grayish with fine dark banding and a somewhat wider dusky to darkish subterminal band.

BASIC II: Similar to adult but head, including throat and neck, and back are blackish. Rump is marked with black and white. Underwings appear rather uniformly pale: white coverts and pale gray flight feathers are narrowly barred dark rufous or black. Belly, flanks, and leg feathers are heavily barred reddish brown or black. Uppertail appears as a mix of dirty white and pale gray feathers.

UNUSUAL PLUMAGES: No unusual plumages have been described, but all immature plumages have not been previously described.

SIMILAR SPECIES

(1) SWAINSON'S HAWK (Pls. 20, 21) light morphs also have two-toned underwings, but their primaries and secondaries are all the same dark gray color. They also have either a dark bib (adult) or a spotted or streaked breast (juvenile and Basic I). Dark-morph Swainson's are similar to juvenile White-tails but are smaller, have more prominent tail banding, dark unbarred leg feathers, and a less distinct white U above tail base, and lack the white breast patch. **(2) FERRUGINOUS HAWK** (Pls. 28, 29) light morph birds are similar to adult White-tails but have white cheeks, pale primaries on underwings, and rufous leg feathers (adult) and lack wide black subterminal wing and tail bands. **(3) HARLAN'S HAWK** (Pls. 25, 27) darker morphs are similar to juvenile White-tails but have dark undertail coverts, silvery flight feathers with wider dark border, more rounded wingtips, and dusky subterminal tail band and lack white U above tail base. **(4) DARK MORPH BUTEOS** of other species lack white U above tail base and have silvery flight feathers.

FLIGHT

White-tailed Hawks are similar to Swainson's Hawks in flight and silhouette. Active flight is more labored than that of Swainson's, with slow, steady wingbeats. Soars with wings in a strong dihedral; glides with wings in a modified dihedral. Hovers and kites frequently.

MOLT

Not studied. Annual molt of all age classes is apparently complete or nearly complete. Onset of molt is not well known but is presumably early in the year, or it is possible that they are in active molt throughout the year. The three immature age classes are juvenile, Basic I, and Basic II.

BEHAVIOR

White-tailed Hawks hunt both from perches and on the wing, either gliding, kiting, or hovering. Their wide variety of prey includes mammals, birds, reptiles, amphibians, crustaceans, and insects, as well as carrion. They gather at prairie fires, sometimes in numbers, to feed on disturbed prey. Talon-grappling has been observed. Nest is usually placed in a single low tree or bush.

STATUS AND DISTRIBUTION

White-tailed Hawks are fairly common but local in relatively undisturbed Texas coastal prairie and chaparral from Brownsville to Galveston. This species is sedentary, but local concentrations, particularly of juveniles, have been noted during winter. Juveniles are casual in Louisiana, and the few sightings in Arizona and New

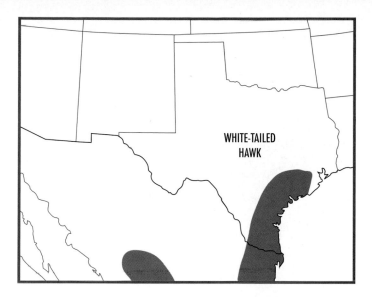

WHITE-TAILED
HAWK

Mexico are most likely from n. Mexican, rather than Texas, populations.

FINE POINTS

Juveniles have two, rarely three, pale spots on sides of face, noticeable when viewed at close range; these are not seen on older immatures. Some paler juveniles show a single large pale area, as the spots merge.

SUBSPECIES

The Texas birds belong to *B. a. hypospodius*.

ETYMOLOGY

Albicaudatus is from the Latin *albus*, "white," and *caudatus*, "tail."

MEASUREMENTS

LENGTH:	46–58 cm (50);	18–22 in. (20)
WINGSPREAD:	126–135 cm (129);	49–53 in. (51)
WEIGHT:	880–1,350 g (1,100);	1.9–3.0 lb. (2.4)

Buteo albonotatus

DESCRIPTION

The Zone-tailed Hawk, a slender-winged and long-tailed blackish buteo, occurs in hills and mountains of the Southwest. Silhouette, underwing pattern, and flight habits are similar to those of Turkey Vultures. Sexes are almost alike in plumage, with females noticeably larger. Juvenile plumage is similar to that of adults. Eyes are dark brown. Face skin is light gray.

ADULT: Head, body, and wing and tail coverts are black with a grayish bloom. Flight feathers are black above. Underwings appear two-toned: black coverts contrast with pale gray flight feathers, which have heavy narrow black barring that includes outer primaries and a wide dark subterminal band. Black tail has one wide white band and either one to four (rarely) narrow white bands or two wide white bands and one narrow one; bands are gray above on outer web and white on inner web and on underside. Females usually have more white bands, but there is overlap in this character. On perched adults, wingtips extend beyond tail tip. Cere and legs are yellow.

JUVENILE: Similar to adult but overall blackish lacking grayish bloom and with a variable amount of white spotting on underparts from none to much. In faded plumage, juveniles appear

Zone-tailed Hawk adult. All appear overall dark above and fly with wings above the horizontal. Adults show gray bands on uppertails. Arizona, April (BKW)

Zone-tailed Hawk juvenile. Most juveniles show some white spotting on underparts. Arizona, July (WSC)

Zone-tailed Hawk juvenile. Juveniles appear much like Turkey Vultures in flight. Arizona, July (WSC)

browner. Flight feathers are whiter below than those of adult, are completely barred, and lack wide dark subterminal band. Tail is gray above, with five to seven narrow black bands, subterminal band wider, and whitish below, with five to seven narrow dusky bands and a wider dusky subterminal band. On perched juveniles, wingtips just reach tail tip. Cere and legs are dull yellow, duller than those of adults.

UNUSUAL PLUMAGES: A juvenile with white forehead and nape was seen and photographed in Arizona.

SIMILAR SPECIES

(1) **TURKEY VULTURE** (Pl. 1) appears quite similar in flight but is larger, has smaller, unfeathered red head (adult) and unbanded tail, and lacks yellow cere and dark trailing edge on underwings. (2) **COMMON BLACK-HAWK** (Pl. 14) adults are almost identical when perched to adult Zone-tails. See under that species for differences. (3) **BROAD-WINGED HAWK** (Pl. 18) dark-morph adults have a similar tail pattern but are dark brown, not black, and smaller and soar and glide with wings level. (4) **DARK-MORPH BUTEOS** of other species lack the wide white tail band, except for adult Broad-winged Hawk and Rough-legged Hawk.

FLIGHT

Active flight is with medium-slow, flexible wingbeats. Soars and glides like a Turkey Vulture, with *wings in a strong dihedral* and constantly teetering. Does not hover or kite.

MOLT

Not studied. Apparently the annual molt of adults is not complete, as adults captured in the breeding season show wave molt in the primaries. Presumably most of the adults' molt is done on the winter grounds. The onset of post-juvenile molt is unknown, but presumably occurs in the second spring.

BEHAVIOR

Zone-tailed Hawks hunt on the wing, apparently mimicking the Turkey Vulture so that they can approach prey close enough for capture before it can flee. They sometimes fly with Turkey Vultures, showing their true identity and rapid flight only when potential prey is sighted. Then they stoop rapidly to snatch a bird, mammal, or lizard. Another hunting method is a wide spiraling descent terminated by a short quick stoop. They are often overlooked because of their similarity to Turkey Vultures.

Talon-grappling between individuals has been reported. Vocalizations are typical of buteos: a drawn-out whistled, *keeer*. This species can be very brave in defense of its nest and has on numerous occasions swooped at, and even soundly smacked, human intruders.

STATUS AND DISTRIBUTION

Zone-tailed Hawks are uncommon and local in hilly riparian habitat and mountain coniferous forests and canyons of w. Texas and parts of New Mexico and Arizona. They are now breeding locally in s. California and casual in s. Texas. Some individuals are resident, but most migrate south for winter. Small numbers have recently been reported in winter in the lower Rio Grande Valley of s. Texas and near Goleta, California.

FINE POINTS

The gray color on uppertail bands is on outer feather web only; bands are white on inner web; the uppertail bands appear white only when tail is fanned.

SUBSPECIES

Monotypic.

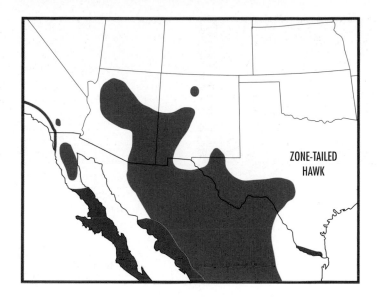

ZONE-TAILED
HAWK

ETYMOLOGY

Named "zone-tailed" for its tail markings; *albo* and *notatus* are Latin for "white" and "marked."

MEASUREMENTS

LENGTH:	48–56 cm (51);	19–22 in. (20)
WINGSPREAD:	121–140 cm (129);	48–55 in. (51)
WEIGHT:	610–1,080 g (830);	1.3–2.4 lb. (1.8)

RED-TAILED HAWK

PLS. 24–27

Buteo jamaicensis
(Harlan's Hawk, *B. j. harlani*, is described separately.)

DESCRIPTION

The Red-tailed Hawk, our most common and widespread buteo, is polymorphic in plumages. Plumages vary in a continuum from whitish to dark, but the *rufous tails* of adults, the *two-toned upperwings* of juveniles, and the *dark patagial marks on underwings* of light-morph birds are diagnostic field marks. There is consider-

Red-tailed Hawk adult B. j. calurus *light morph. All light-morph hawks show dark patagial marks. Arizona, March (WSC)*

Red-tailed Hawk adult B. j. calurus *light morph. Most light-morph hawks show pale* V *on scapulars. Oregon, February (WSC)*

able geographic and individual variation in plumage, nevertheless, six light-morph and three dark-morph forms can be distinguished. The light-morph forms are: Eastern, Florida, Western, Fuertes', Alaskan, and Krider's. The dark forms are dark, dark intermediate, and rufous (intermediate) morphs. Sexes are alike in plumage and overlap considerably in size. Juvenile plumage differs from that of adults in all forms.

Adults have shorter tails and broader wings compared to those of juveniles and thus have different flight silhouettes. On perched adults, wingtips almost reach tail tips in Western and many Florida and Fuertes' adults but fall somewhat short in other adults and juveniles. Adults' eyes are medium to dark brown. Ceres are dull yellow to greenish yellow. Leg color varies from dull yellow to yellow. In subsections that follow, Eastern adults are described first, then other adults are compared to them.

EASTERN ADULT: Head is tawny brown with darker brown malar stripes, white (occasionally dark) throat, and sometimes pale superciliaries. White throat is sometimes offset by a narrow dark collar line. Back and upperwing coverts are dark brown, with whitish mottling on scapulars, usually forming a noticeable V on back, and white spotting on median upperwing coverts. Underparts are white, often with a light rufous wash on sides of upper breast and with an incomplete belly band of short dark streaks, occasionally with little or no belly band. Underwings are white, with coverts lightly washed rufous and with a *dark patagial mark* and a dark comma beyond wrist. Blackish tips of flight feathers

Red-tailed Hawk juvenile B. j. borealis. *Best field mark for juveniles is the two-toned upperwings. Minnesota, September (BKW)*

form a wide dark band on trailing edge of underwings. Whitish undertail coverts and leg feathers are usually unmarked. *Rufous tail* has a narrow dark brown subterminal band (rarely absent) and can appear pinkish from below. Whitish areas of otherwise rufous uppertail coverts form a pale U above tail base on many adults. **NOTE:** Adults with Westernlike characters are found in winter in the eastern United States; their origins are most likely from northeastern Canada.

KRIDER'S HAWKS are a relatively uncommon pale color morph of the Eastern Red-tailed Hawk, breeding in the northern Great Plains.

KRIDER'S ADULT: Similar to Eastern adult but is overall much whiter (see also partial albino under Unusual Plumages). *Head is usually completely white,* but intergrades may have narrow dark malar stripes, dark streaking on crown and nape, and narrow dark eye lines. *Brown back and upperwing coverts are heavily mottled with white.* Patagial marks on underwings are rufous or dark brown and are usually narrow and faint. White underparts are unmarked, lacking a belly band; rufous markings on sides of upper breast often appear as a partial collar on flying birds. *Tail is pinkish to whitish,* often washed with rufous near tip, and usually with a narrow, faint, dusky subterminal band. Intergrades are encountered that show a mixture of both adult Krider's and adult Eastern characteristics.

FLORIDA ADULT: Somewhat similar to Eastern adult (more similar to Western adult), but head and upperparts are a darker brown; throat is dark or heavily streaked; underparts have many dark brown streaks that form a heavy, often solid, belly band; leg feath-

Red-tailed Hawk adult B. j. calurus *dark morph. Body and wing coverts are dark; tail has multiple dark bands. Colorado, January (BKW)*

Red-tailed Hawk adult. Partial albino adults occur occasionally throughout the range. Colorado, November (BKW)

ers are either unbarred or have narrow dark barring; and rufous tail often shows numerous narrow, sometimes incomplete dark bands, subterminal wider. Markings on scapulars and upperwing coverts are darker gray and do not contrast much with upperparts, so the pale V of other forms is usually not noticeable. Axillaries and greater underwing coverts are usually heavily barred.

FUERTES' ADULT: Almost like Eastern adult but has longer wings, lacks dark belly band, and sometimes has dark throat, usually in the areas where it intergrades with Western form. They also show faint rufous barring on flanks and a darker head with a distinct face pattern of dark malar stripes, pale cheeks and superciliary, and narrow dark eye lines. They are more likely than other races to lack a dark subterminal tail band.

WESTERN LIGHT-MORPH ADULT: Somewhat similar to Eastern adult, but throat is usually dark or heavily streaked, brown on head and upperparts is darker, there is a richer rufous wash on underparts and underwing coverts, and patagial marks are larger and darker. A variable amount of short dark streaks form the belly band, which is usually wider and more pronounced but may be narrow or even absent. Flanks, belly, and leg feathers have rufous barring. The pale markings on the scapulars can be either whitish, buffy, or tawny but may be absent on darker birds. Axillaries and greater underwing coverts are often heavily barred. Tail has wider dark subterminal band and may have numerous other narrow, sometimes incomplete dark bands.

ALASKAN ADULTS: Similar to darker Western adults but with a stronger rufous wash on underparts and underwing coverts. Adults in the Queen Charlotte Islands have distinct arrowhead-shaped breast markings. They almost always have dark throats; heavy belly bands; brownish barring on flanks, belly, and leg feathers; and wider dark tail bands. However, some show only the dark subterminal band.

DARK RED-TAILED HAWKS vary in a cline from rufous morph through intermediate dark to dark morph. All dark birds occur within the ranges of Western birds.

RUFOUS-MORPH ADULT: Head is dark tawny with wide dark brown malar stripes, sometimes with narrow dark eye lines. Back and upperwing coverts are dark brown, usually lacking pale markings on the scapulars. Breast varies from pale to dark rufous; belly is uniformly dark brown but often shows whitish spotting. Underwing coverts are rufous, with some dark barring; dark patagial marks are noticeable. Whitish axillaries are heavily barred dark brown. Rufous leg feathers and uppertail coverts have narrow dark brown barring. Rufous tail usually shows numerous narrow dark bands, with subterminal band much wider. Rufous undertail coverts are usually unmarked.

DARK INTERMEDIATE ADULT: Similar to rufous-morph adult but darker, with dark head, smaller and duller rufous breast patch, often with dark streaks, and dark rufous-brown underwing coverts that obscure the dark patagial marks. Legs are dark brown with rufous feather edges.

DARK-MORPH ADULT: Head, upperparts, underparts, wing coverts, and leg feathers are overall dark brown, rarely jet black. Dark brown undertail coverts are barred rufous. Rufous tail usually shows numerous narrow dark bands, with subterminal band much wider. Dark brown uppertail coverts have rufous tips.

JUVENILE RED-TAILED HAWKS of all races and morphs show *two-toned upperwings: pale primaries and coverts contrast with darker secondaries and coverts,* with a sharp line of contrast that extends across entire upperwing. Eyes of juveniles are pale gray, often with a yellowish cast. Ceres are dull greenish to greenish yellow. Backlit underwings show square or trapezoid pale primary panel, a feature shared with other buteo species. Wingtips of perched juveniles fall quite short of tail tip on most forms but extend farther on Western and Fuertes' juveniles. Leg color varies from dull yellow to yellow.

EASTERN JUVENILE: Head is brown, paler than adult's, with pale superciliaries, cheeks, and throat, dark malar stripes, and sometimes faint narrow eye lines. White throat is sometimes offset by a narrow dark collar line. Back and upperwing coverts are brown, with white mottling on scapulars forming a pale V on back and some white mottling on median upperwing coverts. White underparts show an unmarked breast and heavy belly band of short dark streaks. Recent fledglings have a rufous bloom on breast that usually fades quickly. Pale underwings show *dark patagial marks* and dark band on trailing edge that is paler and narrower than that of adult. Dusky tips of outer primaries usually show dark barring. Whitish uppertail coverts form a U at base of uppertail.White undertail coverts are unmarked, but white leg feathers often show rufous spotting. Brown tail usually shows many narrow equal-width dark brown bands, sometimes the subterminal band is somewhat wider than the others; uppersides of tails on some show a rufous cast.

KRIDER'S JUVENILE: Similar to Eastern juvenile but is overall much whiter (see also partial albino under Unusual Plumages). *Head is white,* with narrow dark malar stripes and sometimes dark streaking on crown and nape and narrow dark eye lines. Brown back and upperwing coverts are heavily mottled with white. Dark patagial marks on underwings are reduced and faint. Underparts are white, with a variable amount of dark spots, usually confined to flanks, but can form a sparse belly band. Uppertail appears whitish on base and pale brown toward tip, with dark bands on outer half. Intergrades are encountered that show a mixture of both juvenile Krider's and juvenile Eastern characteristics.

FLORIDA JUVENILE: Identical to Eastern juvenile.

FUERTES' JUVENILE: Very similar to Eastern juvenile but with longer wings. Belly bands average heavier and throat is sometimes streaked or dark.

WESTERN LIGHT-MORPH JUVENILE: Similar to Eastern juvenile, but brown coloration is darker, throat is usually streaked or dark, belly band is wider and more heavily marked, leg feathers have brown barring, and tips of outer primaries are usually uniformly dark, lacking barring. Creamy undertail coverts can show faint narrow rufous barring.

ALASKAN JUVENILE: Similar to Western juvenile, but with head and upperparts more blackish brown, pale streaked throats, and wider dark tail bands.

RUFOUS-MORPH JUVENILE: Similar to Western light-morph juvenile, but with white to buffy breast heavily streaked, wide dark belly band mottled white, dark markings on underwing coverts (which often mask dark patagial mark), and heavily barred leg feathers and undertail coverts. Tips of outer primaries are uniformly dark, lacking barring. Tail is like that of Western light-morph juvenile.

DARK INTERMEDIATE JUVENILE: Similar to dark-morph juvenile but with rufous-tawny patch or streaking on breast, sometimes with dark streaking, and often some rufous streaks on neck and rufous markings on belly, leg feathers, and undertail coverts.

DARK-MORPH JUVENILE: Overall dark brown on head, body, and coverts, sometimes mottled with buff or rufous on underparts and underwing coverts. Tips of outer primaries are uniformly dark, lacking barring. Tail is like that of Western light-morph juvenile but with wider dark bands.

UNUSUAL PLUMAGES: Partial albinos, varying from almost all-white birds to some with just a few white feathers, are fairly common and are reported from almost all areas. Most are more than half white. Most almost completely white individuals often have a dark area on the nape. All partial albinos seen, reported, and in collections are adults. Two dilute-plumage adults in photos were overall whitish with faint rufous barring on flight feathers. One had a pale rufous tail and the other, a whitish tail. A dilute-plumage juvenile specimen is mostly cream colored, with some faint rufous bars and streaks. A light-morph adult specimen that is normal in every other way has a greenish gray, not rufous, tail.

SIMILAR SPECIES

(1) FERRUGINOUS HAWK (Pl. 28) light-morph adult can also have a dark belly band, rufous tail, and dark markings on underwing coverts but has dark rufous leg feathering down to feet, its tail does not have a dark subterminal band, dark on outer primaries is restricted to tips, and underwing markings, if present, are chestnut and not restricted to fore-edge of patagium. Light-morph juvenile (Pl. 29) is similar to Krider's Hawk juvenile but has legs feathered to toes, shows wide dark lines behind eyes and black marks on flanks, has dark primary upperwing coverts, and lacks barring on tips of outer primaries. **(2) SWAINSON'S HAWK** juveniles (Pl. 21) can appear similar; see under that species for differences. **(3) HARLAN'S HAWK** (Pls. 24, 25) light-morph hawks appear similar to Krider's Hawk. See under that form for distinctions. **(4) LIGHT-MORPH BUTEOS** of other species lack dark patagial marks on underwings. **(5) DARK-MORPH BUTEOS** of other species have different tail patterns.

FLIGHT

Active flight is with slow, steady, deep wingbeats. Soars with wings raised somewhat above the horizontal. Glides with wings level or in a slight dihedral. Hovers and kites on moderate wind, especially using deflection updrafts from wood edges and cliffs. Red-tails soar and hover fairly often.

Molt

Annual molt is not complete for adults, as not all of the primaries and secondaries are replaced every year. Most adults retain 2 or 3 old outer primaries and an old secondary or two. Some breeding adults, especially males, may suspend molt for a while. First pre-basic (post-juvenile) molt is also not always complete; it begins in the spring and is suspended by late summer or autumn. First plumage adults usually have 2 or 3 retained outer primaries and retained S4 and S8 or S9.

Behavior

Red-tailed Hawks are birds of both open and wooded areas, particularly wood edges, and are often seen perched conspicuously on a treetop, a utility pole, or other lookout while hunting. Red-tails prey mainly on rodents but also take larger mammals, such as rabbits and squirrels, as well as reptiles and birds, insects and their larvae, and fish. They often pursue prey into dense brush, pirate prey from other raptors, and eat carrion. The most frequently heard vocalization is a long, wheezy *kkeeeeer,* somewhat like the sound of escaping steam.

Courtship and territorial displays are a series of steep dives and climbs and include glides by both adults together with their feet down. Talon-grappling has been reported and is usually an aggressive defense of territory.

Red-tailed Hawks build large stick nests in tall trees, occasionally on cliff ledges.

Status and Distribution

Red-tailed Hawks are widespread and common, occasionally abundant, and occur in every North American habitat except high Arctic and extensive tracts of dense forest. Northern birds are migratory.

EASTERN: Resident from the Great Plains east, south of the Boreal forest.

FLORIDA: Resident on the entire Florida peninsula, but Eastern birds are also present in winter.

KRIDER'S: Found in summer on n. Great Plains, where it is greatly outnumbered by Eastern form. It winters south to Texas, Oklahoma, Arkansas, Louisiana, and Kansas.

FUERTES': Resident from s. Texas west through s. New Mexico and s. Arizona. It intergrades with Eastern and Western forms on northern boundaries of its range.

WESTERN: Resident west of the Great Plains and north of the

RED-TAILED
HAWK

Fuertes' range, north to n. British Columbia and eastward across forested Canada to Labrador, where they intergrade with Eastern Red-tails. They occur in winter on the Great Plains and in the East. Eastern and Western forms intergrade also on the western edge of the Great Plains. Dark-morph hawks are relatively rare but can constitute as much as 10 percent of a local population.

ALASKAN: Resident in Pacific Northwest rain forests, along the Pacific Coast from se. Alaska to the Queen Charlotte Is., with much intergradation with Western hawks inland and farther south into Washington.

FINE POINTS

First plumage adults from northern areas can sometimes be distinguished by the faded retained juvenile outer one or two primaries and several shorter retained juvenile secondaries (see Molt). When viewed flying head-on, many Red-tails show light areas, somewhat like headlights, on the leading edge of each wing.

SUBSPECIES

The AOU (1957) recognized the following races: *B. j. borealis* in e. North America except the Florida peninsula, where it is replaced by *B. j. umbrinus*; *B. j. calurus* in w. North America, except in s. Texas, New Mexico, and Arizona, where it is replaced by *B. j. fuertesi,* and in n. British Columbia and Alaska, where it is replaced by *B. j. harlani.* The range given for *B. j. krideri* is the n. Great Plains. The AOU has not listed subspecies in all checklists since 1957.

ETYMOLOGY

Krider's Hawk was named for John Krider, who collected the first specimens in Iowa. Fuertes' Red-tailed Hawk was named by George Sutton and Josselyn Van Tyne for Louis Agassiz Fuertes, the bird artist. *Jamaicensis* is for Jamaica, where the first Red-tailed Hawk specimen was collected.

MEASUREMENTS

LENGTH:		45–55 cm (49);	17–22 in. (19)
WINGSPREAD:	East	110–132 cm (120);	43–52 in. (47)
	West	120–141 cm (130);	47–56 in. (51)
WEIGHT:		710–1,550 g (1082);	1.5–3.3 lb. (2.4)

NOTE: "East" includes Eastern and Krider's forms; "West" includes others.

HARLAN'S HAWK
PLS. 24–27

Buteo jamaicensis harlani
(Red-tailed Hawk is described separately.)

DESCRIPTION

The Harlan's Hawk, which replaces Red-tailed Hawk in Alaska and nearby Canada, is polymorphic in plumage. There is a stable zone of interbreeding between Harlan's Hawk and western Red-tailed Hawk. Plumages vary in a continuum from whitish to dark, but the *gray tails* of adults, the *two-toned upperwings* of juveniles, and the *dark patagial marks on underwings* of light-morph birds are diagnostic field marks. There is considerable variation in coloration, with five color morphs described herein. Harlan's differ from other Red-tails by the lack of rufous coloration (but see below for adults) and the more blackish coloration of upperparts. Sexes are alike in plumage and overlap considerably in size. Juvenile plumage is different from that of adults.

Adults have shorter tails and broader wings compared to those of juveniles and thus have different flight silhouettes. On perched adult birds, wingtips fall somewhat short of tail tips. Adults' eyes

Harlan's Hawk adult intermediate morph. Adults have gray upper-tails. Undersides of secondaries are often unbanded. Colorado, January (BKW)

Harlan's Hawk adult intermediate morph. All have coal black plumage, lacking warm brown tones of Red-tailed Hawks. Whitish to gray tails usually show blackish mottling. Texas, November (WSC)

are amber; ceres are dull yellow to greenish yellow; and legs vary from dull yellow to yellow.

LIGHT-MORPH ADULT: Head is patterned: dark crown and nape, white face and throat, and dark eye lines and malar stripes. Back and upperwing coverts are blackish brown, with whitish mottling on scapulars usually forming a noticeable V on back. White uppertail coverts often show some rufous patches. Underparts are white, with a lightly to heavily marked belly band of short dark streaks. Underwings are white with wide dark patagial marks; undersides of adult flight feathers can show dark banding or dark mottling or a mix of both. Adult tails vary considerably from whitish to dark gray, usually with a dusky or darker wide subterminal band, a hint of rufous near the tip, and dark mottling or partial banding or both. Some tails show numerous narrow dark bands and a wider dark subterminal band (See Pl. 25).

LIGHT INTERMEDIATE ADULT: Similar to light-morph adult but more heavily marked, with narrow dark streaks on the white breast, heavier belly band, dark mottling on flanks, and some dark markings on white underwing and undertail coverts. Dark patagial marks are noticeable.

INTERMEDIATE-MORPH ADULT: Dark head has white superciliaries and throat, sometimes white cheeks. Upperparts are blackish brown. Breast is streaked dark and white. Blackish brown belly and un-

Harlan's Hawk juvenile dark intermediate morph. Similar to dark juvenile Red-tail but lacking warm brown in plumage. Note dark spike on tail tips and barring on outer primaries. Colorado, November (BKW)

Harlan's Hawk juvenile light intermediate morph. Similar to dark juvenile Red-tail but lacking warm brown in plumage. Note dark tail tip. Colorado, November (BKW)

derwing coverts show white spotting, and blackish brown leg feathers and undertail coverts have white feather edges. Dark uppertail coverts often show rufous patches. Undersides of adult flight feathers can show dark banding or dark mottling or can be unmarked except for wide dark tips. Dark patagial marks are obscured by heavy markings on underwing coverts.

DARK INTERMEDIATE ADULT: Overall blackish brown, but with some white streaking on breast and sometimes a white throat. A few individuals show white speckling on belly and completely dark breast. Undersides of flight feathers are heavily banded. Dark uppertail coverts often show rufous patches.

DARK-MORPH ADULT: Overall blackish brown with no white markings.

Juvenile plumages are similar to those of juvenile Red-tails, but color of head and upperparts is darker, outer primaries are usually barred, dark tail bands are wider on dark juveniles, and they lack tawny coloration on face, neck, and breast. Eyes of juveniles are pale gray, often with a yellowish cast, ceres are dull yellow to greenish yellow. All juveniles show *two-toned upperwings: pale primaries and coverts contrast with darker secondaries and coverts,* with a sharp line of contrast that extends across entire upperwing. Backlit underwings show square or trapezoidal pale primary panel, a feature shared with other buteo species. Wingtips fall quite short of tail tip on perched juveniles. Leg color varies from dull yellow to yellow.

LIGHT-MORPH JUVENILE: Head is patterned, with dark crown and nape, white face and throat, and dark eye lines and malar stripes. Back and upperwing coverts are blackish brown, with whitish mottling on scapulars usually forming a noticeable V on back. White uppertail coverts usually show dark spots. Underparts are white, with a noticeable belly band of short dark streaks. Underwings are white, with wide dark patagial marks. Pale brown to brown tails show many narrow to wide dark bands.

LIGHT INTERMEDIATE JUVENILE: Similar to light-morph juvenile but more heavily marked, with dark streaks on breast, heavier belly band, and some dark markings on white underwing and undertail coverts. Dark patagial marks are occasionally noticeable.

INTERMEDIATE-MORPH JUVENILE: Dark head has white superciliaries and throat, sometimes white cheeks. Upperparts are blackish brown, with some whitish spotting. Breast is streaked dark and white. Blackish brown belly and underwing coverts show white spotting, and blackish brown leg feathers and undertail coverts have white feather edges. Uppertail coverts are usually barred white and dark. Dark patagial marks are obscured by heavy markings on underwing coverts. Brown tails show many narrow to wide dark bands.

DARK INTERMEDIATE JUVENILE: Overall blackish brown, often with white throat, whitish streaks on the breast, and whitish spotting on belly, wing and tail coverts, and leg feathers. A few individuals show white speckling on belly and completely dark breast. Brown tails show many wider dark bands.

DARK-MORPH JUVENILE: Overall blackish brown with few whitish markings. Brown tail shows many wider dark bands, similar to tail of juvenile Western Red-tailed Hawk.

UNUSUAL PLUMAGES: No reported cases of albinism. Intergrades with Red-tailed Hawks occur occasionally; they show a mix of characters of both. Photographs of a dark adult show some characters of Harlan's and some of Rough-legged Hawks; it is most likely a hybrid.

SIMILAR SPECIES

(1) FERRUGINOUS HAWK (Pl. 28) dark-morph adult can also have white mottling on breast like adult Harlan's but has narrow black tips on outer primaries and lacks wide dark band on trailing edge of underwings and dusky subterminal tail band. **(2) ROUGH-LEGGED HAWK** (Pl. 30) dark-morph adult is quite similar to dark-morph adult Harlan's but has mostly to completely dark uppertail; little or no white mottling on breast and underwing coverts; longer, narrower wings; and legs feathered to toes. Pale area in lores doesn't extend to the eyes on dark Rough-leggeds but does on dark Harlan's. **(3) KRIDER'S RED-TAILED HAWK** (Pls. 24, 26) is similar to light Harlan's, but has faint narrow malar stripes and patagial marks. Adult Krider's lack dark spots on belly. Juvenile Harlan's have dark uppertails. **(4) DARK RED-TAILED HAWK** juveniles (Pl. 27) are similar to dark juvenile Harlan's, but the color of their upperparts is a warmer brown, and they usually have dark tips to outer primaries and lack barring. They also do not show dark on tips of tail feathers seen in most juvenile Harlan's (see Fine Points).

FLIGHT

Active flight is with slow, steady, deep wingbeats. Soars with wings raised slightly above horizontal. Glides with wings level or in a slight dihedral. Hovers and kites on moderate wind, especially using deflection updrafts from wood edges and cliffs.

MOLT

Apparently not studied. Presumably annual molt is not complete for adults, similar to more northern Red-tailed Hawks; not all flight feathers are replaced every year. First prebasic (post-juvenile) molt most likely begins when juveniles return to the breeding areas and is suspended but not completed when they migrate in the autumn. Apparently little molt takes place during migration or on the winter grounds, but some active molt has been noted in November.

BEHAVIOR

Similar to Red-tailed Hawk. However, in winter they are much more wary, especially the adults, with much greater flush distances compared to other Red-tailed Hawks.

STATUS AND DISTRIBUTION

Intermediate and dark intermediate morphs are fairly common; light morph is uncommon; and light intermediate and dark morphs are rare.

Harlan's Hawks are found in summer throughout much of Alaska and w. Yukon Territory, overlapping in range with Western Red-tail form in n. British Columbia and se. Alaska. Fairly commonly seen on migration on the n. Great Plains. The main wintering area is e. Colorado, w. Arkansas, e. Texas, Oklahoma, and Kansas. However, they are encountered widely but locally throughout the West.

FINE POINTS

Many juveniles' tails show the dark of the outermost band extending as a spike to the tip in the center of each feather; also a similar spike on some secondaries; this is not shown by other juvenile Red-tails.

SUBSPECIES

See under Red-tailed Hawk.

ETYMOLOGY

Audubon named the Harlan's Hawk for Dr. Richard Harlan (he did not coin the common name but only used *harlani*; he called the bird "Black Warrior").

MEASUREMENTS

See under Red-tailed Hawk.

FERRUGINOUS HAWK
PLS. 28, 29

Buteo regalis

DESCRIPTION

The Ferruginous Hawk, our largest buteo, inhabits much of the arid West. They have long, tapered wings, large heads, wide gapes, and robust chests. They are polymorphic in plumage, with light-morph hawks much more common than dark ones. Dark hawks vary from rufous to dark. Upperwings show whitish primary patch but have dark primary coverts (see juvenile Red-tailed Hawk). Backlit underwings show square or trapezoid pale primary panel, a feature shared with other buteo species. Legs are feathered down to toes. Sexes are alike in plumage, but females are noticeably larger than males. Juvenile plumages differ from those of adults and lack rufous on upperparts, legs, and tails. Wingtips reach tail tip on perched hawks. Cere and feet are yellow.

LIGHT-MORPH ADULT: Head varies from whitish with some narrow gray, tawny, or brown streaking on crown and nape, less heavy on

Ferruginous Hawk adult light morph. Adults have narrow dark tips on outer primaries and dark rufous legs that form a V on undersides. New Mexico, November (WSC)

Ferruginous Hawk adult rufous morph. Breast is rufous, with rufous tones on dark brown belly and underwing coverts. Note whitish comma at wrist. Colorado, July (WSC)

cheeks, to gray-brown or dark brown with some whitish streaking, with dark eye lines, often pale superciliaries, and white throats; they lack wide dark malar stripes. Eyes are light to dark brown. Back and upperwing coverts are rufous with black centers to many feathers, but greater coverts are blackish with some rufous feather edges. *Uppersides of flight feathers are gray* with black banding; inner webs of primaries are white, forming a white panel on upperwings of flying adults. Primary upperwing coverts are dark. White underparts vary from unmarked to lightly marked with dark spots and rufous barring on flanks and belly to heavily marked with dark and rufous barring on flanks and belly, forming a dark belly band like that of the Red-tailed Hawk, and with rufous wash and some streaks on the breast. Underwings are white with a black wrist comma and a variable amount of rufous on coverts, from none to completely rufous, also with some dark barring on heavily marked adults. Undersides of flight feathers are white with *narrow dark tips on outer primaries* and narrow dusky tips on the rest, forming a narrow dusky band on the trailing edge of wings. Completely feathered legs vary from rufous with dark brown barring to white with narrow rufous barring and are visible as a *dark V on the undersides* of most light-morph adults in flight. *Unbanded tail* is sometimes rufous, often with white mixed in at base and inner webs and, less often, light gray on central feathers, and sometimes completely white, occasionally with narrow dark

Ferruginous Hawk adult dark morph. Underparts, including breast, and underwing coverts are dark brown. Note whitish comma at wrist. Texas, February (BKW)

Ferruginous Hawk juvenile light morph. Fledglings show a buffy wash on the breast. Note the large gape. Colorado, July (WSC)

mottling. A few adults show a complete or incomplete dark subterminal band on their tails. Whitish uppertail coverts usually have small dark centers. Wingtips fall just short of tail tip on perched adults.

DARK ADULTS vary from rufous-morph to dark-morph in a continuous cline.

RUFOUS-MORPH ADULT: Head is dark brown or dark gray, sometimes with narrow white streaks on throat. Eyes are light to dark brown. Back and upperwing coverts are dark brown, with wide dark rufous edges on the coverts, but greater coverts are blackish brown with narrow rufous edges. Uppersides of flight feathers are gray with black banding; inner webs of primaries are white, forming a white panel on upperwings of flying adults; and primary upperwing coverts are dark. Uppertail coverts are dark rufous with dark centers. Underparts are a mix of dark brown and dark rufous, often with some white streaks on the breast. Breast or belly can be mostly rufous. Underwing is two-toned; silvery primaries contrast with dark rufous and brown coverts. A *white comma at wrist* and *narrow black tips of outer primaries* are evident on underwings. Trailing edge of underwings has a narrow dusky border. *Unbanded tail* appears gray on uppersides and white on undersides, and often shows some dark spots near the tips of outer feathers. Undertail coverts are paler rufous, usually with some dark spotting or barring.

Ferruginous Hawk juvenile dark morph. All show pale gray primaries and dark primary coverts on upperwings. Colorado, December (BKW)

DARK-MORPH ADULT: Similar to rufous-morph adult but head, body, and wing and tail coverts are blackish brown without any rufous coloration. Intergrades between the morphs show a clinal variation.

LIGHT-MORPH JUVENILE: White head has brown streaking on crown and nape, pale superciliaries, and dark eye lines; *white cheeks do not show dark malar stripes.* Eyes are pale grayish yellow to pale brown. Back and upperwing coverts are dark brown with some inconspicuous narrow rufous feather edging and some more obvious white streaking. Uppersides of flight feathers are brown with indistinct darker bands; inner webs of primaries are white, forming a white panel on upperwings of flying juveniles; and primary upperwing coverts are dark. White underparts show *darkish lines on each flank* that are visible on flying juveniles, occasionally a row of short dark streaks on the breast, and often a sparse belly band of dark spots. Recently fledged birds have a rufous wash on breast that fades by fall. White underwings show black wrist commas, some small black spots on coverts, *narrow dark tips on outer primaries,* and a very narrow dusky band on trailing edge. White leg feathers have black spots. Uppertail is white on basal third, the rest is grayish brown with several indistinct dark bands; undertail appears silvery with a dusky tip. White uppertail coverts show dark spots.

RUFOUS-MORPH JUVENILE: Head and breast are dark brown with a rufous cast and a sharp line of contrast between breast and dark brown belly. Eyes are pale grayish yellow to pale brown. Back and wing and uppertail coverts are dark brown. Flight feathers are like those of light-morph juveniles. Underwing is two-toned; silvery flight feathers contrast with dark coverts. Note *white comma at wrist* and *narrow dark tips on outer primaries.* Uppertail is brown with indistinct darker brown bands; below it is whitish with a dusky tip and 2 or 3 narrow indistinct dark bands near tip. Undertail coverts are dark brown with whitish barring and tips.

DARK-MORPH JUVENILE: Rare. Similar to rufous-morph juvenile but head, breast, and undertail coverts are dark brown.

UNUSUAL PLUMAGES: No unusual plumages have been reported.

SIMILAR SPECIES

(1) RED-TAILED HAWK (Pls. 24–27) can appear similar in many plumages. See under that species for differences. **(2) HARLAN'S HAWK** (Pls. 24–27) dark adults also have white breast streaking and grayish tail. See under that account for differences. **(3) ROUGH-LEGGED HAWK** (Pls. 30, 31) light-morph birds have square dark carpal patches on underwings, wide dark tips on outer primaries, heavily marked underparts, and usually a solid dark belly band. Dark-morph juveniles have tail pattern similar to dark-morph juvenile Ferruginous but have white foreheads, wider dark tips on outer primaries, and smaller gape and lack white wrist commas. **(4) DARK-MORPH BUTEOS** of other species have wider dark tips on outer primaries and different tail patterns.

FLIGHT

Active flight is with slow, strong wingbeats, much like that of a small eagle. Soars with wings in medium to strong dihedral; glides with wings in a slight or modified dihedral. Hovers occasionally.

MOLT

Annual molt of adults is more or less complete, but not all primaries or secondaries are replaced every year. Molt begins in spring and is completed by late autumn. First prebasic (post-juvenile) molt begins when hawks are about a year old and is completed before winter.

BEHAVIOR

Ferruginous Hawks are adept flyers and hunt by a variety of methods: coursing rapidly low over open ground, soaring at height, hovering, or from a perch. Cooperative hunting of pairs has been reported. Their main prey are ground squirrels and jackrabbits, but they occasionally take other mammals and birds.

They construct large stick nests in small trees or on rock outcroppings but also on the ground and sometimes on haystacks when no tree or outcropping is available. Adults are strong in their nest defense against ground predators and chase away mammals as large as coyotes by their relentless attacks.

Vocalizations include a drawn-out *keerrr,* typical of buteos, less wheezy than that of the Red-tailed Hawk. Ferruginous Hawks occasionally form communal night roosts in winter, sometimes with other species, including Bald Eagles.

STATUS AND DISTRIBUTION

Ferruginous Hawks are fairly common, breeding on undisturbed plains, sage grass, high deserts, badlands, or edges of pinyon-juniper woodlands from w. Great Plains north into s. Canada, west to cen. Washington and Oregon and w. Nevada, and south to n. Arizona and nw. Texas. In winter some birds move south, east, and west. They are casual in the East during migration and in winter, with many records from Minnesota and Wisconsin but some also from Illinois, Indiana, Ohio, Tennessee, Virginia, New Jersey, and Florida. Dark-morph birds are not uniformly distributed and make up from 1 percent to 10 percent, rarely as much as 25 percent, of local populations.

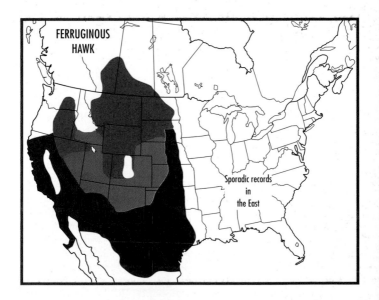

FERRUGINOUS
HAWK

Sporadic records
in
the East

Ferruginous Hawks have large yellow gapes that extend well beneath their eyes. These are thought by some researchers to be used for thermal regulation by allowing rapid air exchange, especially in the case of nestlings and incubating females, which can be in direct sunlight on ground nests during the heat of the day.

SUBSPECIES

Monotypic.

ETYMOLOGY

"Ferruginous" comes from the Latin *ferrugo,* "rust," for rufous color in adult plumage; *regalis* is Latin for "royal," a reference to the bird's large size.

MEASUREMENTS

LENGTH:	50–66 cm (59);	20–26 in. (23)
WINGSPREAD:	134–152 cm (143);	53–60 in. (56)
WEIGHT:	900–1,600 g (1,175);	2.0–3.3 lb. (2.6)

ROUGH-LEGGED HAWK
PLS. 30, 31

Buteo lagopus

DESCRIPTION

The Rough-legged Hawk, a large long-winged buteo, breeds on the Arctic tundra and winters in southern Canada and the northern United States. They have small feet and beaks compared to similar-sized buteos. Pale nape patch with dark spot in center is often noticeable. Most show a *square black carpal patch* on each underwing. Legs are feathered completely to toes. Females are larger than males. Adult plumages differ by sex, but sexes are nearly alike in juvenile plumage. Plumages are dimorphic, with dark-morph hawks occurring more commonly than in other buteos, especially in the East. On perched adults, wingtips extend somewhat past tail tip; wingtips of juveniles reach tail tip. Toes are orange-yellow.

LIGHT-MORPH ADULT MALE: Brown head has white forehead and outer half of lores, white throat with narrow dark streaks, white streaking on crown, pale superciliaries and cheek patches, dark eye

Rough-legged Hawk adult male light morph. Adult males have barred flanks. Wingtips extend beyond tail tip on perched adults. Oregon, February (WSC)

Rough-legged Hawk adult male light morph. Adult males have barred flanks and multiple dark tail bands. Adults lack pale primary patches on upperwings. Colorado, February (BKW)

lines, and wide dark malar stripes. Adult eyes are dark brown. Ceres of males are yellow to orange-yellow. Back is dark brown with a mix of gray, white, and tawny mottling. Upperwings are dark brown, lacking large white primary patches, but often show two or three small white streaks on outer primaries. White, occasionally buffy, underparts show dark breast, darkly barred flanks, and lightly barred or unmarked belly, with a pale unmarked U-shaped area between the markings on breast and belly. Breast often appears as a solid dark bib at a distance but can be marked with white spots or streaks and sometimes with white down the center. Underwings have *black carpal patches*, usually with much white mottling; darkly marked white secondary coverts; unmarked line on median coverts; and secondaries and inner primaries with narrow dark bands and wide dark subterminal band. Outer primaries show either wide dark tips or narrow dark tips and are dusky to the emarginations, in either case appearing as wide dark tips from a distance. White leg feathers have dark barring. White uppertail coverts have wide dark barring. Tail is white but with a wide dusky tip, a dark subterminal band, and usually one to five other narrow dark bands. White undertail coverts vary from unmarked to lightly marked to heavily barred dark.

LIGHT-MORPH ADULT FEMALE: Buffy head shows noticeable dark eye lines and narrow dark streaking on malar area and crown and nape. Eyes of adult are dark brown. Ceres of females are yellow.

Rough-legged Hawk subadult female light morph. Adult females (and juveniles) have uniformly dark flanks. Note retained juvenile flight feathers. Colorado, March (BKW)

Back is dark brown, with some white and buffy streaking. Upperwings are dark brown, usually lacking large white primary patches, but often show two or three small white streaks on outer primaries. Some first-plumage adult females have juvenile-like pale primary panels on upperwings. White uppertail coverts have dark spots. Buffy underparts show narrow dark streaks on breast, sometimes quite heavy, forming a dark bib, and solid wide dark band on flanks and belly, sometimes with white in center of belly, often with a pale unmarked U-shaped area between the breast and belly markings. Underwings have *black carpal patches*

Rough-legged Hawk subadult female light morph. Subadults often show pale primary patch on upperwings. Note dark primary coverts. Colorado, March (BKW)

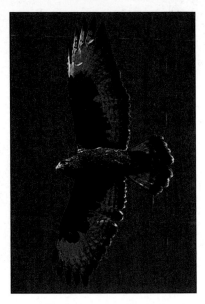

Rough-legged Hawk adult dark morph. Dark brown adult can be male or female. Oregon, February (WSC)

and lightly marked buffy secondary coverts, with an unmarked line on median coverts, and secondaries and inner primaries have a wide dark subterminal band and sometimes other narrower dark bands. Outer primaries show either wide dark tips or narrow dark tips with dusky to emarginations, appearing as wide dark tips from a distance. White leg feathers show dark spotting or barring. Tail is white but with a wide dusky tip and a dark subterminal band, and occasionally one or two other narrow dark bands. White undertail coverts are unmarked. Some males show some or all female characters.

BLACK DARK-MORPH ADULT: All black adults are males. Head, body, and wing and tail coverts are jet black. Eyes of adult are dark brown. Ceres are yellow to orange-yellow. Undersides of flight feathers are silvery with some narrow dark bands and wide subterminal band on trailing edge of wings; outer primaries have wide dark or dusky and dark tips. *Black uppertail shows three narrow white or pale gray bands;* undertails are dark with three narrow white bands and wide darker band near tip.

DARK BROWN DARK-MORPH ADULT: Dark brown adult males and females are alike. Head, body, and wing and tail coverts are dark brown, except for black carpal patches on underwings, pale superciliaries and cheek patches on the head, and some rufous on breast. Ceres of females are yellow. Undersides of flight feathers are silvery with some narrow dark bands and wide subterminal band on trailing edge of wings; outer primaries have wide dark or dusky and dark tips. Some adults show paler heads, sometimes with pale throat, and pale streaking on upper breasts. Some adult females lack narrow pale bands on uppertail. Undertails are pale with a single wide blackish subterminal band, sometimes with three other narrow dark bands.

Rough-legged Hawk juvenile light morph. Juveniles have narrower dusky bands on trailing edges of wings and tip of tail. Oregon, February (WSC)

LIGHT-MORPH JUVENILE: Similar to light-morph adult female but belly band is more brownish and is usually complete; underwing coverts, uppertail coverts, and leg feathers are less heavily marked; white tail lacks dark subterminal band, showing only a wide dusky tip; band on trailing edge of underwings is narrower and dusky; and eyes are pale gray to pale brown. Ceres of juveniles are dull yellow to yellow. Juveniles have whitish panel on the upper primaries, with dark primary coverts. Outer primaries have wide dark tips. Backlit underwings show square or trapezoidal pale primary panel, a feature shared with other buteo species. Some juveniles show two or more narrow, somewhat indistinct dark bands in the tail. Wingtips just reach tail tip on perched juveniles.

DARK-MORPH JUVENILE: Similar to dark brown adults but tail lacks dark subterminal band, showing only a wide dusky tip; band on trailing edge of underwings is narrower and dusky; and eyes are pale gray to pale brown. Ceres of juveniles are dull yellow to yellow. Some dark-morph juveniles are dark brown overall, but others have rather pale heads and whitish and tawny mottling on upper breasts. Juveniles have whitish panel on upper primaries, but primary coverts are dark. Outer primaries have wide dark tips. Backlit underwings show square or trapezoid pale primary panel, a feature shared with other buteo species. Some juveniles show two or three pale bands on brown uppertail. Wingtips just reach tail tip on perched juveniles.

UNUSUAL PLUMAGES: Photographs of a dark adult show some characters of Harlan's Hawks and some of Rough-legged Hawks; it is presumably a hybrid between the two.

Similar Species

(1) **FERRUGINOUS HAWK** (Pl. 29) dark-morph juveniles are quite similar to dark Rough-legged juveniles. See under that species for differences. (2) **HARLAN'S HAWK** (Pl. 25) dark adults are similar to dark-morph Rough-leggeds. See under that account for differences. (3) **SWAINSON'S HAWK** (Pl. 20) adults also show a dark breast or bib like that of adult male light-morph adults. See under that species for differences. (4) **NORTHERN HARRIER** (Pl. 10) also has white on uppertail coverts. See under that species for differences. (5) **DARK-MORPH BUTEOS** of other species have different tail patterns, except for adult Harlan's Hawk and juvenile Ferruginous Hawk.

Flight

Active flight is with slow, flexible wingbeats. Soars with wings in a medium dihedral. Glides with wings in a modified dihedral. Hovers and kites frequently; sometimes with deep wingbeats, sometimes with wings fluttering, often with legs dangling.

Molt

Annual molt is not complete; not all flight and tail feathers are replaced every year. Molt occurs only during the short Arctic summer. Juveniles molt into adult plumage in their second summer, usually showing retained outer primaries and several middle secondaries. First-plumage adults usually have retained juvenile outer primaries and some secondaries. Apparently little molt takes place during migration or on the winter grounds.

Behavior

Rough-legged Hawks are birds of open country, breeding above tree line on open tundra. The entire population moves south and in winter frequents open areas such as farmlands, marshes, and airports. They hunt from lower perches, hover and kite in lighter winds, and perch on smaller trees and limbs than do Red-tailed Hawks. Rough-legged Hawks prey almost exclusively on small to medium-sized mammals and often eat carrion in winter. Communal night roosts are formed in winter. On migration, concentrations occur at water barriers, however, Rough-legs appear less hesitant than other buteos to cross open water.

Status and Distribution

Rough-legged Hawks breed on Arctic tundra and in mixed tundra-Boreal forest from the Aleutian Is. and w. Alaska to Newfoundland. They are a common winter visitor across North America from south of the Boreal forest to the cen. United States and to Mexico in the Southwest. Large numbers are encountered in spring migration around the Great Lakes. A few juveniles linger into June in n. United States and s. Canada.

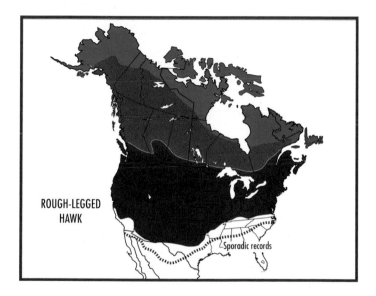

ROUGH-LEGGED
HAWK

Sporadic records

Fine Points

Dark brown adults have slightly darker bellies than breasts, whereas dark-morph juveniles have paler breasts or breast and belly the same color. Adult males usually show a white band on underwing coverts; adult females show a buffy band.

Subspecies

The North American race is *B. l. sancti-johannis*.

Etymology

Named "Rough-legged" for its completely feathered legs; *lagopus* is from the Greek *lagos*, "hare," and *pous*, "foot."

Measurements

LENGTH:	46–59 cm (53);	18–23 in. (21)
WINGSPREAD:	122–143 cm (134);	48–56 in. (53)
WEIGHT:	745–1,380 g (1,026);	1.6–3.0 lb. (2.2)

BOOTED EAGLES
GENUS *Aquila*

One species of booted eagle, the Golden Eagle, is widespread in North America. Booted eagles have legs feathered to the toes and are often seen soaring or gliding. They are large and dark, with proportionally longer wings than the smaller buteos, which they resemble in flight. Golden and Bald Eagles are similar in size; in both species, females are larger than males and northern birds larger than southern ones. Golden Eagles have longer tails and wider wings in their first (juvenile) plumage than in older immature and adult plumages.

"Eagle" comes from the Middle English *egle* and the Old French *egle* or *aigle,* which in turn is derived from the Latin word *aquila,* which also means "eagle."

GOLDEN EAGLE   PLS. 32, 33

Aquila chrysaetos

DESCRIPTION

The Golden Eagle, one of two large brown North American eagles, breeds in hilly and mountainous areas of the West and northern Canada. On flying eagles, *head and neck projection is less than half the tail length*. In all plumages, head, body, and coverts are dark brown, except for golden crown and nape, buffy leg feathers, and rufous undertail coverts. Eagles approaching head-on show a rufous line on leading edge of inner wings. *Golden nape and crown* vary from straw yellow to deep orange-brown among individuals but do not vary with age. *Bill and cere are tricolored:* beak tips are dark, bases are horn-colored, and ceres are yellow. *Legs are feathered to the toes*. Feet are yellow. They have four recognizably different plumages: Adult, older im-

Golden Eagle adult. Note pale inner primaries and secondaries with dark tips and pale bands in undertail. California, February (WSC)

Golden Eagle older immature. All show golden crown and nape. Older immatures have white on base and grayish marbling on dark tails. Colorado, December (BKW)

matures (Basic II–IV), Basic I, and juvenile. Sexes are alike in plumage; females average larger than males. Wingtips almost reach tail tip on perched adult and older immatures, but fall somewhat short of tip on perched juveniles. Adult plumage is usually acquired by four or five years of age.

ADULT: Head, body, and wing and tail coverts are dark brown. Plumage often appears mottled because new dark feathers contrast with old paler, faded ones. Eyes vary from amber to pale brown, occasionally darker brown. Median secondary upperwing coverts are heavily marked with tawny, resulting in a more or less noticeable diagonal bar on folded wings of perched eagles and across upperwings on flying eagles. Dark brown flight and tail feathers show a variable amount of grayish marbling except on tips, resulting in a dark subterminal band on wings and tail. Marbling is not as noticeable on uppersides of flight feathers. Underwings appear somewhat two-toned: dark brown underwing coverts contrast with paler flight feathers. Undertail coverts are rufous.

JUVENILE: Similar to adult, but plumage is darker and more uniform in color, with white bases on tail and often on flight feathers. Eyes are dark brown. Recently fledged birds appear a darker blackish brown. Upperwing coverts show only a hint of the tawny bar. Undersides of flight feathers lack grayish marbling and wide dark tips but some show white bases, resulting in variably sized *white patches at base of inner primaries and outer secondaries*. Smaller white patches are visible on upperwings of juveniles that have large underwing patches. Longer tail is two-toned: white

Golden Eagle juvenile. Variant with much white on base of flight and tail feathers. California, February (WSC)

Golden Eagle juvenile. Some juveniles show no white on flight feathers. Juveniles have uniformly colored secondaries that lack dark tips and lack gray marbling in dark area of tails. Colorado, November (BKW)

base, including *white edges,* and wide dark brown terminal band. Border between white and dark areas is relatively even. White on tail is more easily seen from above, as it is usually concealed on undertails by the long undertail coverts.

OLDER IMMATURES: Golden Eagles in Basic I through III plumages gradually attain adult characters in their flight and tail feathers. It is usually not possible to age most older immatures to specific age class in the field, however, many Basic I eagles can be distinguished by molt. All differ from juveniles by their overall mottled appearance due to a mix of old faded and new darker feathers on body and coverts and *tawny bar on upperwings.* The molt of flight and tail feathers is not complete; see below under Molt. Replacement secondaries differ in being shorter and having adultlike grayish marbling and dark band on tips, however they can have white on the bases. Replacement tail feathers are shorter than juveniles', have gradually less white, show a more ragged border between the white and dark areas, and have grayish marbling in the dark. Some Basic I eagles have undergone minimal molt, replacing only some inner primaries, central tail feathers, and no secondaries and appear very juvenile-like, except for mottled body, a mix of new darker and old faded feathers. Basic I eagles that have undergone considerable molt and Basic II and III eagles show ragged trailing edges to wings because of a mix of longer retained juvenile and shorter replacement secondaries; white on under-wings, if present, is a series of streaks or spots rather than the single oval patches of juveniles. Some eagles (Basic III or IV) appearing otherwise adult show a little white in their tails. **NOTE:** The amount of white on the underwings is *not* an age character for immature eagles because of individual variation.

UNUSUAL PLUMAGES: A few cases of partial albinism have been reported. Adults with white scapulars, "epaulets," have been reported.

SIMILAR SPECIES

(1) BALD EAGLE (Pls. 7, 8) immatures can appear similar to Golden Eagles. See under that species for differences. **(2) DARK-MORPH BUTEOS** are much smaller, have relatively shorter wings, and, in flight, show whitish flight feathers that contrast with darker underwing coverts.

FLIGHT

Active flight is with slow, deep wingbeats. Soars with wings usually held in a dihedral but sometimes flat. Glides with wings held flat or in a modified dihedral. They are masterful flyers and often hunt from the air, soaring or kiting on strong upcurrents. After sighting prey, they stoop at high speeds; Darling (1934) and others report that, in a dive, they are faster than Peregrine Falcons.

MOLT

Golden Eagles undergo an incomplete annual molt, actively molting from March into November. They replace about half of their flight, tail, covert, and body feathers each year, but with considerable individual variation in amount. Breeding adults often suspend molt for a time. Juveniles begin post-juvenile molt in late spring and replace their flight feathers in the typical accipitrid pattern. Adult plumage is attained after four or five molts.

BEHAVIOR

Golden Eagles are agile flyers for their size and are able to take mammalian prey much larger than they are, including (rarely) adult coyotes, deer, pronghorn antelope, fox, and bighorn sheep. They also capture large birds, such as Sage Grouse, Canada Geese, and even Whooping Cranes. Their usual prey, however, are jackrabbits, rabbits, marmots, or ground squirrels, and other small mammals. In winter they also feed on carrion and associate with Bald Eagles in waterfowl concentration areas. They hunt from perches and on the wing, gliding slowly or kiting on an up-draft while searching the ground below. When they spot prey, they stoop rapidly and directly. Mated adults often hunt as a pair. Most prey is captured on the ground, although Goldens also take birds in flight. They have been reported dropping live turtles from a considerable height, no doubt to break the shells open.

Flight displays include undulating flight and mutual soaring. They construct typical raptor stick nests on cliff faces, where they raise 1 to 3 eaglets, but sometimes they build on old tree nests of ravens or other raptors or use man-made platforms atop power pylons.

In winter, a few roost communally at night with Bald Eagles.

STATUS AND DISTRIBUTION

Golden Eagles are fairly common in summer in western and northern hilly and mountainous areas as far east as Maine. They formerly nested in New York and New Hampshire. The only con-firmed nests in the Appalachian Mts. are in Tennessee in the mid-1990s, most likely by eagles hacked in Georgia and Tennessee. In autumn, northern birds move southward, and many immatures

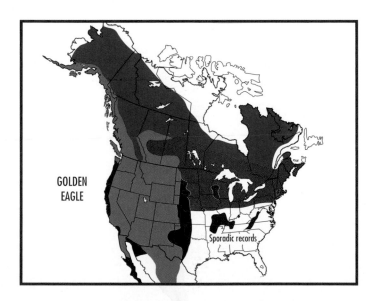

GOLDEN EAGLE

Sporadic records

move away from mountains. In winter they are found throughout the continent as far south as (rarely) Florida. Their worldwide range also includes mountainous areas of Asia, Europe, the Middle East, and n. Africa.

Golden Eagles have been persecuted in the past by shooting, trapping, and poisoning, but population levels have nevertheless remained fairly stable. Reported local population declines are likely due to habitat modification, usually the encroachment of suburbia.

FINE POINTS

Golden Eagle's crown and nape do not change color throughout the eagle's life; color varies among individuals, however, and these feathers are faded somewhat by sunlight.

SUBSPECIES

The North American race is *A. c. canadensis*.

ETYMOLOGY

"Golden" refers to the color of crown and nape feathers. *Aquila* is Latin for "eagle," and *chrysaetos* is from the Greek *chrysos*, "golden," and *aetos*, "eagle."

MEASUREMENTS

LENGTH:	70–90 cm (80);	27–35 in. (31)
WINGSPREAD:	185–225 cm (205);	72–88 in. (80)
WEIGHT:	3–6.4 kg (4.5);	6.6–14 lb. (10)

FALCONS
FAMILY FALCONIDAE

Eight species of falcons of the genus *Falco* and one species of caracara in the genus *Caracara* occur in our area. Five of the falcons are regular breeders; two others, Northern Hobby and Eurasian Kestrel, are vagrants; and Aplomado Falcon was extirpated as a breeder but is now being reintroduced.

Falconidae is not closely related taxonomically to Accipitridae; members of these two raptor families nevertheless share many characteristics, including sharp, curved talons; hooked beaks; excellent eyesight; and both predatory and scavenging habits. Their differences are mainly structural and behavioral.

The true falcons of *Falco* are characterized by long, pointed wings, dark eyes, and medium to long tails. In all species the orbital skin (eye-ring) is bare and usually the same color as the cere. Beaks are horn colored on bases and blackish on tips; they are notched for killing their vertebrate prey by severing the spinal column at the neck. Falcons molt into adult plumage at approximately one year of age.

Falcons are all active predators but many will, on occasion, eat carrion. There are accounts of piracy by falcons, but more often they lose prey to other raptors through piracy. Falcons have two distinctive behaviors when they are excited, bobbing their heads and, in some species, especially kestrels, pumping their tails up and down. Accipitrine raptors wag their tails from side to side when excited.

Falcons do not build their own nests. Instead they use tree cavities or cliff ledges or appropriate stick nests constructed by other raptors or corvids. Man-made structures, such as nest boxes, bridges, and building ledges and crevices, are also used.

Caracaras are quite different from true falcons. They have large heads and beaks, pale eyes, long necks, long legs, and wide, rounded wings. They are more piratical and vulturine and less predatory than falcons. Unlike falcons, they construct their own nests.

Falco and "falcon" are derived from the Latin *falx,* meaning "sickle," referring to the falcon's wing shape in flight or, according to another source, to the shape of their beaks and talons.

CRESTED CARACARA PL. 34

Caracara cheriway

DESCRIPTION

The Crested Caracara, a large, unusual, long-legged falconid, occurs in central Florida, south and central Texas, and south-central Arizona. Their bold plumage, colorful face skin, large horn-colored beak, large *crested head,* and *long neck in flight* are distinctive. They have three age-related plumages: juvenile, Basic I, and adult. Sexes are alike in plumage, but females are slightly larger. Wingtips reach tail tip on perched Caracaras.

ADULT: *Large, crested head* consists of black crown and nape, white cheeks and throat, and bare face skin, whose color usually varies from yellow to orange but can quickly change from yellow to vivid red, depending on mood. Adults' eyes are medium brown; their large beaks are horn colored. Upper back is black with fine white barring; lower back and upperwing coverts are blackish brown. Long neck and breast are buffy, with narrow black barring

Crested Caracara adult. Large head and beak and bright face skin are distinctive. Texas, May (WSC)

Crested Caracara Basic I. Similar to adult, but browner, with less-well-defined barring on breast and back. Texas, January (WSC)

Crested Caracara juvenile. Plumage is buffy and brown, with streaking on breast and back. Texas, January (WSC)

on lower neck and breast. Belly has wide black band. Wings are blackish except for mostly white outer primaries that form *large white wing panels*. Underwing coverts are blackish and contrast with paler dark gray undersides of secondaries. Tail coverts are white. White tail has many narrow black bands and a wide black terminal band. Leg feathers are blackish, and long legs are yellow to yellow-orange.

JUVENILE: Similar in pattern to adult, but crown, body, wing coverts, tail bands, and leg feathers are dark brown; face, neck, and breast are buffy; and buffy breast, lower neck, and upper back are streaked with brown rather than barred with black. Facial skin is gray to pink, eyes are dark brown, and legs are pale yellowish gray.

BASIC I: Almost like adults, but crown, body, wing coverts, tail bands, and leg feathers are brownish black rather than black, barring on back and breast is less well defined, face skin is pink to yellow, neck is buffy, and legs are yellow. Dark crown has fine rufous streaking, visible only when seen up close.

UNUSUAL PLUMAGES: A dilute-plumage specimen that was overall mottled buffy was collected in Argentina.

SIMILAR SPECIES

Caracaras are quite different from other raptors; nothing is similar.

FLIGHT

Active flight is with medium slow, steady, almost mechanical wingbeats. Soars with wings held flat, with leading and trailing edges straight. Caracaras appear eaglelike when soaring because of long neck and straight wings. Glides with wings crooked; wrists are cocked forward and above the body, and wingtips are pointed down. When pursuing other raptors on the wing, they are agile and acrobatic.

MOLT

Annual molt of adults is complete, beginning from January to April and completed by winter. Molt into juvenile and Basic I plumages begins and ends at about the same times.

BEHAVIOR

Caracaras are primarily scavengers, but they also pirate prey from other birds, including other raptors, especially vultures, forcing them to give up or disgorge food. They prey occasionally on live birds, small mammals, reptiles and amphibians, and insects. They regularly harass other raptors and dominate Black and Turkey Vultures at carcasses. Caracaras spend considerable time on the ground foraging for food and cruise highways searching for road-killed animals.

Allopreening by adults has been observed. Unlike falcons of the genus *Falco,* they build their own nests. Vocalizations include a low rattle and a single *wuck* note. When excited they throw their head back and snap it forward or roll the back of the head across the shoulders while at the same time giving a rattle call.

STATUS AND DISTRIBUTION

Caracaras are fairly common on the prairies of cen. Florida and s. Texas, common along the Texas Gulf Coast, and rare in s.-cen. Arizona. They are nonmigratory, but individuals wander into states adjacent to their breeding range; there are curious records from points as distant as Washington, Wyoming, New York, and even Ontario — possibly escapees.

FINE POINTS

This species sometimes continues to flap when soaring.

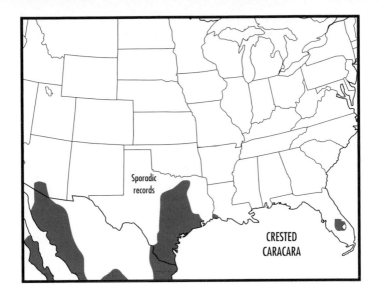

Sporadic
records

CRESTED
CARACARA

SUBSPECIES

The North American race is *C. c. auduboni.*

ETYMOLOGY

"Caracara" most likely comes from a South American native ono-matopoeic name; *cheriway* is the Carib (Native American) name for this species. **NOTE:** "Audubon's Caracara" is another name for our race. Former scientific names are *Caracara plancus* and *Polyborus plancus.*

MEASUREMENTS

LENGTH:	54–60 cm (58);	21–24 in. (23)
WINGSPREAD:	118–132 cm (125);	46–52 in. (49)
WEIGHT:	800–1,300 g (1,006);	1.8–2.8 lb. (2.2)

Falco sparverius

DESCRIPTION

The widespread American Kestrel, the smallest North American falcon, is one of our most common and colorful raptors. *Underwings appear pale* on flying falcons. Females are slightly larger and heavier, but there is considerable overlap in size. Plumages of adult and juvenile males are similar and differ from plumages of females. Wingtips do not reach tail tip on perched kestrels. Eyes are dark brown. Cere, eye-ring, and leg colors are yellow to orange, paler on juveniles.

ADULT MALE: Head has blue-gray crown, usually with a variably sized rufous crown patch; white cheeks and throat separated by *two black mustache marks,* one below the eye and the other on the auriculars; and *buffy to rufous nape with black spots forming false "eyes" or ocelli.* Rufous back is narrowly barred black on lower half. *Upperwing coverts are blue-gray* with small black spots. Uppertail coverts are unbarred rufous, occasionally with some blue-gray and black feathers intermixed. Uppersides of primaries are black, with *a row of white spots noticeable on trailing edge of outer wings,* more noticeable on backlit underwings. Whitish underwings have fine dark markings. Whitish to deep rufous breast is usually unmarked but can show some fine dark streaks; paler belly has a variable number of black spots, heavier on flanks. Unmarked leg feathers and undertail coverts vary from white to creamy. Typical tail is rufous with a wide black subterminal band and a narrow terminal band that is either white, rufous, blue-gray, or a combination of these, however, outer tail feathers are usually white with black banding. Tail pattern and color vary considerably; a few tails are banded black, white, and gray, with little or no rufous. **NOTE:** Males of the race *paulus* in Florida are smaller and differ from the nominate race by showing few markings on back and upperwing coverts.

ADULT FEMALE: Head is like that of adult male, with narrow dark gray streaking in crown patch. Back and upperwing coverts are reddish brown with even-width dark brown barring. Uppertail coverts are reddish brown with narrow dark brown barring. Creamy underparts are heavily streaked reddish brown. Creamy to white leg feathers and undertail coverts are unmarked. Uppersides of primaries are dark brown with a row of buffy spots on trailing edge, less noticeable on backlit wing than the white spots of males. Tail is reddish brown with numerous narrow dark brown bands; subterminal band is noticeably wider.

American Kestrel adult male. Males have blue-gray upperwing coverts. Note row of white spots on tips of primaries. Colorado, November (BKW)

American Kestrel female. Females have streaked underparts. All show pale underwings. Colorado, August (BKW)

JUVENILE MALE: Similar to adult male but whitish breast is streaked with black, back is barred up to the nape, and crown patch has black shaft streaks. They usually molt into adult body plumage during late summer or fall, but some retain juvenile body characteristics into the next summer. Napes of some juveniles are buffy or whitish.

JUVENILE FEMALE: Like adult female, but often with dark subterminal tail band only as wide as or slightly wider than other dark bands. Napes of some juveniles are buffy or whitish.

American Kestrel juvenile male. Juvenile males have streaked breasts and backs barred to the neck. All show two black mustache marks. Florida, November (BKW)

UNUSUAL PLUMAGES: Kestrels have been reported that were completely white or had some white feathers. Specimens exist of gynandromorphs, showing plumage characters of both sexes. A juvenile with a completely black-and-white banded tail and gray uppertail coverts has been described. An adult male captured for banding in Michigan had black primary and greater secondary upperwing and uppertail coverts, mostly black back, and black tail with narrow white bands. White spots on its black primaries were smaller. Its head and underparts appeared normal.

SIMILAR SPECIES

MERLIN (Pl. 36) appears somewhat similar to females. See under that species for differences.

FLIGHT

Active flight is light and buoyant; however, Kestrels can fly in a direct, rapid, Merlin-like fashion when chasing birds. Soars on flat wings, often with tail fanned. Glides on flat wings or with wrists lower than body and wingtips curved upward. It is the only North American falcon to hunt regularly by hovering (wings flapping) or, in strong winds, by kiting (wings held steady).

MOLT

Annual molt of adults is complete. Juveniles begin a more or less complete body molt in late summer to early autumn but do not renew their flight and tail feathers until the next summer.

BEHAVIOR

American Kestrels are usually found in open areas, where they are usually seen hovering or kiting on the wind or sitting on exposed perches, such as poles, wires, or treetops, where they hunt for rodents, insects, birds, lizards, or snakes. Females tend to hunt in more open areas than males, especially during winter.

Kestrels nest in tree cavities but will readily use holes in cliffs, crevices in barns and buildings, or nest boxes. They are fairly common in cities and towns. They can be vociferous, and their easily recognized *killy-killy* call carries some distance.

STATUS AND DISTRIBUTION

American Kestrels are widespread and common throughout North America south of the Arctic tree line in most habitats; they

AMERICAN
KESTREL

prefer more open country. Northern populations are migratory, with some birds moving as far south as Central America. They are abundant in s. United States in winter.

FINE POINTS

Kestrels possess a pair of false eyes, or ocelli, on the nape. This is thought to be protective coloration in that the watching "eyes" will deter potential predators.

SUBSPECIES

The race *F. s. sparverius* occupies most of North America north of Mexico, except for the Florida peninsula, where it is replaced by the smaller-sized race *F. s. paulus*, in which only males are distinguishable from nominate race kestrels (by having little or no dark barring on their backs and a richer coloration overall).

ETYMOLOGY

"Kestrel" is an old English name for *F. tinnunculus,* the Common Kestrel. Formerly called "Sparrow Hawk"; *sparverius* in Latin means "pertaining to a sparrow."

LENGTH:	Male	22–26 cm (24);	8–10 in. (9)
	Female	23–27 cm (25);	9–11 in. (10)
WINGSPREAD:	Male	52–57 cm (55);	20–22 in. (21)
	Female	54–61 cm (57);	21–24 in. (22)
WEIGHT:	Male	97–120 g (109);	3.4–4.5 oz. (3.8)
	Female	102–150 g (123);	3.6–5.3 oz. (4.3)

MERLIN   PL. 36

Falco columbarius

DESCRIPTION

The Merlin of northern forests and prairies is a small, stocky, dashing falcon. They *lack the bold dark mustache marks* of other falcons, having at most only faint ones. There are three distinct forms: Taiga, Prairie, and Black Merlins, corresponding to recognized races. Sexes differ in adult plumage and size, with females noticeably larger. Juvenile plumages are similar or identical to those of adult females. Wingtips do not reach tail tip on perched Merlins. Eyes are dark brown.

TAIGA MERLINS *(F. c. columbarius)* are darkest in the East and become gradually paler westward. In all plumages *underwings are uniformly dark.*

TAIGA ADULT MALE: Head consists of slate-blue crown and nape with fine black streaking, narrow whitish to buffy superciliary lines, buffy cheeks with fine dark streaking, dark eye lines and auriculars, faint dark mustache marks, faint whitish or rufous markings on hindneck, and white, unmarked throat. Back and upperwing and uppertail coverts are slate blue, with fine black shaft streaking. Whitish underparts are heavily streaked dark brown, with dark barring on flanks and usually with a rufous wash on the breast. Underwings of blackish brown flight feathers and dark brown coverts show white spotting. Undertail coverts and leg feathers have dark streaks, latter also show a strong rufous wash. Black tail shows three slate-blue bands on upperside, three white bands on underside, and a wide white terminal band. Cere, eyering, and leg colors are orange-yellow (nonbreeding) to bright orange (breeding).

TAIGA ADULT FEMALE: Head is like that of adult male, except that crown and nape are dark brown and superciliaries are buffy. Back and upperwing coverts are dark brown, sometimes with a grayish cast, and brown uppertail coverts have a grayish cast. Underwings

Merlin adult male F. c. columbarius. All show heavily streaked underparts. Taiga Merlins show single dark mustache mark and dark underwings. Adult males have rufous leg feathers. New Jersey, October (BKW)

Merlin adult female F. c. columbarius darker variant. Some appear almost as dark as Black Merlins. Wisconsin, July (WSC)

of dark brown flight feathers and dark brown coverts show buffy spotting. Creamy underparts are heavily streaked dark brown, with dark barring on flanks. Creamy leg feathers and undertail coverts are lightly streaked dark brown. Dark brown tail has three sometimes incomplete buffy or gray bands and a wide white terminal band. Cere and eye-rings are dull greenish yellow to yellow. Legs are bright yellow.

TAIGA JUVENILE: Very similar to Taiga adult female and difficult to separate in the field. Uppertail coverts are dark brown without the grayish cast of adult females. Dark brown tail shows three buffy (females) or whitish to gray (males) bands on upperside and a white terminal band.

PRAIRIE MERLINS (*F. c. richardsonii*) are overall much paler and somewhat longer winged than other Merlins, and their underwings appear quite pale compared to those of other races; they have more and larger pale spots on dark flight feathers and underwing coverts.

PRAIRIE ADULT MALE: Plumage pattern is like that of Taiga adult male, but they are overall much paler. Mustache marks are faint or absent. Streaked crown, back, and upperwing and uppertail coverts are pale blue-gray. Pale areas on hindneck form a collar and often show a rufous wash. Whitish underparts are streaked reddish brown. Pale leg feathers have a rufous wash and fine dark streaking. Black tail has three or four wider whitish to light gray bands and wide white terminal band.

Merlin adult male
F. c. richardsonii. *Prairie Merlins are much paler than other races; some show a faint mustache mark. Adult males have rufous leg feathers. Colorado, March (BKW)*

PRAIRIE ADULT FEMALE: Plumage pattern is like that of Taiga adult female, but they are overall much paler. Crown, back, and upperwing and uppertail coverts are medium to sandy brown. Many adult females lack a gray wash on their uppertail coverts. Creamy underparts are streaked reddish brown. Leg feathers and undertail coverts show fine dark streaking, but this is sometimes lacking. Medium brown tail has three or four (when closed) or five (when spread) wider buffy bands and white terminal band.

PRAIRIE JUVENILE: (Sexes alike.) Not separable from Prairie adult female in the field.

BLACK MERLINS (*F. c. suckleyi*) are much darker than the other forms, because of pigment saturation. Heads appear brownish black, with some streaking on the throat. *Underwings appear almost uniformly dark,* as the flight feathers have little or no pale markings. Undertail coverts have dark barring. Pale tail bands are reduced or absent. Some Merlins show characters intermediate between Black and Taiga.

BLACK ADULT MALE: Is similar in plumage pattern to Taiga adult male but appears overall much darker. Blackish head shows little or no pale superciliaries and dark cheeks that mask dark mustache marks. Back and upperwing coverts are slaty black, with blue-gray cast visible on lower back and uppertail coverts only in good light. Underparts are dark brownish black, with some rufous-buff streaking. Heavily streaked dark leg feathers have a strong rufous wash. Creamy undertail coverts are heavily barred black. Black tail has a narrower whitish terminal band and other pale bands reduced or absent.

BLACK ADULT FEMALE AND JUVENILE: Like Black adult male but with blackish brown upperparts that lack the blue-gray cast, also lack rufous wash on leg feathers. Dark underwings show tawny and sometimes whitish markings.

UNUSUAL PLUMAGES: Two dilute-plumage Merlins, one adult male and one female, and one partial albino adult male have been captured for banding. There is a report of a mostly white bird that also had some tan feathers. There are records of albinism in the European race.

SIMILAR SPECIES

(1) KESTREL (Pl. 35) is smaller, has a lighter, more buoyant flight, and in flight shows smaller head and narrower wings with pale undersides. Kestrels have rufous tails and backs and two distinct black mustache marks on each side of the face. **(2) PEREGRINE** (Pl. 38) is larger and has relatively longer wings; wider, more distinct mustache marks; and larger head. Juvenile male Peale's Peregrine may appear similar to female Black Merlin when perched, but wingtips reach or almost reach the tail tip on perched Peregrines. **(3) PRAIRIE FALCON** (Pl. 40) can appear similar to Prairie Merlin. See under that species for distinctions. **(4) SHARP-SHINNED HAWK** (Pl. 11) juveniles are similar to adult female and juveniles. See under that species for differences.

FLIGHT

Active flight is rapid and direct, with strong, quick wingbeats. Soars on flat wings with tail somewhat fanned. Glides on flat wings or with wrists lower than body and wingtips curved upward. Does not hover.

MOLT

Annual molt of adults is usually complete; however, sometimes an outer secondary on one or both wings is retained, less often also an outer primary. Molt begins in summer and is completed before autumn migration, but some adults still show signs of molt in September and even into October. First prebasic (post-juvenile) molt also begins in summer and is usually complete.

BEHAVIOR

Merlins are dashing falcons that hunt birds on the wing. Their rapid hunting flight is typically in a direct line over open areas. They use speed to quickly approach and surprise a flock of birds and snatch out of the air one that is slow to react. They also hunt from exposed perches, making rapid forays after prey. Merlins fly fast enough to tail-chase swallows, swifts, and shorebirds and are capable of very sudden changes in direction and spectacular aerial maneuvers. They often capture and eat insects, especially dragonflies, in flight. They force small birds to fly up to a great altitude and capture them when they try to drop back to earth. Merlins have an unusual flight mode when attacking a bird from low altitude. They flap their wings in quick bursts interspersed with glides on almost closed wings, producing an undulating but rapid flight that appears like that of woodpeckers. This mode of attack may allow them to be mistaken for a nonraptor until it is too late for the prey to escape. Like many other raptors, they have been reported hunting cooperatively. They regularly harass larger birds, including gulls and other raptors. Their primary vocalization is a rapid, high-pitched *ki ki ki ki ki ki ki.*

STATUS AND DISTRIBUTION

Merlins are widely but sparsely distributed as a breeding bird in Canada and Alaska in open areas of Boreal forests, in western mountains south to Oregon and Colorado, on the Great Plains south to the Dakotas, and in Pacific Coast rain forests.

TAIGA MERLIN: Uncommon breeder in Boreal forests from New-

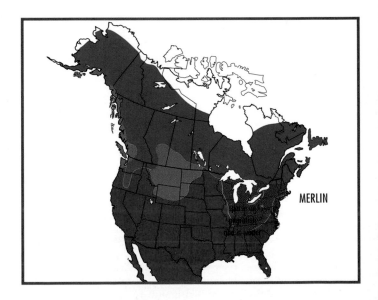

MERLIN

foundland to w. Alaska, and south into the United States in n. New England, New York, n. Great Lakes states, and the western mountains. They are highly migratory, moving to coasts, the Caribbean, Central America, and South America as far as Peru. Migration takes place throughout the contiguous states on a broad front. They are fairly common along the ocean coasts in migration, where some remain in winter.

PRAIRIE MERLIN: Fairly common but local breeder in prairie-parkland areas, especially along rivers and more recently in cities, of s.-cen. Canada and n. prairie states. Some birds move south in fall and winter to n. Mexico, east to Minnesota, and west to Pacific Coast. However, some birds also winter throughout the breeding range, especially in cities, where they feed on sparrows and waxwings.

BLACK MERLIN: Uncommon to rare resident in the Pacific Coastal forest of British Columbia and se. Alaska. Some individuals move as far as s. California, New Mexico, and Texas in fall and winter. Some darker Taiga Merlins breeding in n. Minnesota and n. Wisconsin and seen occasionally elsewhere in the East appear much like Black Merlins.

FINE POINTS

Tail bands on uppertails of juvenile Taiga Merlins differ by sex: buffy and often incomplete on females; pale grayish and more noticeable on males.

SUBSPECIES

The three North American races correspond to the forms described. Taiga is *F. c. columbarius*, Prairie is *F. c. richardsonii*, and Black is *F. c. suckleyi*.

ETYMOLOGY

"Merlin" derives from the Old French *esmerillon*, the name for this species. Formerly called "Pigeon Hawk," after its resemblance in flight to the Common Pigeon (Rock Dove); *columbarius* in Latin means "pertaining to a dove (pigeon)."

MEASUREMENTS

(Taiga Merlins; others similar).

LENGTH:	Male	24–27 cm (26);	9–11 in. (10)
	Female	28–30 cm (29);	11–12 in. (11)

WINGSPREAD:	Male	53–58 cm (57);	21–23 in. (22)
	Female	61–68 cm (64);	24–27 in. (25)
WEIGHT:	Male	129–187 g (155);	4.5–6.6 oz. (5.5)
	Female	182–236 g (210);	6.4–8.3 oz. (7.4)

APLOMADO FALCON   PL. 37

Falco femoralis

DESCRIPTION

The Aplomado Falcon, a colorful, narrow-winged, long-tailed, medium-sized falcon, formerly bred along the Mexican border from southeastern Arizona to southern Texas. They were extirpated in the early 1900s in southern Texas but are now being reintroduced there. *Silhouette, bold head pattern, and hourglass-shaped dark belly band are distinctive.* Sexes are almost alike in plumage, with female noticeably larger. Juvenile plumage is similar to that of adults. Eyes are dark brown. On perched falcons, wingtips extend three-quarters of way down the tail.

ADULT: *Head has distinctive pattern* of blackish crown and nape, wide black eye lines, and narrow black mustache marks that separate whitish to creamy cheeks and throat, with whitish to creamy superciliary lines that begin behind the eyes and join together on hindneck to form a V. Back and upperwing coverts are lead gray. *Trailing edge of dark wings has noticeable narrow pale edge* that extends from body to primaries. Whitish to creamy breast of males is unmarked, but those of females have a few narrow dark streaks; breast is separated from rufous belly by *blackish hour-*

Aplomado Falcon adult male. All show dark hourglass-shaped belly bands. Adult males show no breast streaking. Mexico, February (WSC)

Aplomado Falcon adult female. All show narrow pale line on trailing edge of wings. Adult females have narrow dark breast streaks. Texas, May (BKW)

glass-shaped belly band, which shows narrow white barring. Underwings appear uniformly dark. Leg feathers and undertail coverts are rufous, brighter on males. *Long black tail* shows five to seven narrow white bands. Cere, eye-rings, and legs are bright yellow to orange-yellow.

JUVENILE: Similar to adult, but back and upperwing coverts are dark brown with narrow buffy feather edges, breast is buffier with more and wider dark streaks, dark belly band lacks white barring, and leg feathers and undertail coverts are rufous-buff to buff. Dark tail has five to seven narrow buffy bands. Cere and eye-rings are initially pale blue-gray but become pale yellow, and legs are pale yellow to yellow.

UNUSUAL PLUMAGES: No unusual plumages have been reported.

SIMILAR SPECIES

Aplomado Falcons are quite distinctive when seen well, but confusion with other species is possible with quick or distant looks. **(1) AMERICAN KESTREL** (Pl. 35) is smaller, has rufous tail and back, and lacks dark belly band. In flight, their tails appear shorter and underwings paler than those of Aplomados. **(2) MERLIN** (Pl. 36) is smaller, has completely streaked underparts, and lacks distinct facial pattern and dark belly band. In flight, their tails appear shorter than those of Aplomados. **(3) CRESTED CARACARA** (Pl. 34) has similar pattern on body but is much larger and has different head pattern, much longer neck, and different wing shape. **(4) MISSISSIPPI KITE** (Pl. 6) is similar in size and silhouette, and adults also have a narrow pale line on trailing edge of wings, but they lack strong face pattern and dark belly band.

Active flight is rapid and direct, with light, quick wingbeats, but when it is not pursuing avian prey, flight is slower, buoyant, and more Kestrel-like. Glides on flat wings or with wrists below body and wingtips curved upward. Soars on flat wings. Hovers when prey goes under cover.

MOLT

Not studied. Presumably the annual molts of adults and juveniles are complete.

BEHAVIOR

Aplomado Falcons feed primarily on birds, which are captured after a rapid direct flight from a perch, sometimes including a long tail chase or pursuit through heavy brush on foot. They also take many insects and hunt from both exposed and inconspicuous perches. Reptiles, rodents, and even bats are also taken, and some prey are pirated from raptors and other birds. Hunting from soar and cooperative hunting by pairs have also been reported. They regularly gather at grass fires to hunt displaced birds, insects, reptiles, and mammals. Breeding pairs remain together throughout the year and often perch close together.

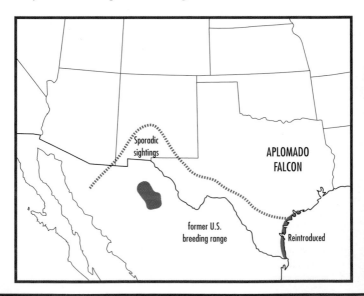

Sporadic sightings

APLOMADO FALCON

former U.S. breeding range

Reintroduced

Aplomado Falcons formerly bred from s. Texas to se. Arizona in savanna grasslands with yucca, mesquite, and cacti. Last breeding record was in 1952 from New Mexico. The reason for the extirpation is most likely habitat loss and was probably not due to pesticides.

However, sightings and photographs of Aplomado Falcons, apparently from a breeding population in adjacent Chihuahua, have been reported recently from s. New Mexico. Captive-bred falcons are now being released within their former range in s. Texas; numerous pairs have now successfully raised young there.

FINE POINTS

Adult's dark belly band has fine white barring, which is heavier on males and lacking on juveniles.

SUBSPECIES

The North American race is *F. f. septentrionalis*.

ETYMOLOGY

Aplomado in Spanish means "lead-colored," a reference to their back color. In Latin, *femoralis* means "referring to the thighs," for the rufous coloration of the leg feathers.

MEASUREMENTS

LENGTH:	Male	35–39 cm (37);	14–16 in. (15)
	Female	41–45 cm (43);	16–18 in. (17)
WINGSPREAD:	Male	78–84 cm (81);	31–33 in. (32)
	Female	93–102 cm (97);	37–40 in. (38)
WEIGHT:	Male	208–305 g (265);	8.4–10.7 oz. (9.3)
	Female	310–460 g (391);	12.0–16.0 oz. (13.8)

GYRFALCON   PLS. 39, 40

Falco rusticolus

DESCRIPTION

The Gyrfalcon, the largest falcon, is a rare winter visitor from the Arctic to southern Canada and northern United States. They oc-

cur in three color morphs: white, gray, and dark. (Juvenile gray-morph falcons appear dark brown.) Some falcons are intermediate in the cline between gray and dark morphs. Gyrfalcons are *heavier bodied, broader winged, and longer tailed* than other large falcons, with *wide, noticeably tapered tails*. Sexes are alike in plumage; females are noticeably larger. Juveniles have different plumages than those of adults. *Wingtips reach only about two-thirds down tail* on perched falcons. Eyes are dark brown.

WHITE-MORPH ADULT: *Unmistakable*. White head usually has narrow dark eye lines, often with fine dark streaking on crown and nape, and lacks dark mustache marks. White back, upperwing coverts, and uppersides of flight feathers have short brownish to blackish barring. Underparts are white, sometimes with a few dark spots or bars on flanks or leg feathers. Underwings are white except for dark tips on outer primaries, faint dusky banding on secondaries, and sometimes sparse dusky spotting on coverts. White tail often, but not always, has narrow brown to black banding, with either complete or partial bands in the center of feathers. Cere, eye-ring, and legs of adult are yellow to orange.

GRAY-MORPH ADULT: Slaty gray head has pale forehead, narrow pale superciliary lines, pale markings on hindneck, and paler gray cheeks and white throat separated by faint narrow dark mustache marks. Back and upperwing coverts are dark slate gray with many short pale gray crossbars. Underparts are white, usually with dark spotting forming streaks on breast, dark barring on flanks, and dark spotting on belly. Underwings show dark secondaries and paler primaries and coverts, the latter with some dark markings. Whitish leg feathers and undertail coverts are darkly barred. Tail has even-width light and dark gray bands; uppertail coverts are

Gyrfalcon juvenile gray morph. Juveniles usually show two-toned underwings. Note the broad base of tail. Ontario, February (Tony Beck)

the same color as uppertail. Whitish undertail coverts sometimes show narrow dark streaks.

DARK-MORPH ADULT: Head, back, and upperwing coverts are dark slate gray with some faint narrow pale markings on upperparts. Dark underparts show short whitish streaking on breast and belly and short whitish barring on flanks, leg feathers, and undertail coverts. *Underwings are two-toned:* paler grayish unbarred flight feathers contrast with dark coverts, which show pale spotting. Tail has even-width light and dark gray bands; uppertail coverts are the same color as uppertail but are paler than the upperparts. **NOTE:** There is a clinal variation in color between dark and gray morphs, with dark falcons much less common than gray ones, and intergrades even less common.

WHITE-MORPH JUVENILE: Similar to adult, but back and upperwing coverts are dark brown with white spotting and feather edges; however, some juveniles appear whiter because their upperparts are white with dark brown blobs in the center of feathers. White underparts and leg feathers have a variable amount of short dark brown streaking; juveniles with whiter upversides tend to have fewer markings on underparts and unbanded tails. Cere, eye-ring, and legs of juvenile are dull blue-gray.

GRAY-MORPH JUVENILE ("BROWN" MORPH): Head has narrow pale and dark brown streaking, except for narrow pale superciliary lines, wider dark eye lines, faint narrow dark mustache marks, and white throat. Back and upperwing coverts are medium to dark gray-brown, with narrow pale feather edges. Creamy underparts have heavy dark brown streaking. *Underwings are two-toned:* darker coverts contrast with paler flight feathers, but secondaries are usually somewhat darker than primaries. Whitish leg feathers have dark streaking. Tail is dark brown with numerous narrow pale bands.

DARK-MORPH JUVENILE: Head is uniformly dark brown, with whitish throat and sometimes with faint narrow superciliary lines. Upperparts are uniformly dark brown. Dark brown underparts have whitish spotting and streaking. Leg feathers are uniformly dark brown. *Underwings are two-toned:* paler flight feathers contrast with dark coverts, which show pale spotting. Upperside of tail is usually unbanded dark brown and is paler on underside and can show faint bands. Dark undertail coverts have pale barring.

UNUSUAL PLUMAGES: No unusual plumages have been reported. **NOTE:** See under this heading in the Peregrine account about captive-bred falcon hybrids.

SIMILAR SPECIES

(1) PEREGRINE FALCON (Pl. 38), especially Peale's Peregrine, can appear similar. See under that species for distinctions. **(2) PRAIRIE FALCON** (Pl. 40) is smaller and overall paler and show dark axillaries when flying. **(3) NORTHERN GOSHAWK** (Pl. 13) adults in flight appear similar to Gyrfalcons. See under that species for distinctions. **(4) RED-TAILED HAWK** albinos or partial albinos can appear similar to perched white-morph Gyr but usually have dark markings on nape or some rufous in tail and their wingtips almost reach tail tip.

FLIGHT

Active flight is rapid, with stiff, shallow, powerful wingbeats; in level flight, Gyrs are faster than Peregrines. Soar and glide on level wings. Gyrs hover occasionally for short periods, particularly when looking for prey that has taken cover.

MOLT

Not studied in North America. Annual molt of Eurasian adults is complete (presumably the same for North American Gyrs), but some body feathers and wing coverts are retained. Molt begins after breeding for males and during egg laying for females. Post-juvenile molt is usually complete, except for some body feathers and wing coverts, and begins earlier than that of adults.

BEHAVIOR

Gyrfalcons prey on birds and mammals, especially ptarmigan and ducks, but also seabirds, lemmings, and ground squirrels. They hunt from exposed perches and, after sighting quarry, begin a tail chase, sometimes continuing for a considerable distance. Hunting is also done by rapid flight low over the ground, occasionally while soaring higher. They seldom stoop from heights as Peregrines do. Nests are usually on cliffs, but tree nests have been reported. Wintering Gyrs are usually found near bird concentrations, often coastal dunes or airports.

STATUS AND DISTRIBUTION

Gyrfalcons are uncommon to rare breeders in Arctic tundra and subarctic mountain areas of Alaska and n. Canada (and also in Eurasia). In winter, juveniles and some adult females are uncommon and local but regular in s. Canada and n. border states, and occasionally appear farther south to New Jersey, Pennsylvania, Nebraska, Oklahoma, Colorado, and California. Many adults, especially males, remain throughout the winter on their breeding territories.

FINE POINTS

Gyrfalcons have longer belly feathers than other falcons and, when perched, are able to cover their feet by spreading these feathers. Some gray-morph adults have pale gray upperparts, little

GYRFALCON

extreme
winter limit

or no spotting on white underparts, and appear much like white-morph adults; they are distinguished by their faint dark mustache marks and gray bands in their tails.

SUBSPECIES

Monotypic.

ETYMOLOGY

Common name derives from Latin *gyrfalco* or *girofalco,* thought to be either a corruption of *hierofalco,* meaning "sacred falcon," for its exalted place in falconry, or from the Old German *gir,* meaning "greedy," for its rapacity. In Latin, *rusticolus* means "living in the country," probably a reference to the tundra habitat.

MEASUREMENTS

LENGTH:	Male	50–54 cm (52);	19–21 in. (20)
	Female	57–61 cm (59);	22–24 in. (23)
WINGSPREAD:	Male	110–120 cm (115);	43–47 in. (45)
	Female	124–130 cm (127);	49–51 in. (50)
WEIGHT:	Male	1,000–1,300 g (1135);	2.2–2.9 lb. (2.5)
	Female	1,400–2,100 g (1703);	3.1–4.6 lb. (3.8)

PEREGRINE FALCON   PL. 38

Falco peregrinus

DESCRIPTION

The Peregrine Falcon, a large, long-winged dark falcon, is widespread but local. In most plumages, *dark head appears hooded*. They have *one wide dark mustache mark* under each eye. Underwings in flight appear uniformly dark. The three recognizable North American forms differ in plumage. The highly migratory Tundra Peregrine is the palest in color, the mainly western Anatum Peregrine is darker, and the mainly sedentary Peale's Peregrine is darkest. Females are noticeably larger than males. Sexes are almost alike in adult plumage. Juvenile plumage is different from that of adult. Eyes are dark brown. This is the only North American falcon whose *wingtips extend to, or almost to, tail tip on perched falcons.* **NOTE:** The forms described below do not relate strictly to races but are general types that are recognizably different in the field. Falcons of more than one type can occur within a race's breeding range.

Peregrine Falcon adult F. p. anatum. *All show wide dark mustache marks and uniformly dark
underwings. Adults of this race
usually show a rufous wash on the
breast. Colorado, June (BKW)*

Peregrine Falcon adult F. p. anatum. *Adults have uppertail coverts
contrastingly paler than uppertails. Colorado, June (BKW)*

TUNDRA ADULT: Slate gray head has pale forehead, dark mustache mark narrower than those of other forms, large white area on cheek, and white throat. Slate gray back and upperwing coverts have blue-gray barring and fringes, heavier on lower back. Upper-tail coverts appear a paler blue-gray. Upperwings are slate gray. Underwing coverts are evenly barred black and white, and slate undersides of flight feathers have some pale barring. White underparts have, at most, a faint rufous wash on the belly, heavier on females. Breast is unstreaked or lightly streaked, and flanks and undertail coverts have black barring; all these markings are heavier on females. Belly shows black spots. White leg feathers are finely barred black. Blackish uppertail has eight or more narrow blue-gray bands and a wide white terminal band and contrasts with paler blue-gray uppertail coverts. Adult eye-ring, cere, and legs are yellow to yellow-orange, brighter on males.

ANATUM ADULT: Similar in plumage to Tundra adult, but head is blackish with dark forehead, wider mustache mark, much smaller whitish area on cheeks (sometimes absent), and usually a stronger rufous wash on underparts. Upperback and upperwing coverts are more blackish.

PEALE'S ADULT: Similar to Anatum adult but overall darker on underparts. Their white cheeks are streaked, white breasts are heavily spotted, bellies and flanks are heavily barred, and underparts lack a rufous wash. Back and upperwing coverts have a grayish powdery bloom, noticeable at close range. Adults from Aleutian

Peregrine Falcon juvenile F. p. tundrius. Juveniles have streaked underparts, and their wingtips almost reach tail tip. Juveniles of this race can be quite pale-headed. New Jersey, October (WSC)

Islands have more heavily marked underparts than those from southeastern Alaska and the Queen Charlotte Islands.

TUNDRA JUVENILE: Head has distinctive pattern: buffy forehead, dark brown crown, buffy superciliary lines, dark eye lines, and buffy cheek and throat separated by narrower dark mustache marks. Some juveniles have completely buffy crowns and narrower dark eye lines and mustache marks. Dark brown back and upperwing and uppertail coverts have wide buffy-rufous feather edges. Upperwings appear dark brown. Dark brown underwing coverts have buffy markings, and dark brown undersides of flight feathers have buffy banding. Creamy underparts are narrowly streaked dark brown. Creamy leg feathers have narrow dark streaks. Creamy undertail coverts are barred or streaked dark brown. Dark brown uppertail has 10 or more usually incomplete narrow buffy bands and a wide whitish terminal band. Juvenile's tail is longer and wings are wider than that of adult. Juvenile's eye-rings and ceres are pale blue-gray, occasionally dull yellow; legs vary from pale blue-gray to yellow.

ANATUM JUVENILE: Similar to Tundra juvenile, but head is mostly dark with smaller rufous-buff cheek patches, upperparts have fewer and narrower tawny edges, streaking on rufous-buff underparts is wider and heavier, and dark markings on leg feathers are chevron-shaped. Undertail coverts are usually darkly barred.

PEALE'S JUVENILE: Similar to Anatum juvenile but is overall darker, with narrow dark streaking on pale cheek patches and throat, few or no pale edges on back and upperwing coverts, dark underparts that have narrow whitish streaking, very dark underwings, and dark leg feathers that have narrow whitish edges. Pale bands in the tail are narrower — often some are incomplete or even absent — but tail always has a wide whitish tip. **NOTE:** Peregrines reintroduced into eastern North America are similar to one of the above forms.

UNUSUAL PLUMAGES: A Tundra juvenile captured for banding in Texas was overall café-au-lait, with narrow mustache marks noticeable. Two other specimens of dilute-plumage juveniles have many cream-colored (normally dark brown) feathers. Sight records exist of birds with a few white feathers. Albinism has been reported from the British Isles. **NOTE:** Peregrines are being cross-bred in captivity with Prairie Falcons, Gyrfalcons, and exotic falcons for use in falconry. These sometimes escape, and when seen, pose field identification problems beyond the scope of this guide; they appear different from our usual falcons in a bewildering mix of characters.

SIMILAR SPECIES

(1) PRAIRIE FALCON (Pl. 40) is paler and has narrower mustache marks than Peregrine, but Tundra juvenile can be similarly pale. Peregrines lack white area between eye and dark cheek found on all Prairies. In flight, Prairies show dark axillaries and median coverts on pale underwings, and uppertails appear paler than backs and upperwings. When perched, Prairie's wingtips fall short of tail tip, but Peregrine's reach or almost reach tail tip. **(2) GYRFALCON** (Pls. 39, 40) is larger; bulkier; has longer, wider, more tapered tail; broader wings; and fainter, narrower mustache marks. Underwings of many Gyrfalcons are overall pale or two-toned: dark coverts contrast with pale flight feathers. On perched Gyrfalcons, wingtips extend about two-thirds down tail. Juvenile Peale's can appear similar to dark-morph juvenile Gyrfalcon but shows uniformly dark underwings in flight and, when perched, has wingtips that extend nearly to tail tip. **(3) MERLIN** (Pl. 36) Juvenile Peale's can appear similar to Black Merlin; see under that species for differences. **(4) MISSISSIPPI KITE** (Pl. 6) is similar in shape to flying Peregrines. See under that species for differences.

FLIGHT

Active flight is with shallow but stiff and powerful wingbeats, similar to those of cormorants. When actively chasing prey, Peregrine often uses deeper wingbeats. Soars on flat wings with widely fanned tail; outer tail feathers almost touch trailing edge of wing, making tail appear diamond-shaped. Wingtips appear broad and rounded when soaring and narrower and pointed when gliding.

Glides with wings level or with wrists below body and wingtips up. Wingtips bow upward noticeably when falcon is executing a high-speed turn.

Molt

Annual molt of adults is complete, beginning in spring and completed by autumn for Peale's and Anatum adults, but is suspended for migration and completed on winter grounds for Tundra adults, which breed and begin molt later due to the short Arctic summer. Adult females begin molt before their mates. Post-juvenile molt begins in the spring of their second year and is usually not quite complete; Tundra falcons complete this molt on the winter grounds.

Behavior

Peregrine Falcons are awe-inspiring raptors to watch because of their power, grace, and speed in flight. They perform spectacular vertical dives (stoops) from great heights, with wings held tight against body, diving at and striking birds at high speeds. They eat birds almost exclusively, capturing them usually in the air but occasionally on the ground.

Peregrines nest primarily on cliffs but have used stick nests in trees, on building ledges, and, recently, on level sites under bridges. Fledglings often chase after and catch flying insects, such as dragonflies.

Water is no barrier to Peregrines on migration, and they are frequently observed far at sea capturing birds, eating them on the wing, and perching on ships to eat and rest.

Status and Distribution

Peregrine Falcons are worldwide in distribution, mainly in Arctic to temperate areas. One or another of the three forms described above occurs in almost all parts of North America sometime during the year.

Tundra Peregrines are uncommon to rare as breeding birds in the Arctic areas of Canada and Alaska. Many migrate into South America. Autumn concentrations are noted at coastal areas such as Cape May, New Jersey, Assateague Island, Maryland and Virginia, and Padre Island, Texas. This population now appears stable but was somewhat reduced in the recent past by pesticide contamination.

Anatum Peregrines were formerly widespread but local breeding birds throughout the rest of continental North America, ex-

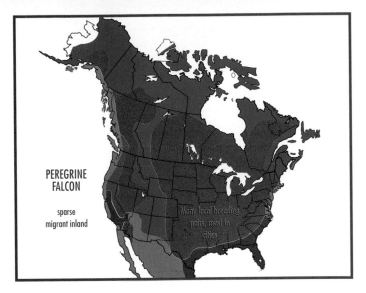

PEREGRINE
FALCON

sparse
migrant inland

Many local breeding
pairs, most in
the cities

cept the Southeast and Great Plains. The breeding population in e. North America south of the Arctic was extirpated by DDT and other persistent pesticides. As a result of reintroduction efforts, Peregrines now breed throughout the East. Breeding pairs occur in all western states and w. Canadian provinces and cen. Alaska. These falcons can also be migratory, with more northern ones moving south as far as Central America. Many remain in North America, especially along the coasts.

Peale's Peregrines are fairly common and sedentary on the coast and on islands from British Columbia north to se. Alaska and the entire Aleutian Is. chain. Some individuals, particularly juveniles, move south along the Pacific Coast in winter. This population is stable.

FINE POINTS

Peregrines have proportionally longer primaries than do other North American falcons: as a result, in flight the bend at the wrist appears relatively closer to the body.

SUBSPECIES

There are three North American subspecies, which correspond generally with the forms described. Tundra with *F. p. tundrius,* Peale's with *F. p. pealei,* and Anatum with *F. p. anatum.*

Peregrine and peregrinus from Latin for "wandering," for their long-distance migrations and dispersals. Formerly called "Duck Hawk" in North America, presumably for one of its prey.

Measurements

(Tundra Peregrine; other forms are slightly larger).

LENGTH:	Male	37–41 cm (39);	14–16 in. (15)
	Female	42–46 cm (44);	16–18 in. (17)
WINGSPREAD:	Male	94–100 cm (97);	37–39 in. (38)
	Female	102–116 cm (111);	40–46 in. (44)
WEIGHT:	Male	453–685 g (581);	1–1.5 lb. (1.3)
	Female	719–952 g (817);	1.6–2.1 lb. (1.8)

PRAIRIE FALCON   PL. 40

Falco mexicanus

Description

The Prairie Falcon, a large, pale, long-tailed falcon, occurs in hilly and mountainous areas of the West. *White area between eye and dark ear patch* and *dark axillaries* are distinctive. Large head appears blocky. Adult and juvenile plumages are similar. Sexes are almost alike in plumage; females are noticeably larger. Eyes are dark brown. On perched falcons, wingtips fall somewhat short of tail tip.

Prairie Falcon adult female. All show dark axillars. Adult females have uniformly dark median underwing coverts. Wyoming, June (BKW)

Prairie Falcon adult male. Adult males show pale banding on upperparts. Uppertail on all usually appears paler than upperparts. Wyoming, April (BKW)

Prairie Falcon juvenile. Juveniles are similar to adults, but with streaked underparts. Wyoming, June (BKW)

ADULT: Brown head has pale superciliary lines, narrow dark eye lines, pale markings on hindneck, and whitish cheeks and throat separated by narrow dark mustache marks. *Small white area between eye and dark ear patch* is unique. Back and upperwing coverts are medium brown, with buffy bars and edges on most feathers, and appear overall sandy, paler than those of juveniles, with males averaging paler than females. *Underwings appear pale except for dark brown axillaries and median coverts;* the latter are paler on males. Whitish underparts are marked with a few short streaks on breast, rows of spots on belly, and barring on flanks. Whitish leg feathers have dark spots or bars. Long tail often appears paler on upperside compared to back and upperwings and shows incomplete buffy banding. Cere, eye-rings, and legs are yellow-orange, averaging brighter on males.

JUVENILE: Similar to adult, but back and upperwing coverts appear darker because most feathers lack buffy barring. Buffy underparts are heavily marked with dark brown streaks and fade to creamy by spring. Creamy leg feathers have narrow dark streaks. Uppertail is brown and unbanded, with wide white tip. Cere and eye-rings are blue-gray, becoming pale yellow by spring. Legs are pale lead gray, becoming pale yellow by spring.

UNUSUAL PLUMAGES: Records exist of two partial albinos and a dilute-plumage adult female with some cream-colored and some normal feathers. Natural hybrids with Peregrines have been re-

Prairie Falcon juvenile. Fledgling in fresh plumage. Juveniles have pale blue-gray cere and eye-rings. Wyoming, July (WSC)

ported, but no descriptions are given of the offspring. **NOTE:** See under this heading in the Peregrine account about captive-bred hybrid falcons.

SIMILAR SPECIES

(1) PEREGRINE FALCON (Pl. 38), especially juvenile Tundra Peregrine, is similar in size and appearance. See under that species for differences. **(2) SWAINSON'S HAWK** (Pl. 21), especially pale juveniles, have a similar face pattern and appear similar to Prairie Falcons when perched. See under that species for differences. **(3) PRAIRIE MERLIN** (Pl. 36) is much smaller, has faint mustache marks and noticeable pale bands in tail, and lacks dark axillaries. **(4) GYRFALCON** (Pls. 39, 40) can appear somewhat similar. See under that species for differences.

FLIGHT

Active flight is with shallow, stiff, powerful wingbeats, with wings mostly below the horizontal. Soars on flat wings, with tail somewhat fanned. Glides on flat wings or with wrists below body and wingtips curved upward. Occasionally hovers, sometimes for 10 seconds or so.

MOLT

Annual molt of adults is complete, beginning in May and completed by October. Post-juvenile molt begins earlier in the spring and is also completed by autumn.

Prairie Falcons hunt from either a high perch or in flight. Their favorite prey is small mammals, especially ground squirrels, and ground-dwelling birds, especially Horned Larks, but they also take lizards and flying insects. They fly fast and low over open country and surprise prey, which they capture as it attempts to escape. From either perch or soar, Prairie Falcons stoop to pick up speed and then close rapidly on prey in a ground-hugging flight. Birds that flush are often tail-chased a considerable distance. Unlike Peregrines, Prairies readily take prey on the ground. On occasion, they hover, often for many seconds, looking for prey that was lost from sight. Prairies nest almost exclusively on cliffs, but tree nests and a building ledge nest have been reported. During winter they inhabit areas where birds concentrate; here they are often robbed of prey by other raptors.

Status and Distribution

Prairie Falcons are fairly common breeders in hilly and mountainous deserts and grasslands west of the Great Plains from s. Canada (British Columbia, Alberta, and Saskatchewan) south to n. Mexico. In late summer, after breeding, some falcons move up

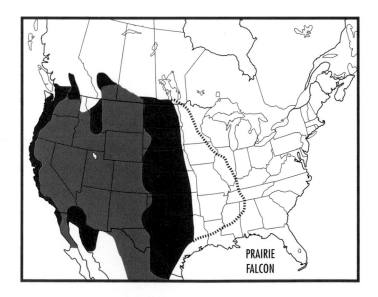

PRAIRIE FALCON

to the mountain tundra. Some birds disperse in winter south, east, and west to the coast, where they inhabit grasslands, deserts, and farmlands. They are casual in e. United States with records from Wisconsin, Illinois, Tennessee, Mississippi, both Carolinas and Alabama, although some records could be of escaped falconry birds.

FINE POINTS

Prairie Falcon's eyes are larger and their tails are longer than those of Peregrines. First-plumage adults, especially males, have a grayish cast to upperparts, lacking on juveniles and usually lacking on older adults.

SUBSPECIES

Monotypic.

ETYMOLOGY

Mexicanus for Mexico, where the first specimen was collected.

MEASUREMENTS

LENGTH:	Male	37–40 cm (38);	14–16 in. (15)
	Female	42–47 cm (44);	16–18 in. (17)
WINGSPREAD:	Male	90–98 cm (95);	35–39 in. (37)
	Female	102–114 cm (109);	40–45 in. (43)
WEIGHT:	Male	420–635 g (524);	0.9–1.4 lb. (1.2)
	Female	675–1,140 g (926);	1.5–2.5 lb. (2)

VAGRANTS
FAMILIES ACCIPITRIDAE AND FALCONIDAE

Twelve species of diurnal raptors have been recorded as vagrants in North America north of Mexico. They originated from Europe, Asia, or Mexico.

There are three or more records of the following species, which are native to both Europe and Asia: White-tailed Eagle, Common Kestrel, and Eurasian Hobby. All are recognized by the AOU. The Steller's Sea Eagle is a vagrant from Asia and is also recognized by the AOU.

Three species have occurred in extreme southern Texas as vagrants; they are the Crane Hawk and the Collared Forest Falcon, once each, and the Roadside Hawk, three times. All have been recognized by the AOU.

Five European species have occurred once each in eastern North America and were seen and described well but have not been recognized by the AOU. They are Black Kite (Newfoundland), Eurasian Honey Buzzard (Delaware), Egyptian Vulture (Virginia), Marsh Harrier (Virginia), and Booted Eagle (Bermuda). All are migratory species in Europe and most were probably ship-assisted in crossing the Atlantic Ocean, however, the possibility that one or more of the observed vagrants may have escaped from a zoo or other captivity cannot be dismissed.

EURASIAN HONEY BUZZARD   *Pernis apivorus*

DESCRIPTION

The Eurasian Honey Buzzard, a large buzzardlike kite, has occurred as a vagrant in Delaware. They lack bony projections over the eyes (supraorbital ridges) and *appear somewhat pigeon-*

Eurasian Honey Buzzard adult male. Long narrow head and neck, oval dark carpal patches, and narrow dark tips on flight feathers are distinctive. Israel, May (WSC)

headed. Small head, long neck, and long tail with rounded corners are distinctive on flying birds, which show an oval or rectangular dark carpal patch on each underwing. Plumages are polymorphic, but variations in base coloration of body and underwing coverts are similar for adult males, adult females, and juveniles. Age and sex are easily determined, however, using eye, cere, and face colors and extent of black on outer primaries. Base color of underparts is uniform and varies from white to creamy to pale brown to rufous to dark brown to black, with many intergrades between these. Wingtips fall short of tip of long tail on perched birds. When perched on the ground, they appear horizontal because of short legs.

ADULT MALE: Sides of face are gray. Eyes are bright yellow, and cere is gray. In good light, brown upperparts have a grayish cast and upperwings show dark trailing edges and dark tips to primary coverts. Undersides of outer primaries show narrow black tips with a sharp line of contrast with rest of whitish feathers. Undersides of secondaries are whitish with wide dark terminal band and a wide unbanded space between it and the other bands. Underparts show a variable amount of dark spotting or narrow streaking on breast and dark barring on belly and flanks but can be completely unmarked. Uppertail shows wide dark subterminal band and two narrower dark bands near base.

ADULT FEMALE and **JUVENILE** are described in European bird and raptor field guides.

FLIGHT

Active flight is with slow, deep wingbeats of somewhat flexible wings. Soars on flat wings, occasionally with a small dihedral; glides with wrists level but wingtips noticeably drooped. They never hover.

Honey Buzzards in flight actively twist their heads from side to side in a snakelike manner and twist their tails in a kitelike fashion while maneuvering.

BEHAVIOR

Honey Buzzards are specialized kites that feed mainly on larvae, pupae, nests, and adults of various wasps and bees. But they also feed at times on other insects, reptiles and amphibians, small mammals, and eggs and nestlings of birds, as well as some fruit and berries. They hunt from low perches, searching for movements of insects to and from nests, and have been reported to follow flying insects back to their nests. They are comfortable walking around on the forest floor.

Adults begin migration in northern Europe in early August. While migrating, they are more likely to continue flying using active flight in absence of thermals than are buteos.

STATUS AND DISTRIBUTION

An adult male Eurasian Honey Buzzard was seen and described well by several competent observers at Little Creek, Delaware, on August 11, 1997. This record has not been considered by the AOU.

ETYMOLOGY

Common name was coined by Willughby, who, in the 1600s, found combs of wasps in their nests. *Pernis* is thought to be a corruption of the Greek *pternis* for "a bird of prey"; *apivorus* comes from Latin *apis* and *voro* for "bee" and "devour," for its food preference.

MEASUREMENTS

LENGTH:	51–57 cm (54);	20–22 in. (21)
WINGSPREAD:	115–136 cm (130);	45–54 in. (51)
WEIGHT:	510–1,050 g (790);	1.1–2.3 lb. (1.7)

Description

The Black Kite, a large dark kite, has occurred as a vagrant in Newfoundland. Their buoyant flight and flight silhouette are distinctive. Most kites show whitish crescent-shaped to squarish primary panel on each otherwise dark underwing. Tail appears forked, as outer tail feathers are somewhat longer than central ones but can appear square when fully fanned. They are one of many raptors that have a pale bar across each upperwing. Sexes are alike in plumage; females are noticeably larger. Juvenile plumage is different from that of adult. Wingtips reach beyond central tail feathers to near tail tip on perched kites.

ADULT: Dark brown head has gray face and crown. Eyes vary from pale yellow to pale brown. Upperparts are dark brown with paler median secondary coverts forming a pale wing bar on each upperwing. Underparts vary from sooty brown to dark brown, with narrow black shaft streaks on breast and sooty rufous wash on belly, leg feathers, and undertail coverts. Tail above is dark reddish brown with darker brown banding but appears whitish below with dark brown bands.

JUVENILES: Similar to adults but usually lack sooty rufous tones on underparts. They have pale brown heads with dark brown shaft streaks and a dark brown rectangular area behind each eye. Back feathers and wing coverts have pale edges; upperparts appear more speckled than those of adults. Whitish feather edges of greater wing coverts form narrow pale lines across middle of upper- and underwings when plumage is fresh. Pale primary underwing panels are usually larger than those of adults. Underparts show brown breast with wide pale shaft streaks and paler belly, leg feathers, and undertail coverts.

Flight

Black Kite's graceful flight is usually with few wingbeats but with constant minor adjustments of wings and twisting of tail. Active flight is with slow, almost floppy wingbeats of somewhat flexible wings. Soars with wings cupped, with wrists up and tips down; glides with wings more cupped.

*Black Kite adult.
Forked tail tip is distinctive. Israel,
March (WSC)*

BEHAVIOR

Black Kites are wonderful flyers, often remaining airborne for
hours without a wingbeat. They are usually found near water.
They take a wide array of food, including birds, mammals, insects, reptiles, and especially fish, but also garbage, refuse, and
offal. They will chase each other or smaller raptors, or even other
birds, trying to steal a morsel. Food is often snatched from the
ground or the water's surface without alighting after a short steep
dive, after which the bird rises rapidly.

They are somewhat vociferous, particularly when interacting
with each other. Their drawn-out tremulous call can be heard for
some distance.

STATUS AND DISTRIBUTION

A Black Kite was observed and photographed at Bonavista, Newfoundland, on August 21, 1995. The kite was not seen on following days, in spite of the many observers searching for it. This
record has not been considered by the AOU.

ETYMOLOGY

Milvus is Latin for "kite," *migrans* is Latin for "migrating."

MEASUREMENTS

LENGTH:	46–59 cm (53);	18–23 in. (21)
WINGSPREAD:	130–155 cm (143);	51–61 in. (56)
WEIGHT:	560–1,210 g (875);	1.2–2.7 lb. (1.9)

EGYPTIAN VULTURE

Neophron percnopterus

Description

The Egyptian Vulture, a small Old World vulture, has occurred as a vagrant once in Virginia. *Long narrow beak and wedge-shaped tail are distinctive in all plumages.* Five plumages corresponding to age are recognizable. Sexes are nearly alike in plumage and size. Eyes are dark brown. Wingtips reach tail tip on perched vultures.

ADULT: Very distinctive and shown well in most European bird field guides.

JUVENILE: Head consists of bare gray face skin, pale yellow basal half of dark beak, dark down on crown that comes to a point in a distinctive "widow's peak" on forecrown, and blackish nape and neck feathers that are shorter than those of adults. Body and wing coverts vary from gray-brown to brown to brownish black, with a variable amount of pale diamond-shaped markings. Colorations of upperparts and underparts are quite variable; some birds appear overall creamy on underparts or upperparts or both. Undertail and uppertail coverts are creamy and contrast with darker body. Bare crop patch on chest is pale grey. Flight feathers are dark brown, with a pale brown cast to uppersides of secondaries. Tail is grayish brown with paler tip. Legs are pale gray, often with a pinkish or pale yellow cast.

BASIC I: Essentially like juveniles, except new uppertail and undertail coverts are the same brownish color as body feathers, uppersides of new flight feathers have a grayish cast, upperparts lack pale diamond-shaped markings. Forehead is covered with a mixture of new short whitish down and old blackish down and is lacking dark "widow's peak." Bare crop patch on chest of older immature is usually the same color as its face. The older immature plumages are described in European bird and raptor field guides.

Flight

Egyptian Vultures soar with wings level or slightly cupped and glide with wings slightly cupped and tips held lower than body. Active flight is with strong, deep wingbeats of stiff wings.

Behavior

Egyptian Vultures are primarily scavengers but utilize a wide variety of food sources, including capture of live prey such as turtles and insects. They are less dependent on large carcasses than are large vultures and feed on these after other vultures have eaten

Egyptian Vulture juvenile. Juveniles are overall dark, with long wedge-shaped tail. Oman, November (WSC)

the soft parts. A variety of small mammals, birds, reptiles, and insects are reported as staple food items. They also feed on birds' eggs. They use stones as tools to break large eggs (e.g., those of the Ostrich); they break smaller eggs by lifting them in their beaks and smashing them on ground.

Most European Egyptian Vultures migrate, wintering south of the Sahara, but a few individuals are reported in Europe almost every winter. In late spring or summer, some wander afield into northern Europe. A few immatures remain on winter grounds during the northern summer. Small populations in Canary and Cape Verde Islands are resident.

STATUS AND DISTRIBUTION

A juvenile or Basic I Egyptian Vulture was seen well at Cape Charles, Virginia, in late December, 1985. This record has not been considered by the AOU.

ETYMOLOGY

Neophron was a character from the pseudo-Greek mythological *Metamorphoses*; he was changed into a vulture by Zeus; *percnopterus* comes from the Greek *percnos* and *pteros* for "dusky" and "wing."

MEASUREMENTS

LENGTH:	55–65 cm (60);	22–26 in. (24)
WINGSPREAD:	148–171 cm (159);	58–67 in. (63)
WEIGHT:	1.4–2.3 kg (1.8);	3–5 lb. (4)

Haliaeetus albicilla

DESCRIPTION

The White-tailed Eagle, a large sea eagle, occurs as a rare vagrant in North America. Plumages are similar to those of the Bald Eagle. They are approximately the same size as Alaska Bald Eagles. In flight, head and neck project more than half the length of tail. Adults are distinguished from Bald Eagle by creamy to pale brown, not white, heads; shorter, more wedge-shaped tails; and *dark brown tail coverts*. Juveniles and older immatures are similar to Bald Eagles of like age but appear somewhat darker on underwings, with less prominent white axillaries and diagonal white lines; the *tips of their tail feathers have white spikes*. Sexes are alike in plumage, with females noticeably larger than males. Juveniles have wider wings and much longer tails than do adults. Adult plumage is acquired in four or five years.

ADULT: Head and neck vary from light brown to buff to cream, paler on some (older?) adults, with a variable amount of narrow brown streaking, *lacking a sharp line of contrast with brown breast and back*. Head usually shows narrow dark eye lines. Beak and cere are lemon yellow, eyes are yellow. Body and coverts are dark brown with a variable amount of buffy feather edging that is wider, thus appearing paler, on breast, upper back, and upperwing coverts. Flight feathers, leg feathers, and *undertail coverts are dark brown*. Short white tail has wedge-shaped tip; some adults show black spots on a tail feather or two throughout their lives. Wingtips reach or almost reach tail tip on perched adults. Legs are yellow to yellow-orange.

JUVENILE: Head and neck are dark brown. Body and wing and tail coverts are tawny with variably sized dark brown spoon-shaped markings on most feathers, heavier on the breast. Uppersides are somewhat two-toned: dark flight feathers contrast with tawny back and upperwing coverts. Undersides of dark flight feathers can show a limited amount of whitish wash on inner primaries and inner secondaries. Greater secondary upperwing coverts are buffy to tawny and usually lack dark brown spotting. Tawny leg feathers and undertail coverts show dark brown spotting. Dark underwings show whitish axillaries and usually a white bar (median secondary coverts); these features are shown on the first three plumages. Tail is longer and less wedge-shaped than that of adults, and feathers have dark outer webs and (usually) white inner webs with triangular dark tips resulting in an arrow-shaped

White-tailed Eagle adult. Similar to adult Bald Eagle, but undertail coverts are dark. Japan, February (WSC)

white area on the tip of each feather (a feature shown on the first three plumages). Trailing edge of wings appears serrated due to pointed tips of secondaries and is more curved than that of adults. Wingtips fall short of tail tip on perched juveniles. Beak and cere are blackish, eyes are dark brown, and legs are pale yellow.

OLDER IMMATURES (BASIC I–III): The next three annual plumages are similar to that of juvenile, but heads are paler, often with dark ear patches; dark brown backs and upperwing coverts are mottled whitish; and underparts are whitish with dark brown markings. Basic I eagles show ragged trailing edge of wings like that of Basic I Bald Eagles. Beak and cere gradually lighten and begin to turn yellowish, and eyes lighten to light brown. Flight feathers are blackish, with only an occasional faint whitish mottling on inner secondaries. Tail is like that of juvenile but shorter and more wedge-shaped. Leg feathers are uniformly dark brown.

UNUSUAL PLUMAGES: Completely albino specimens exist that are overall grayish white with a yellow beak. Partial albinos have also been reported.

SIMILAR SPECIES

(1) BALD EAGLE (Pls. 7, 8) adults have white heads and necks, with sharp line of contrast with brown body; white undertail coverts; and longer, less wedge-shaped white tail. Juveniles and older immatures have tails of similar length with dark terminal band as if dipped in ink, in contrast to spiked appearance of those of White-tails; immature Balds show a sharp line of contrast between darker breast and paler belly. On whitish tails of immature Balds, only outer tail feathers have dark outer webs, whereas on similar White-tailed Eagle tails, every feather has a dark outer web. **(2) STELLER'S SEA EAGLE** (Pl. 9) Juvenile and older immatures have mostly white, extremely wedge-shaped tail and massive all-yellow beak. Adult Steller's is unmistakable, with its huge yellow beak and white wing patch.

FLIGHT

White-tailed Eagle is a large, heavy, often cumbersome predator but at times can be surprisingly agile in flight. Active flight is with heavy but shallow, rather quick wingbeats. Soars with wings held level or in a slight dihedral. Glides with wings held level or slightly depressed.

MOLT

White-tailed Eagles undergo an incomplete annual molt, actively molting from March into November. They replace only some of their flight, tail, covert, and body feathers each year. Adults may also suspend molt for a time while raising young. Juveniles begin post-juvenile molt in late spring; it is also not complete. Adult plumage is attained after four or five molts.

BEHAVIOR

White-tailed Eagles are similar in habits to Bald Eagles, sharing their preference for fish and aquatic habitats. They too are superb fishermen and accomplished pirates.

STATUS AND DISTRIBUTION

White-tailed Eagles are rare vagrants in the Aleutian Is. of Alaska but have bred on Attu. Vagrants have also been recorded on Kodiak Is., Alaska, off the Massachusetts coast, in the e. Canadian Arctic, and, most recently, at Derby Hill, New York. Their primary range is most of n. Eurasia. The resident race in sw. Greenland is characterized by larger size.

FINE POINTS

When White-tailed Eagles soar, seven fingerlike emarginated primaries are visible on the wingtips; Bald Eagles show only six.

Eurasian race is *H. a. albicilla;* Greenland race is *H. a. groenlandicus.*

ETYMOLOGY

Albicilla is from Latin *albus,* "white," and *illus,* a Latin diminutive suffix, used mistakenly to mean "tailed." The error probably originated from the name of the wagtail genus, *Motacilla.*

MEASUREMENTS

LENGTH:	77–92 cm (84);	30–36 in. (33)
WINGSPREAD:	208–247 cm (231);	82–97 in. (91)
WEIGHT:	3.1–6.9 kg (4.8);	6.8–15.2 lb. (10.6)

STELLER'S SEA EAGLE   PL. 9

Haliaeetus pelagicus

DESCRIPTION

The Steller's Sea Eagle, a rare vagrant to North America, is larger and heavier bodied than the Bald Eagle. Unmistakable, with *huge beak, adult's white wing patches and legs, and long, deeply wedge-shaped white tail.* Trailing edge of wings is more curved than those of Bald and White-tailed Eagles. Sexes are alike in plumage, but females are noticeably larger. Plumages of juveniles and older immatures are different from adult's. Wingtips fall quite short of tip of long tail on perched eagles. Adult plumage is acquired after four or five years.

ADULT: Unmistakable. Black head usually shows small white forehead patch and fine pale gray streaking on crown and neck. *Huge beak, cere, and face skin are orange-yellow.* Eyes are pale yellow. Body is black, with pale gray streaking on the breast. White lesser and median upperwing and underwing coverts form *white patches on leading edge of upper and lower wings* of flying birds and *white shoulder* of perched ones. Flight feathers and greater coverts are black. Leg feathers, uppertail and undertail coverts, and long wedge-shaped tail are white. Legs are orange-yellow to orange.

JUVENILE: Head, body, leg feathers, and wing and tail coverts are dark blackish brown. *Huge yellow beak is tinged with brown. Cere and face skin are yellow.* Eyes are dark brown. Neck and upper

Steller's Sea Eagle adult. Huge unmistakable eagle with long white wedge-shaped tail. Japan, February (WSC)

breast have pale streaking. Upperwing and uppertail coverts are mottled with white. Flight feathers are blackish. Dark underwings show white axillaries, white bar on median coverts, and, usually, mostly white inner three primaries. *Long, extremely wedge-shaped tail is white* and sometimes shows dark mottling or dark tips or both. White undertail coverts are heavily marked dark brown. Legs are yellow to orange-yellow.

OLDER IMMATURES (BASIC I–III): The next three plumages are similar to those of juveniles but with more whitish mottling on upperwing coverts, legs, and tail coverts. Basic I eagles are like juveniles but with newer shorter inner secondaries. Basic II eagles show ragged trailing edge of wings and whitish leg feathers and undertail coverts. Basic III eagles appear more adultlike but with some immature characters. Eye color gradually lightens, and beak and cere become more orangish.

UNUSUAL PLUMAGES: Adults of the rare dark color morph lack white patches on forehead and wing and white leg feathers.

SIMILAR SPECIES

(1) BALD EAGLE (Pls. 7, 8) adult is smaller; has white head, smaller beak, more rounded wingtips, and square-tipped tail; and lacks white patches on wings. Juvenile and older immatures are smaller and have smaller beaks, dark tails or dark border on whitish tails, and straighter trailing edge of wings. **(2) WHITE-TAILED EAGLE** (Pl. 9) adult is smaller; has pale head, smaller beak, more rounded wingtips; and lacks white patches on wings. Juvenile and older immatures are smaller and have smaller beaks, dark tails or dark tip on whitish tails, and straighter trailing edge of wings.

Flight

Active flight is with heavy, powerful wingbeats. Soars with wings in a strong dihedral and glides on flat wings.

Molt

Not well studied. Apparently annual molt of adults is not complete; only some of the flight and not all of body feathers are replaced each year. Only a few of the flight feathers are replaced in post-juvenile molt and subsequent molt, with three molts required to replace all juvenile flight feathers.

Behavior

Steller's Sea Eagles are typical sea eagles and eat mainly fish and birds but also seal pups and hares.

Status and Distribution

Steller's Sea Eagle is a rare vagrant to North America, occurring in the Aleutian and other Alaskan islands, with sight records from Attu and Unalaska and specimen records from St. Paul and Kodiak Is. An adult had been observed associating with an adult Bald Eagle near Juneau for many years. Their breeding range is along the n. Pacific Coast of Asia from Bering Sea Coast south to Kamchatka peninsula and n. coast of Sea of Okhotsk. They winter south to Korea and the Japanese island of Hokkaido.

Fine Points

Steller's Sea Eagles have 14 tail feathers; other sea eagles have 12.

Subspecies

Monotypic.

Etymology

Named after George Wilhelm Steller, a German naturalist, who accompanied Bering on his explorations of the n. Pacific; *pelagicus* is from the Greek *pelagos*, for "sea," and the Latin suffix *-icus*, "belonging to."

Measurements

LENGTH:	85–105 cm (95);	33–41 in. (37)
WINGSPREAD:	220–245 cm (232);	87–96 in. (91)
WEIGHT:	5–9 kg (7);	11–20 lb. (15)

MARSH HARRIER *Circus aeruginosus*

Description

The Marsh Harrier, a large dark harrier, has occurred as a vagrant once in Virginia. They have relatively wider wings than other harriers and *lack white uppertail coverts*. Adults have sexually dimorphic plumages; females are noticeably larger than males and have proportionally wider wings. Juvenile plumage is alike for the sexes and is similar to that of the adult female. A rare and local dark-morph plumage exists for all age and sex classes. On perched harriers, wingtips fall short of tail tip. Adult males and females and dark-morph plumages are described in European bird and raptor field guides.

JUVENILE: Plumage is almost completely dark brown, but with creamy to whitish unstreaked crown and throat patches; some birds have adult femalelike creamy patches on the breast or upperwing or underwing coverts. Underwings usually show a small white crescent at base of outer primaries. Uppertail coverts are dark brown but may be rufous in spring due to molt. Tail is dark brown without rufous mottling (but replacement feathers may have rufous mottling). Eyes are dark brown on females and paler brown to yellow on males.

Flight

Hunting flight is typical of harriers. Active flight is with heavy, slow wingbeats. Soars with wings in a medium dihedral; glides usually with wings held with less dihedral than other harriers, often held in a modified dihedral.

Behavior

Marsh Harriers hunt in typical harrier fashion, quartering slowly over reed beds and fields searching for birds or mammals. While hunting, they will sometimes stop and hover with legs dangling for a second or more. Range of prey is large and includes most animals that occur in reed beds, including fish. In winter they also eat carrion.

Eurasian Marsh Harrier juvenile female. Large dark harrier. Adult females and juveniles show creamy head with wide dark eye stripe. Israel, May (WSC)

STATUS AND DISTRIBUTION

A juvenile female Marsh Harrier was seen and described well by numerous observers at Chincoteague NWR on December 4, 1994. The harrier was not seen on following days, in spite of the many observers searching for it. This record has not been accepted by the AOU.

ETYMOLOGY

Aeruginosus is Latin for "rusty colored," in reference to adult's belly and leg feathers.

MEASUREMENTS

LENGTH:	42–53 cm (47);	17–21 in. (19)
WINGSPREAD:	115–139 cm (128);	45–55 in. (50)
WEIGHT:	375–755 g (540);	13–27 oz. (19)

CRANE HAWK

PL. 34

Geranospiza caerulescens

DESCRIPTION

The Crane Hawk, a slender medium-sized, long-legged, small-headed Neotropical raptor, has occurred once in the lower Rio Grande Valley of Texas. Wings are broad and rather short, with rounded tips. Outer primaries each have a white spot; these appear as a *curved line of white dots near the wingtips* of flying

hawks. Sexes are alike in plumage; females are larger. Juvenile plumage is similar to adult's. Wingtips extend about a third of the way down tails of perched hawks.

ADULT: Overall slate gray, with red to orange-red eyes and long orangish legs. Underwing coverts, base of flight feathers, undertail coverts, and leg feathers show narrow white barring, and long dark tail has two white bands. Cere and lores are slate gray.

JUVENILE: Similar to adult but with a brownish cast to uppersides; white superciliaries, forehead, and throat; pale streaking on cheeks; amber eyes; narrow buffy barring on underparts and leg feathers; white base to tail; and orange-yellow legs.

UNUSUAL PLUMAGES: No unusual plumages have been reported.

SIMILAR SPECIES

(1) **COMMON BLACK-HAWK** (Pl. 14) perched adults also appear overall dark, but they have more robust bodies, larger heads, yellow ceres, dark eyes, shorter and yellow legs, and only one wide white band on shorter tails. In flight they do not show the curved row of white spots on wings. (2) **ZONE-TAILED HAWK** (Pl. 23) perched adults also appear overall dark, but they have more robust bodies, larger heads, yellow ceres, dark eyes, shorter and yellow legs, longer primary projection, and only one wide white band on shorter tails. In flight they do not show the curved row of white spots on wings.

FLIGHT

Active flight is with loose, floppy wingbeats, interspersed with periods of glide. They occasionally soar only for a short time on level wings and glide on level wings.

Molt

Not studied. Presumably they have a complete annual molt and juvenile plumage is worn for about a year.

Behavior

This curious raptor has double-jointed legs for probing in holes, crevices, and epiphytes in search of prey, often flapping its wings while doing so. They forage along large branches of trees but also on the ground and with harrier-like flight.

Status and Distribution

An adult was seen over a three-month period (December 20, 1987 to March 17, 1988) in Santa Ana NWR on the Mexico border in Texas. They occur in a variety of habitats, usually near water, from ne. and nw. Mexico south through Central America to South America to Peru and n. Argentina.

Subspecies

The subspecies in Mexico is *G. c. nigra*.

Etymology

Geranospiza is from the Greek *granos* meaning "crane," and *spizias*, "a hawk"; *caerulescens* is Latin for "dark blue," in reference to South American hawks, which are more blue-gray and were described first.

Measurements

LENGTH:	43–51 cm (47);	17–20 in. (19)
WINGSPREAD:	92–105 cm (99);	36–41 in. (39)
WEIGHT:	225–358 g (292);	8–13 oz. (10.4)

ROADSIDE HAWK   PL. 16

Buteo magnirostris (or *Asturina magnirostris*)

Description

The Roadside Hawk, a rare vagrant in the lower Rio Grande Valley of Texas, is a small, long-legged, and long-tailed tropical buteo.

Roadside Hawk adult. All show paddle-shaped wings. Mexico, October (BKW)

Roadside Hawk juvenile. Juveniles have streaked breasts and pale superciliaries. Mexico, October (WSC)

Birds from northern Mexico lack or have greatly reduced rufous wing patches that are characteristic of this species in other parts of its range. *Buffy greater uppertail coverts form a pale U above tail base,* visible on flying birds. Sexes are alike in plumage, with females somewhat larger. Adult and juvenile plumages of this accipiter-like raptor are similar. Cere is yellow-orange to orange. Wingtips reach about halfway to tail tip on perched birds.

ADULT: Head is gray to gray-brown; eyes are pale lemon yellow. Back and upperwing coverts are dark brown, with a strong grayish cast in fresh plumage. *Underparts' pattern of brown to gray-brown bib on breast and belly barred rufous and buffy* is diagnostic. Underwings show buffy coverts and white flight feathers with numerous narrow dark bands, subterminal band somewhat wider. Buffy uppertail coverts form a pale U above base of tail, noticeable on flying birds. Buffy leg feathers are finely barred rufous. White to creamy undertail coverts are unmarked. Long tail has equal-width dark and light brown bands. Legs are orange.

JUVENILE: Similar to adult, but head and upperparts are browner, lacking gray tones; head shows noticeable wide creamy superciliary lines and orange-yellow eyes. Buffy breast shows a variable amount of long dark streaks. Underwings are also heavily banded but lack a wider dark subterminal band. Tail has more and narrower bands than that of adult, and legs are more yellowish.

UNUSUAL PLUMAGES: No unusual plumages have been reported.

Similar Species

(1) **GRAY HAWK** (Pl. 15) juvenile has bold face pattern; dark eyes; un-equal-width tail bands; whiter, more extensive U above tail base; and lacks dark bib and barred belly. (2) **BROAD-WINGED HAWK** (Pl. 18) has more pointed wings, adults have dark eyes, and juvenile lacks dark bib and barred belly. (3) **RED-SHOULDERED HAWK** (Pls. 16, 17) has crescent-shaped wing panels, unequal-width tail bands, and dark eyes and lacks dark bib and barred belly. (4) **HOOK-BILLED KITE** (Pl. 3) adult female appears similar to adult Roadside Hawk. See under that species for differences.

Flight

Active flight is accipiter-like, with three to five rapid, stiff, shallow wingbeats followed by a glide. Soars with wings level and tail folded; soaring is usually not very high, most often just above the treetops. Glides with wings somewhat cupped, with wrists up and wingtips down. Does not hover.

Molt

Annual molt of adults is complete. Juveniles molt directly into adult plumage in about a year.

Behavior

Roadside Hawks are conspicuous because of their habit of perching in open places, often on poles and wires along roadways. They are a general feeder, eating mainly insects and reptiles but also rodents and sometimes birds. They hunt from perches and glide down to the ground to capture prey.

Pairs in courtship flights glide together with fluttering wings held in a V, loudly calling. Vocalizations include a drawn out *ke-eerrr* and a staccato *kek-kek-kek* and once heard are seldom forgotten.

Status and Distribution

Roadside Hawks have occurred three times as vagrants in the Rio Grande Valley of Texas. A 1901 specimen exists from Cameron County, Texas. A live hawk was seen and described well in 1979, and another overwintered at Bentsen-Rio Grande Valley State Park in 1982–1983. Nine sight records since have not been accepted by the Texas bird records committee. Their extensive

Neotropical range extends northward to cen. Tamaulipas, where much of their habitat has been lost in recent years.

FINE POINTS

Adults usually have four dark tail bands; juveniles have five. Outer primaries are barred to tips.

SUBSPECIES

The northern Mexico race is *B. m. grisocauda*. Palmer (1988) placed this species, along with Gray and Red-shouldered Hawks, in the genus *Asturina;* see comment under this heading in the account of Gray Hawk.

ETYMOLOGY

Magnirostris is from the Latin *magni* for "large" and *rostrum* for "beak."

MEASUREMENTS

LENGTH:	33–38 cm (36);	13–15 in. (14)
WINGSPREAD:	72–79 cm (75);	28–31 in. (30)
WEIGHT:	230–440 g (318);	8–15 oz. (11)

BOOTED EAGLE   *Hieraaetus pennatus*

DESCRIPTION

The Booted Eagle, a small polymorphic, aerial-hunting eagle, has occurred once as a vagrant on Bermuda. Unique white spots or "landing lights" are usually visible at the bases of the forewings, and all but the darkest eagles show pale inner primaries. All show pale bars across upperwings and usually a whitish U at base of uppertail, as well. They have light, dark, and rufous color morphs. Sexes are alike in plumage. Adults and juveniles of all three morphs differ little and are not distinguishable in the field except by eye color: golden yellow in adults and dark to medium brown in juveniles, which change gradually to adult color by their first molt. Wingtips fall somewhat short of tail tips on perched eagles.

DARK MORPH: Golden to pale brown head has darker brown cheeks and throat. Back and upperwing coverts are dark brown, except for paler median coverts, which form a noticeable pale bar across

Booted Eagle dark morph. Small dark eagle. All show white "headlights" at base of forewings. Israel, May (WSC)

each upperwing. Underparts and underwing coverts are dark brown, usually with narrow darker streaking visible on breast when seen in good light. Undersides of flight feathers are somewhat paler than coverts but still appear darkish. On darker eagles, the three inner primaries may not be noticeably paler than the others, likewise, their uppertail coverts may not be noticeably paler. Pale undertail often appears rufous because of long dark rufous undertail coverts and shows a darker band on tip. Buffy leg feathers are contrastingly paler than dark underparts. Light morph and rufous morph are described in European bird and raptor field guides.

FLIGHT

Active flight is with deep, deliberate wingbeats of somewhat elastic wings. Soars with wings held slightly cupped, not flat, and tail somewhat spread. Glides with wings held in a cupped position, with wrists held up and thrust forward and wingtips down, and with tail folded.

BEHAVIOR

Booted Eagles are aerial hunters, soaring up to heights and then gliding forward slowly while searching the ground directly below until prey is sighted, when they fold up to a teardrop shape and hurtle downward, finishing the stoop with legs and talons outstretched. Sometimes they lower slowly from on high on spread wings and tail to view their prey better, then begin their stoop from a lower height. They do not hover.

A dark-morph eagle was reported on Bermuda by several experienced observers on September 8–13, 1989. It was theorized by the observers that the eagle was carried to the island by a hurricane that formed off the African coast and moved west, passing near Bermuda on September 7. This record has not been considered by the AOU.

ETYMOLOGY

Hieraaetus comes from the Greek *hierax* for "hawk" and *aetos* for "eagle"; *pennatus* is Latin for "feathered" in reference to the completely feathered or "booted" legs.

MEASUREMENTS

LENGTH:	42–50 cm (46);	17–20 in. (18)
WINGSPREAD:	113–134 cm (124);	44–53 in. (49)
WEIGHT:	555–965 g (735);	1.2–2.1 lb. (1.6)

COLLARED FOREST-FALCON   PL. 34

Micrastur semitorquatus

DESCRIPTION

The Collared Forest-Falcon, a slender, medium-sized, long-legged secretive Neotropical raptor, has occurred once in the lower Rio Grande Valley of Texas (white-morph adult). Wings are broad and relatively short, with blunt wingtips. They occur in white, buffy, and dark morphs. Sexes are alike in plumage; females are larger. Juvenile plumages are similar to those of adults. Wingtips barely extend beyond secondaries on perched Forest-Falcons.

WHITE-MORPH ADULT: Crown and nape are black, with an attached *dark half-collar separating white cheeks from white collar* across hindneck. Adults' eyes are brown. *Bare face skin, eye-rings, and cere are dull greenish yellow*. Back and upperwing coverts are black; black uppertail coverts have white tips. Throat, cheeks, and underparts are whitish. Long graduated black tail shows three narrow white bands and narrow white tips; outer feathers are progressively shorter. Long legs are dull yellow.

TAWNY-MORPH ADULT: Like white-morph adult, but throat, cheeks, collar, and underparts are buffy to tawny instead of white. Tail as in white-morph adult.

Collared Forest-Falcon adult light morph. Note dark half-collar and white collar. Peru, September (George Jett)

DARK-MORPH ADULT: Overall sooty black except for some white barring on flanks, belly, and leg feathers, black barring on white uppertail coverts. They never show the pale collar. Face color and tail as in white-morph adult.

WHITE- AND TAWNY-MORPH JUVENILES: Similar to adults but have dark brown eyes, crown, and upperparts with narrow buffy feather edges, and collar, cheeks, and underparts that are coarsely barred dark brown, all washed with cinnamon.

DARK-MORPH JUVENILE: Similar to dark-morph adult but overall dark brown with white barring on belly and leg feathers. Juvenile's eyes are dark brown.

UNUSUAL PLUMAGES: No unusual plumages have been reported.

SIMILAR SPECIES

No other raptor is similar.

FLIGHT

Active flight across open areas is rather jaylike, recalling Brown Jay. Never reported to soar.

MOLT

Not studied. Presumably they have a complete annual molt and juvenile plumage is worn for about a year.

BEHAVIOR

Collared Forest-Falcons are secretive forest raptors that usually perch in inconspicuous places. They are bold predators, taking a wide variety of food, including many birds. They hunt usually from a perch, but also by walking along large branches and on the ground. Vocalization most often heard is a drawn-out repeated *cooww, cooww, cooww.*

STATUS AND DISTRIBUTION

A white-morph adult was seen for several weeks in January and February 1994 at Bentsen-Rio Grande Valley State Park on the Mexico border in Texas. They occur in a variety of forested habitats, from ne. and nw. Mexico south through Central America to South America to Peru and n. Argentina.

SUBSPECIES

The subspecies that occurs in Mexico is *M. s. naso.*

ETYMOLOGY

Micrastur is from the Greek *mikros* for "small" and *Astur,* formerly the genus of the Goshawk; *semitorquatus* comes from the Latin *semi* for "half" and *torquatus* for "collared."

MEASUREMENTS

LENGTH:	54–64 cm (59);	21–25 in. (23)
WINGSPREAD:	76–94 cm (85);	30–37 in. (34)
WEIGHT:	584–820 g (700);	1.3–1.8 lb. (1.5)

COMMON KESTREL   PL. 35

Falco tinnunculus

DESCRIPTION

The Common Kestrel, a long-tailed, medium-sized falcon, occurs in North America as a vagrant. It is somewhat similar to the American Kestrel but is much larger. *The two-toned pattern on upperwings in flight is diagnostic*: reddish brown or rufous secondaries and their upperwing coverts have a sharply demarcated line of contrast with dark brown primaries and their coverts. (Upperparts appear more uniform in color on American Kestrels, lacking sharp line of contrast.) *Noticeably long tail has wedge-shaped tip* when folded. Adults have different plumages by sex, but females are only slightly larger. Juvenile plumage of both

Common Kestrel adult male. All show two-toned upperwings. India, March (WSC)

sexes is similar to that of adult female. Underwings appear pale in all plumages. Eyes are dark brown. Cere, eye-ring, and leg colors are yellow to orange-yellow, paler on juveniles. On perched falcons, wingtips fall short of dark subterminal band on central tail feathers.

ADULT MALE: Head is blue-gray with fine black shaft streaks and whitish cheeks, short dark lines behind the eyes, a narrow dark mustache mark below each eye, and a white throat. Rufous back and upperwing coverts are lightly marked with dark diamond-shaped spots. Creamy to buffy-rufous underparts are streaked on breast, spotted on belly and flanks. Creamy undertail coverts and buffy-rufous leg feathers are unmarked. Uppertail coverts are unmarked blue-gray. Blue-gray tail is usually unbanded except for wide black subterminal band but can have numerous narrow black bands on inner webs, noticeable when tail is spread.

ADULT FEMALE: Head is buffy brown, with fine black shaft streaks, short dark lines behind each eye, whitish cheeks, a narrow dark mustache mark under each eye, and a white throat. (Head can show a grayish cast on some [older?] females.) Back and upperwing coverts are reddish brown with short dark brown triangular bars. Buffy underparts are streaked dark brown, tending to spotting on belly and barring on flanks. Creamy undertail coverts and leg feathers are usually unmarked but latter may show some fine short dark shaft streaks. Uppertail coverts are reddish brown, usually with faint dark barring and a blue-gray cast, but can be uniform blue-gray like those of adult males, without dark barring, but with narrow black shaft streaks. Tail is usually reddish brown, with wide dark brown subterminal band, numerous narrow dark brown bands, and often with a blue-grayish cast to uppertail.

Some females, however, have an adult male–like blue-gray tail, but with many narrow dark bands.

JUVENILE: Similar to adult females, but back and upperwing coverts have wide, even-width dark brown barring, and streaking on underparts is thicker and heavier. New adult feathers of the proper sex begin showing on back and uppertail coverts by their first autumn; body molt is often completed by late spring. Creamy leg feathers and undertail coverts are usually unstreaked, but former may show a few dark shaft streaks. Juvenile male's tail is like that of the adult female but is never completely gray. Juvenile female's tail is reddish brown with wider dark brown bands and never shows a grayish cast. Many juvenile males have a grayish cast to their uppertail coverts, always lacking on those of juvenile females.

UNUSUAL PLUMAGES: A dilute-plumage adult male specimen exists. Albinism has been reported; most accounts are from Britain. Adult males with a rufous (not blue-gray) head and an adult female with a blue-gray (not reddish brown) head have been captured or collected. An alleged melanistic Common Kestrel is illustrated in Harris et al. (1990).

SIMILAR SPECIES

AMERICAN KESTREL (Pl. 35) is smaller, has two dark mustache marks, lacks crisply demarcated two-toned upperwings in flight, and has noticeably shorter tail with a more rounded tip. American Kestrel males have rufous tails and grayish wing coverts; Common Kestrel adult males have grayish tails and rufous wing coverts.

FLIGHT

Active flight is with rapid, shallow, loose, almost fluttery wingbeats. Soars on flat wings with tail somewhat fanned. Glides on flat wings or with wrists below body and tips curved up. Hovers and kites frequently while hunting.

MOLT

Annual molts are complete. Juveniles begin molting body feathers in their first autumn, especially uppertail coverts and back feathers, but flight feathers are not renewed until the next summer.

BEHAVIOR

Common Kestrels act very much like American Kestrels. They take a variety of prey, but small mammals are their staple. They also eat insects, reptiles, and birds, including nestlings. They hunt both from elevated exposed perches and by hovering and kiting on the wind.

STATUS AND DISTRIBUTION

Common Kestrels occur in North America as vagrants; there are single records from Massachusetts, Nova Scotia, New Brunswick, New Jersey, Washington, and British Columbia, six records from the Aleutian Is., and two more from the seas off Alaska. One individual was recorded on Martinique in the West Indies.

FINE POINTS

Some (older?) adult females appear much like adult males, with blue-gray heads, tails, and uppertail coverts and rufous backs, but their tails are usually heavily banded, their gray uppertail coverts have narrow black shaft streaks, and their back markings are wider flattened triangles, not diamond-shaped as on adult males.

SUBSPECIES

The most likely races to occur in North America are the European race *F. t. tinnunculus* and the similar ne. Asian race *F. t. interstinctus*.

ETYMOLOGY

"Kestrel" comes from the Old French *crecerelle*, a name for this species that derived from *crecelle*, meaning "to rattle," for the falcon's vocalizations; *tinnunculus* is Latin for "little bell-ringer," also for its call.

MEASUREMENTS

LENGTH:		29–38 cm (34);	11–15 in. (13)
WINGSPREAD:		68–82 cm (76);	27–32 in. (30)
WEIGHT:	Male	127–220 g (170);	4.5–7.8 oz. (6)
	Female	142–280 g (190);	5–9.9 oz. (6.7)

Falco subbuteo

DESCRIPTION

The Eurasian Hobby, a medium-sized, long-winged, swift and elegant falcon, occurs as a vagrant in North America. Wing proportions are rather Peregrine-like, with short arms and long hands, but they are smaller, with more slender body, narrower wings, shorter tail, and narrower mustache marks. *Flight silhouette is particularly sickle-like,* with wingtips usually pulled back, and, when gliding, they appear somewhat swiftlike. Sexes are alike in plumage, with females only slightly larger. Juvenile plumage is similar to that of adult. Eyes are dark brown. On perched hobbys, wingtips extend just beyond tail tips.

ADULT: Head has gray crown, short narrow pale superciliary lines, creamy cheeks and throat separated by narrow black mustache marks, and creamy areas on sides of nape partially separated from cheeks by second set of shorter black mustache marks. Back and upperwing and uppertail coverts are dark blue-gray; falcons in worn plumage, especially females, appear somewhat dark brown on upperparts. Uppersides of flight feathers are blackish. Whitish underparts have wide, well-defined black streaking; *individual streaks often extend from throat to lower belly.* Because of heavy markings, underparts can appear uniformly dark on distant hobbys, with contrasting white throat and cheeks noticeable. Underwings appear uniformly dark. Leg feathers and undertail coverts are bright rufous. Upperside of folded tail appears unbanded, with a blue-gray cast (central feathers), but underside appears banded, with eight or more sets of even-width dark brown and rufous-buffy bands. Central tail feathers often project beyond the others. Cere, eye-rings, and legs vary from yellow to bright yellow.

JUVENILE: Similar to adult, but upperparts are dark brown, showing buffy feather edges in fresh plumage, and cheeks, throat, and underparts are creamy. Leg feathers and undertail coverts are buffy, with narrow dark streaks. Folded tail appears unbanded dark brown on upperside, with a wide pale terminal band, but on underside shows more distinct even-width dark brown and buffy bands. Cere, eye-rings, and legs are yellowish green, later becoming yellow.

UNUSUAL PLUMAGES: An adult specimen from Russia showed two all-white primary upperwing coverts. A dilute-plumage specimen from Ethiopia had pale whitish-gray tail and flight feathers and underparts, but normally colored upperparts.

Eurasian Hobby adult. Long nar-row underwings are uniformly dark. Israel, October (WSC)

SIMILAR SPECIES

(1) PEREGRINE FALCON (Pl. 38) is larger and has broader-based wings and tail and wider mustache marks. Peregrines have a heavier, less buoyant flight. **(2) AMERICAN KESTREL** (Pl. 35) has rufous back and tail and two mustache marks. In flight it shows pale underwings. **(3) MERLIN** (Pl. 36) is smaller, has shorter wings and banded uppertails, and lacks well-defined mustache marks. Wingtips fall quite short of tail tip on perched Merlins.

FLIGHT

Active flight when hunting is rapid with fast, stiff wingbeats, but hobby also has a light, buoyant, more leisurely flight. Soars on flat wings, usually with wingtips pulled back, wings bent at wrist, and tail somewhat fanned. They usually glide swiftlike, with wrists lower than body and wingtips pointing downward below the horizontal. Leading edge of wing appears somewhat curved. They will hover, especially when prey goes to cover.

MOLT

Annual molt of adults is complete; it begins in late summer after breeding, is suspended during autumn migration, and is completed on winter grounds. Juveniles begin post-juvenile molt by replacing body feathers in early spring while still on winter quarters and complete during the summer.

BEHAVIOR

Hobbys are graceful, elegant, and acrobatic falcons that capture insects and birds on the wing. They hunt birds with Peregrine-like lightning stoops, sometimes with a short upward swoop at end. They hunt insects in a less dramatic, more leisurely fashion, again often ending with a short upsweep; insects are usually eaten on the wing. They also eat bats and, less frequently, small mammals and reptiles. Hobbys are often active at dawn and dusk. In winter and on migration, they are social, forming feeding flocks and night roosts.

STATUS AND DISTRIBUTION

Hobbys occur as vagrants in North America — a few sight, photographic, and specimen records exist from the Pribilof and Aleutian Is. and the adjacent Alaskan seas; a sight record exists from British Columbia; an unsubstantiated sight record comes from New Jersey; and a photograph was taken of a vagrant on a ship off of Newfoundland. The Eurasian population is highly migratory.

FINE POINTS

On folded tail, tip appears wedge-shaped because of the shape of the tips of the feathers. Juvenile's tail has a wide buffy terminal band; adult's has a thin one.

SUBSPECIES

The Eurasian race is *F. s. subbuteo*.

ETYMOLOGY

"Hobby" comes from the Old French *hobe*, meaning "to jump about," for the falcon's agility in capturing flying insects. In Latin, *sub* means "somewhat," and *buteo* is "a kind of hawk or falcon."

MEASUREMENTS

LENGTH:		29–32 cm (30);	11–13 in. (12)
WINGSPREAD:		74–83 cm (78);	29–33 in. (31)
WEIGHT:	Male	131–223 g (193);	4.6–7.9 oz. (6.8)
	Female	141–325 g (237);	5.0–11.5 oz. (8.9)

REFERENCES
INDEX

References

Amadon, D., and J. Bull. 1988. *Hawks and Owls of the World: A Distributional and Taxonomic List.* Proceedings of the Western Foundation of Vertebrate Zoology. Vol 3. no. 4:295–357.

AOU. 1998. *Check-list of North American Birds.* Am. Ornith. Union. Lawrence, Kans.

Clark, W. S., and R. Banks. 1992. The taxonomic status of the White-tailed Kite. *Wilson Bulletin* 104:571-579.

del Hoyo, J., A. Elliot, and J. Sargatal, eds. 1994. *Handbook of the Birds of the World.* Vol. 2. Lynx Edicions, Barcelona.

Edelstam, C. 1984. Patterns of moult in large birds of prey. 1984. *Ann. Zool. Fennici* 21:271–276.

Humphrey, P. H., and K. C. Parkes. 1959. An approach to the study of molts and plumages. *Auk* 76:1–31.

Jollie, M. 1947. Plumage changes in the Golden Eagle. *Auk* 64:549–576.

Miller, A. H. 1941. The significance of molt centers among the secondary remiges in the Falconiformes. *Condor* 43:113–115.

Palmer, R. S. 1988. *Handbook of North American Birds.* Vols. 4 and 5. Yale Univ. Press, New Haven, Conn.

INDEX

We provide the page number on which each species account begins and (in bold face) the number of the plate(s) that portray the species. Maps and photographs are placed within the species accounts.

THE PETERSON SERIES®

PETERSON FIELD GUIDES®

BIRDS

ADVANCED BIRDING (39) North America 97500-X
BIRDS OF BRITAIN AND EUROPE (8) 0-618-16675-0
BIRDS OF TEXAS (13) Texas and adjacent states 92138-4
BIRDS OF THE WEST INDIES (18) 0-618-00210-3
EASTERN BIRDS (1) Eastern and central North America
    91176-1
EASTERN BIRDS' NESTS (21) U.S. east of Mississippi River 93609-8
   HAWKS (35) North America 67067-5
      WESTERN BIRDS (2) North America west of 100th meridian
       and north of Mexico 91173-7
       WESTERN BIRDS' NESTS (25) U.S. west of Mississippi
        River 0-618-16437-5
        MEXICAN BIRDS (20) Mexico, Guatemala, Belize, El
        Salvador 97514-X
        WARBLERS (49) North America 78321-6

FISH

PACIFIC COAST FISHES (28) Gulf of Alaska to Baja California 0-618-00212-X
ATLANTIC COAST FISHES (32) North American Atlantic coast 97515-8
FRESHWATER FISHES (42) North America north of Mexico 91091-9

INSECTS

INSECTS (19) North America north of Mexico
    91170-2
BEETLES (29) North America 91089-7
EASTERN BUTTERFLIES (4) Eastern and central North
    America 90453-6
WESTERN BUTTERFLIES (33) U.S. and Canada west of 100th meridian, part of
    northern Mexico 79151-0

MAMMALS

MAMMALS (5) North America north of Mexico 91098-6
ANIMAL TRACKS (9) North America 91094-3

ECOLOGY

EASTERN FORESTS (37) Eastern North America 92895-8
CALIFORNIA AND PACIFIC NORTHWEST FORESTS (50) 92896-6
ROCKY MOUNTAIN AND SOUTHWEST FORESTS (51) 92897-4
VENOMOUS ANIMALS AND POISONOUS PLANTS (46) North America north of
    Mexico 93608-X

PETERSON FIELD GUIDES® continued

PETERSON FIRST GUIDES®

PETERSON FIELD GUIDE COLORING BOOKS

AUDIO AND VIDEO

EASTERN BIRDING BY EAR
cassettes 97523-9
CD 97524-7

WESTERN BIRDING BY EAR
cassettes 97526-3
CD 97525-5

EASTERN BIRD SONGS, Revised
cassettes 53150-0
CD 97522-0

WESTERN BIRD SONGS, Revised
cassettes 51746-X
CD 975190

BACKYARD BIRDSONG
cassettes 97527-1
CD 97528-X

EASTERN MORE BIRDING BY EAR
cassettes 97529-8
CD 97530-1

WATCHING BIRDS
Beta 34418-2
VHS 34417-4

PETERSON'S MULTIMEDIA GUIDES: NORTH AMERICAN BIRDS
(CD-ROM for Windows) 73056-2

PETERSON FLASHGUIDES™

ATLANTIC COASTAL BIRDS 79286-X
PACIFIC COASTAL BIRDS 79287-8
EASTERN TRAILSIDE BIRDS 79288-6
WESTERN TRAILSIDE BIRDS 79289-4
HAWKS 79291-6
BACKYARD BIRDS 79290-8
TREES 82998-4
MUSHROOMS 82999-2
ANIMAL TRACKS 82997-6
BUTTERFLIES 82996-8
ROADSIDE WILDFLOWERS 82995-X
BIRDS OF THE MIDWEST 86733-9
WATERFOWL 86734-7
FRESHWATER FISHES 86713-4

PETERSON FIELD GUIDES can be purchased at your local
bookstore or by calling our toll-free number, (800) 225-3362.

When referring to title by corresponding ISBN number,
preface with 0-395, unless title is listed with 0-618.